Saltwater Angler's Guide to™

The Southeast

**Flyfishing and Light Tackle
in the Carolinas and Georgia**

Saltwater Angler's Guide to™

The Southeast

Flyfishing and Light Tackle
in the Carolinas and Georgia

Bob Newman

Wilderness
Adventures
Press™

Belgrade, Montana

This book was made with an easy opening, lay flat binding.

Cover Photograph © 1999 Barry and Cathy Beck
Photographs contained herein © 1999 Bob Newman or as noted,
    except photo page 163 © 1993 Joel Arrington.
Fish description artwork © 1999 Duane Raver
Forage Species artwork © 1999 Susan Newman

Maps, book design and cover design © 1999 Wilderness Adventures Press
Saltwater Angler's Guide to™

Published by Wilderness Adventures Press
45 Buckskin Road
Belgrade, MT 59714
800-925-3339
Website: www.wildadv.com
email: books@wildadv.com

10 9 8 7 6 5 4 3 2 1

Printed in the United States of America

Library of Congress Cataloging-in-Publication Data

Newman, Bob, 1958–
    Saltwater angler's guide to the Southeast : flyfishing and light tackle in the Carolinas and
    Georgia / Bob Newman.
       p. cm.
    ISBN 1–885106–81–5 (alk. paper)
    1. Saltwater fly fishing—North Carolina. 2. Saltwater fly fishing—South Carolina. 3.
Saltwater fly fishing—Georgia. I. Title.

SH531 .N48 1999
799.1'6'09756—dc21
                                                                99–050031

Table of Contents

Acknowledgments

Well, here I go again. Every time I write a book, I feel funny once the manuscript is done and heading to the publisher. Funny because I know I have so many people to thank. Yes, my name is on the cover, but a book is always, at least in my experience, a group effort.

I must thank the publisher of Wilderness Adventures Press, Chuck Johnson, for the idea in the first place. No, this book wasn't even my idea. However, I usually know a good idea when I hear one, and this was one.

Darren Brown, my editor, was patient during the writing process, probably more so than he should have been. The book is a better one because of Darren.

My friends in the flyfishing world all provided encouragement. They include Lefty Kreh, Bob Popovics, Ed Jaworowski, Tom Earnhardt, Captain Tyler Stone, Captain Joe Shute, Captain Bill Harris, Jon Cave, Joe Albea, Bob Clouser, Captain Brian Horsley, Joel Arrington, George Poveromo, Captain Larry Kennedy, John Martyn, and Captain Richard Stuhr, among others.

Rick Pelow, George Misko, and Fred Kluge provided me with many hours of entertainment on the water.

And finally, my wife, Susan, who did the forage fish illustrations, came through as always.

Introduction

This book came to be written by me in a somewhat unusual manner, which has to do with a friend of mine getting into a fist fight with a large and rather cantankerous Tanzanian lion many years ago. You see, John Kingsley-Heath was a professional hunter in East Africa and Botswana for about 30 years and one day a lion decided to call him on it. The huge cat mangled him badly in an epic fight. John broke his rifle over the top of the cat's massive head and then he punched it in the mouth (John's arm went straight down the cat's throat; the lion opened its mouth just as John threw the punch). The lion broke John's arms and removed part of his scalp, then grabbed him by the foot and broke that. Naturally, John, calling for his gunbearer to shoot the cat before it killed him, was annoyed to find that his gunbearer had fled in terror, leaving our erstwhile professional hunter to his fate. But it didn't work out as you might expect, as John, too, can be a scrappy fellow.

The lion died. John didn't.

In any case, I edited John's first book, *Hunting the Dangerous Game of Africa* (Sycamore Island Books; Boulder, CO), and Chuck Johnson, publisher of Wilderness Adventures Press, and I came into contact this way, with Chuck buying some of John's books from us to sell to his customers. Chuck learned of my having written 16 or so books and asked me to write this one because of my familiarity with the Carolinas' and Georgia's saltwater fly- and light-tackle fishing from the Outer Banks to St. Mary's Entrance. So you see, this is all John Kingsley-Heath's doing. Well, his and that poor lion's.

The littorals of the Carolinas and Georgia are some of the most intricate, rich, and fascinating in North America. For instance:

- Did you know that the world-record red drum was taken on the Outer Banks?
- That Charleston Harbor offers some of the best crevalle jack fishing in the country?
- That North Carolina's Pamlico Sound offers huge tarpon?
- That ladyfish behind Fort Sumter go wild once the water warms up in the late spring?
- That Georgia's coast is lightly developed and offers tremendous game fish?

Here flyfishers and light-tackle enthusiasts can take on spotted seatrout in a creek along the Bogue Banks, tripletail off Morehead City, red drum in Albemarle Sound, tarpon off Hilton Head, ladyfish around Charleston, king mackerel near Cape Lookout, sheepshead close to Myrtle Beach, flounder in the Atlantic Intracoastal Waterway, crevalle jack around Little St. Simon's Island, tarpon in the mouth of the Altamaha River, and many other great game fish in locations that usually only see the "locals" testing. The Carolinas' and Georgia's salt waters are very accessible, and this book is designed to get you into those waters armed with the tackle and tactics it takes to fool a great many game fish.

An angler prepares to throw a cast net for menhaden and finger mullet in
Mile Hammock Bay on the Atlantic Intracoastal Waterway.

We will discuss in detail what saltwater flyfishing and light tackle is appropriate and recommended. This information is broad, encompassing rods, reels, lines, flies, lures, and other matters of critical importance to the flyfisher and light-tackle lover hitting the salt in this region. You will find very specific recommendations here and the reasons for those recommendations, and you may be assured that the suggested tackle is proven. There is nothing worse (well, almost nothing) than using the wrong tackle in a situation that will quickly show you just how wrong a selection you have made.

The specifics of game fish of the region are also covered. Every species of saltwater game fish hereabouts that can be safely (quickly enough to be properly released by the average angler) fought by flyfishers or with light tackle is covered, including habitat preferences, prey, habits, current, weather, and seasonal effects. This is where you will get to know the game fish.

In the trip planning chapter you will learn how to set up a trip and greatly minimize problems on the way and once there. Airlines and road info, fishing pressure, guides, tides, accommodations, self-guiding advice, restaurants, historical weather patterns, and much more is revealed here.

The weather can be a bigger factor than you might think. Coastal North Carolina suffered the wrath of Hurricanes Bertha and Fran in the summer of 1996. The Christmas House in Swansboro did not survive.

Licenses and natural seasons (when the fish are there) are also covered, but I do not cover legal seasons and regulations such as length and creel limits because these rules change frequently. It is always a good idea to call for current regulations.

Three chapters on the waters of the region allow a very close look at the waters between Currituck and St. Mary's Entrance, and it includes saltwater rivers. Yes, this is the skinny on precisely where you cast flies and other tackle at game fish. Whether you want to fish Rodanthe, Avon, Nags Head, Ocracoke, Portsmouth Island, Morehead City, Cape Lookout, Wrightsville Beach, Cape Fear, Myrtle Beach, Charleston, Beaufort, Hilton Head Island, St. Simon's Island, Brunswick, and any-where in between, these chapters will help you.

Finally, an examination of the threats to our marine fisheries, primarily in North Carolina, and what is being done to protect the precious ecosystems that comprise these waters. This section is frank, and it needs to be, because these waters are not safe from every threat. Far from it.

Let's get going.

Game Fish

The Southeast's saltwater, from Currituck to St. Mary's Entrance, is some of the most diverse on the planet, providing excellent habitat for the many species of game fish that call these waters home, and I do mean the many species. Given this, let's examine these game fish so that we can come to truly know each of them, for knowledge is power, without which our flies and lures will go unmolested—a most unsatisfactory thought.

The game fish of the Southeast coast include:

- Tarpon
- Striped bass
- Red drum
- Black drum
- Spotted seatrout
- Cobia
- Flounder
- Great barracuda
- Weakfish
- Spadefish
- Tripletail
- Crevalle jack
- Ladyfish
- False albacore
- Dolphin
- Croaker
- Spanish mackerel
- King mackerel
- Wahoo
- Yellowfin tuna
- Skipjack tuna
- Sheepshead
- Greater Amberjack
- Bluefish
- Pompano
- Atlantic bonito

Descriptions of a few species will be brief since this book is primarily directed at inshore and near-shore game fish, and not game fish that are usually found offshore and which only occasionally wander into near-shore waters. Nor is this a surf-fishing manual—such manuals have already been written ad nauseum. The yellowfin tuna will be gone over comparatively lightly because it is primarily an offshore species, although some do come in fairly close to shore under the right conditions. We will not discuss the bluefin tuna or billfish—marlin and sailfish—because they are beyond the tightly defined scope of this book. (While these species can be caught on the fly and on light tackle—I have done so myself—the vast majority of anglers who buy this book aren't going to be using a fly rod or light spinning gear to battle a 1000-pound blue marlin or 800-pound bluefin tuna.)

We won't go to great lengths in our discussion of croakers, whiting, black sea bass, pompano, or spadefish (pretty things that look like giant angelfish, caught on bluebird days over near-shore wrecks and rocks by dropping a piece of cannonball or blueball jellyfish down), because these species are hardly ever a challenge to find or entice to strike and require comparatively little forethought.

Offshore bottom fish, such as grouper, gray triggerfish, and snapper, will not be discussed in this chapter because most Southeast anglers will never go after them with anything but heavy bottom gear. They may, however, be covered in other chapters, although lightly. Nor will I discuss in any detail tactics for weakfish (gray trout) because they are under extremely heavy pressure by commercial fishermen and shouldn't be intentionally targeted by anglers at this time. Suffice it to say that the same general tactics for spotted seatrout will work for gray trout. And when it comes to great barracuda, which are excellent game fish with attitude, I will only discuss them topically because they are so easy to catch. I will say, however, that more anglers should seek these marvelous game fish. They are strong, acrobatic, and apparently a little crazy.

Before we start, a word on terminology, namely what I mean by a soft plastic curltail jig. This is a flexible jerkbait, such as that made by Mister Twister, Kalin's, and Berkley. The tail curls when at rest and flutters behind the jig when moved forward. I call them jigs, as do most other anglers along the coast of the Carolinas and Georgia. A colored lead head with a hook is attached to this bait, thus making it sink; otherwise, it will float. These versatile lures are an important addition to every tackle box.

Let's begin our study of the region's saltwater game fish with none other than the silver king.

TARPON

Fanaticism best describes the effect that tarpon have on flyfishers. The mighty tarpon, known by its innumerable admirers and pursuers as the silver king, is a game fish of legendary abilities and traits, for no other game fish is quite like it, or anything like it, for that matter. Untold millions of words have been written about the tarpon, and no doubt many millions more will be penned before I finally break off. Once you hook your first tarpon, you will understand this, for the silver king is a game fish of sheer might, determination, and athletic ability matched by few, if any. Couple these traits with their ability to grow very large—well in excess of 200 pounds —and their armored-chrome appearance, and it becomes clear why the tarpon is perhaps the most addicting game fish that swims. The old guard of saltwater flyfishing—Kreh, Sosin, Apte, and Fernandez—are all admitted tarpon junkies who twitch and become slack-jawed when a big tarpon turns toward their fly. Yes, the tarpon is a game fish that stuns the mind and shatters one's nerves.

Habitat

Truly fishable populations of the silver king generally range from the sounds of North Carolina to northern South America, although they do sometimes wander farther north during the heat of summer. Nevertheless, the tarpon is a subtropical and tropical game fish that prefers water temperatures from the 70s well into the 80s, making North Carolina's Pamlico Sound nearly perfect, at least insofar as water temperature goes in summer. When you add large populations of baitfish and other forage species to the equation, such as menhaden, mullet, crabs, and shrimp, you get tarpon that sometimes appear to be so numerous that it boggles the mind.

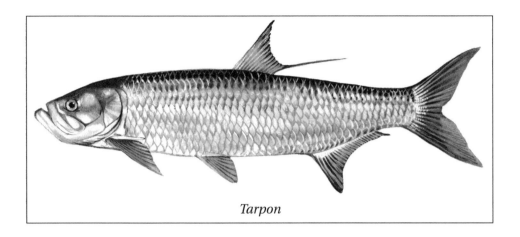

Tarpon

Once, when fishing with Captain George Beckwith, we found thousands of big tarpon north of Cedar Island in Pamlico Sound, a few miles behind Ocracoke Inlet. George and I had been catching some nice specks off Raccoon Island and had decided to go look for some tarpon. We found them rolling in the middle of the sound —huge fish that were flashing in the hot afternoon sun like windshields spread out over the surface of the water. This was the first time that George and I really understood just how many tarpon came to North Carolina during the summer. As far as the eye could see, there were bright flashes of light reflecting off the chrome sides of the great fish; a genuine revelation. We knew that tarpon came to the sound starting around June, but we—no one—had any idea just how great their numbers were.

Tarpon are thought by many to be fish of the flats—and they are—but tarpon do not spend nearly as much time on the flats as many folks think. The classic tarpon flyfishing situation entails casting to pods of the giant fish from the forward deck of a flats boat (such as an Action Craft or Hewes) on a Florida Keys flat, your guide poling from the elevated stern platform and excitedly pointing out tarpon coming your way. But the truth is that tarpon spend more time in channels and cuts and sounds than anywhere else.

For flyfishers and spin casters, the tarpon's preference for deeper water is somewhat problematic: seeing and casting to tarpon on the flats isn't all that difficult, but when they are in deeper water and can't be seen, just how are you supposed to get a fly or lure in front of the fish? The answer is coming up in the tarpon tactics section.

Tarpon also like to hang out under overhanging branches; in bays; quiet backwaters; under docks; in rivers (especially around bridge abutments, such as where North Carolina's Neuse River passes under the Route 17 bridge in New Bern); in the surf and just outside of it (one can spot tarpon cruising the beaches of Georgia and the Carolinas in midsummer, looking for goodies to munch); and even in harbors.

So, you might find a tarpon anywhere in southeastern saltwaters, from Currituck Sound to St. Mary's Entrance. All this means that you had better be ready.

Prey

The silver king has a fairly eclectic diet, including crustaceans such as blue crabs (surely one of their favorites, especially when a swimming crab happens by), shrimp, ladyfish, menhaden, mullet, croakers, pinfish, silversides, mummichogs, lizardfish, seatrout, catfish, Spanish mackerel, and sea robins, among other things.

So, with so many things on the menu, it should be easy to get the tarpon to eat something you have to offer, right? Wrong.

Flyfishing: Tactics, Techniques, and Tackle

I would like to be able to tell you that flyfishing for tarpon is just as effective in the Carolinas and Georgia as it is in the Keys, but that just isn't the case. The thing is, flats with crystalline water such as those in the Keys are not found here, and situations like that in Boca Grande Pass on Florida's west coast, where great mobs of tarpon are found in the spring throughout the water column, are unheard of in the Carolinas and Georgia.

Is this to say tarpon can't be caught on the fly along the Southeast coast? No, but most that are caught with fly tackle are taken in very specific situations, such as in the golf course ponds of Georgia's Golden Isles. And if everything works just right, you might be able to hook up to a tarpon that has come into your chum slick if you get the fly right in front of it very quickly. Other than these situations, due substantially to more murky water, tarpon on the fly are tough to come by.

The minimum weight tarpon rod is an 8-weight, which should only be used when targeting baby tarpon of 30 pounds or less. Any lighter and you run the serious risk of fighting the tarpon too long, tiring it so badly that it will not survive release, and all tarpon should be released. A 10-weight is more efficient, and a 12-weight isn't too heavy. Rod lengths should be in the 9-foot range with a fast action that allows the delivery of large, heavy flies, even in the wind.

I also prefer tarpon fly rods to have an extra powerful butt for turning the fish at every opportunity so that it becomes tired more quickly, thus facilitating a safe release.

My two favorite tarpon rods are a 12-weight, 9-foot 4-piece Orvis Saltrodder, which can handle even the most deranged tarpon, and a 10-weight, 9-foot 2-piece St. Croix Legend Ultra, which I like for midsize tarpon.

Fly reels for tarpon simply must have outstanding drags that can take great heat. They must also have substantial line capacities with the ability to hold 200 yards of 30-pound backing. (I have never seen or even heard of a tarpon that spooled a fly-fisher with average skills and decent gear. Most tarpon will not run off more than 100 yards of backing. A good flyfisher with a rod that can do the job, provided the flyfisher has the nerve to use the rod properly to turn the fish, will never be spooled.) There are many such reels on the market today, so get the facts from knowledgeable fly-fishers and make your choice.

Light Tackle: Tactics, Techniques, and Tackle

The vast majority of tarpon caught in the Carolinas and Georgia are taken on fairly light tackle, at least when compared to offshore jigging gear. A fast, 6½- to 7½-foot rod with a good butt is the ticket.

Chum slicks can bring tarpon in from a long way off.

The reel has got to be top notch. It must have the most dependable of drags and have a line capacity of at least 250 yards of 20-pound test. Never use a reel that has a discount drag! You will regret it. Line rated at 20 pounds is the minimum, with 30 being the max. (One of the best reels for fishing live bait is the Shimano Baitrunner because it allows line to be taken off the reel without the bail being open.) You should also use a shock leader of at least 6 feet, and a heavy one at that. This 80-pound shock helps prevent the tarpon from rubbing the line to the breaking point with its rough mouth and abrasive shoulders. But to tell you the truth, there are many theories when it comes to tarpon leaders. What one angler finds very effective, another will say is useless.

Running a chum line is one of the most popular ways of getting a tarpon hooked up in the Southeast. A mesh bag filled with menhaden chum left soaking and the occasional few pieces of chum tossed into the steady slick are effective. The slick should be run so that the pieces of bait drift to where the tarpon are known or suspected to be feeding (watch for rolling fish). Amid the slick goes a piece of menhaden impaled on a very sharp hook. Tuna "circle" hooks have become very popular as their shape results in more good hookups. Whatever your hook style preference, sizes generally run from 3/0 to maybe 6/0. Also, never bury the hook's point. Leave it exposed so that you can hit the fish instantly and get a hookup. Tarpon do not examine baits for hooks. And skip the treble hook; you need a hook with one directed entry point, not three points spread out.

Live bait can work great—pinfish, mullet, croakers, menhaden, and the largest shrimp you can find are five choices. Fished a few feet below a large popping cork right inside the slick can bring fast and wild results.

For both live bait and cut bait fishing, set the hook soon after the tarpon picks it up—don't let him swallow it. When you feel the line tighten and the rod begins to bend, nail him! If the tarpon swallows the bait, it will almost surely die and will fight poorly at best.

Large bucktail or soft plastic jigs work well in deep water, such as channels and holes in sounds. Menhaden oil applied to the jig is always a good idea. Tarpon have a sense of smell and use it all the time. If it smells good, the chances of them eating it are increased.

Seasons

Tarpon first hit Georgia in any numbers in spring when the water warms to at least the mid-70s, preferably warmer. As water warms up farther north, the silver kings slowly move up the coast and eventually into the sounds of North Carolina, with the heaviest concentrations remaining in the Pamlico Sound watershed, which includes the sound's rivers. Here they stay until September or so, when they head south again as the water cools.

Tarpon tournaments have become popular in the Southeast. Participating in one of these with a good guide will really let you know just how many big tarpon come up here in the summer. The Oriental (North Carolina) Rotary Club's annual tarpon tournament has become a big thing. Give it a try.

COBIA

Cobia are an outstanding game fish in many ways, and no angler turns his back on one if the situation presents itself. They are extremely strong, curious, very predictable, and delicious game fish. Mark Sosin calls them "the man in the brown suit."

Habitat

Structure is absolutely crucial to cobia. They like buoys, piers, wrecks, rocks, bridges, and other heavy structure. Happily, cobia live in rivers and inlets, but also inhabit deep water out where the grouper and snapper live. Never be surprised when a cobia shows up.

Prey

Cobia are another great opportunist, eating crabs (a favorite of every cobia; one of their nicknames is crabeater), shrimp (a nice big fat one is often irresistible), and baitfish (nearly any species, from mullet to pinfish to menhaden to anchovies).

Flyfishing: Tactics, Techniques, and Tackle

Most flyfishers who catch cobia on fly rods do so by sightcasting. Buoys are one of a flyfisher's best friends when it comes to cobia, so always check out every buoy you pass—approaching slowly and watching carefully. Take a good long look, too. Sometimes you will see one or more right away, but sometimes they can remain hidden for a few minutes. Remember, don't get too close to the buoy—stand off and look. Better yet, get up high and look down on the buoy (possibly from the flying bridge). Also, get up high and watch for cobia moving along the beach outside the surf.

Cobia

When a cobia is spotted, figure the drift. Get some line out and cast so that your fly lands several feet away from it. Let the cobia spot it and continue your steady retrieve until the cobia comes to get it. Some attacks are fast and direct, and other times a cobia just takes its time. Be ready for anything.

Use a strip strike and a waist twist to set the hook and hang on tight. The fight these rascals put up is most impressive, and they can weigh more than 60 pounds!

Use your 10-weight false albacore rod and reel for cobia under 15 pounds but go up to a 12- or 13-weight fast rod (and tough reel) for anything larger.

Warning: Never, never, never put a "green" cobia in your boat—that is, a cobia that isn't all that tired. Wear the fish out before you put it in the boat. If you intend to release it, get it up beside the boat and remove the hook with a hook remover without lifting the fish from the water. If a green cobia gets into your boat, it could destroy rods and other gear, and even seriously injure someone. This is no joke.

Light Tackle: Tactics, Techniques, and Tackle

Flyfishing tactics also work on light tackle. For bait, a live crab is a killer. Try drifting them past the structure with the current. Cobia love crabs and will often run out for a passing crab. Sometimes, when there is more than one cobia, others will come out, too, and then start looking around for another crab, which they seem to expect to come by at any second. A large live shrimp is also a killer for cobia. Present it just as you would a crab. Ditto for a baitfish.

For lures, a bucktail jig is very hard to beat, especially a large one that is yellow, chartreuse, or gold. Add a Mister Twister tail for extra action.

When it comes to tackle, go with false albacore tackle for cobia under 15 pounds. For anything bigger, use yellowfin tackle.

Seasons

Cobia like water between the mid-70s and mid-80s, but they can go a little bit either way. Therefore, spring, summer, and fall are the best seasons to find them.

STRIPED BASS

Stripers are a very significant game fish in North Carolina but less so in South Carolina and Georgia. North Carolina's Roanoke River striper fishery—unless the state government allows it to be completely destroyed by a proposed pulp mill to be built right on the river's shores—is the most important such fishery in the state. The sounds behind the Outer Banks, with Albemarle and Pamlico being of special note, are also important.

Habitat

Stripers are inshore and near-shore game fish and are found in inlets, surf zones, estuaries, rivers and creeks, bays, sloughs, cuts, and channels.

Prey

Eclectic is the best way to describe striped bass eating habits. They prey on sardines, anchovies, menhaden, cigar minnows, striped killifish, mummichogs, sticklebacks, silversides, herring, needlefish, gobies, mullet, Spanish mackerel, croakers, whiting, flounder, crabs, lobsters, marine worms, clams and other bivalves, pinfish, alewives, seatrout, and weakfish.

While this is a very long grocery list of edibles, it is surely only partial. What it all means is that you probably have something with you that they would eat. The bad news is that you have to figure out what they want at the moment. But there is good news with the bad: stripers may be willing to eat a variety of things at the moment.

Flyfishing: Tactics, Techniques, and Tackle

Sometimes you can see stripers feeding and other times you may simply suspect they are in the area. This is what dictates your tactics and techniques.

I love to watch stripers eat a fly on the surface, so I go heavy with poppers when the stripers are feeding up top. Standard pencil poppers (pencil poppers aren't a specific pattern but rather a general design; somewhat thin like a pencil with a slightly rounded head), Crystal Poppers, Flexo Poppers, and Foam Boilermakers are my four heavy hitters.

If stripers are not on the surface, I throw Deceivers, Clousers, Abel Anchovies, Conehead Minnows, Sar-Mul-Macs, Baby Bunkers, and the like. If I know precisely what they're eating, I use a fly that mimics it. For example, if stripers are attacking menhaden, I throw a Baby Bunker. If they're after silversides, I throw a standard Silverside or a Peterson's Silverside. And if they're hitting finger mullet, I use a Silicone Mullet. Despite their wide range of prey, in certain situations stripers can get choosy, and determining exactly what they are eating can be crucial to success.

Most stripers can be handled on a 9-weight rod that has a fairly fast tip. The reel should be good but it need not cost $600. A note on lines: Stripers can go down, so have a sinktip or full-sinking line at hand. Better yet, have a few of differing densities to cover various situations. Stripers love to sit in a rip and eat well below. A high-density sinking line will get down to them. Otherwise they might never see your fly.

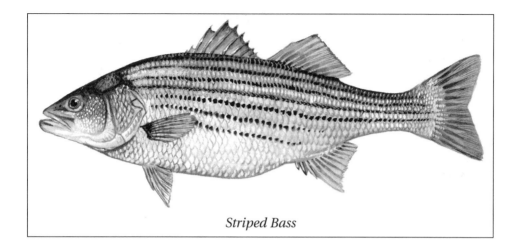

Striped Bass

Light Tackle: Tactics, Techniques, and Tackle

Spotted seatrout tackle works just fine for most Roanoke River and Sound stripers. Big ones in the surf call for a false albacore rig.

Lures for stripers are many and quite varied and include all sorts of crankbaits, jerkbaits, and jigs, but I have found one type of lure to be better than others most of the time, and that is a 5½-inch Storm Shallostick in silver scale. Captain Bill Harris first introduced me to this particular lure, color, and presentation years ago in North Carolina's Neuse River in New Bern. We were fishing just south of the Highway 70 West bridge along a seawall. Bill insisted that we (Rick Pelow and I) throw only that lure and that we retrieve it only in a slow, steady manner with no hesitation, twitches, or jerks. The stripers pounded that thing! And if I switched baits or presentation, nothing would happen.

Over the years I have learned that two other colors also work well with the Shallostick, and these are blue fade and metallic blue scale with a red lip.

If I am out of Shallosticks in such a situation, I go with a Smithwick Rattlin' Rogue. Floating models in chrome with a blue back (4½ inches long) are very productive.

Deep-diving lures, such as Fat Free Shads, Deep Thundersticks, and Shad Raps, can be retrieved through rips where you suspect stripers are cruising at depth. Bucktail jigs are also good for this.

When stripers are feeding heavily on the surface, try a surface plug that makes a lot of noise and splashes a lot. I like Rapala's new Skitterpop.

Seasons

Stripers stage in the sounds, Albemarle in particular, in late March to early April and are ready to move up the rivers to spawn. They stay in the rivers in very good numbers right into summer, then they begin to filter out.

Red Drum

The legend—red drum, a.k.a. channel bass, spot-tail bass, red bass, redfish, puppy drum (small ones of a few pounds or so—a term most often used in North Carolina), and bull reds (the big daddies often found in the surf of the Outer Banks) are one of the most respected and hotly pursued game fish in the region. They are beloved because they are beautiful, usually crafty, grow to huge proportions (more than 90 pounds), often travel in schools, fight like Trojans, and taste superb when properly prepared.

Habitat

Redfish are masters at adapting to various habitats. They can be found rummaging in flooded spartina marshes; on broad flats (over sand or mud bottoms); in channels (hence one of their monikers); in surf zones; working in the hook of a cape; in rivers and creeks; in sloughs and backwaters; hanging around piers; and hunting near jetties.

I have spoken with divers who have even found them (usually bull reds of at least 40 pounds) many miles offshore in the dead of winter in 120 feet of water over a wreck. If the red drum is anything, it's versatile.

Prey

Redfish are as diverse in their selection of forage as they are versatile in where they choose to live and hunt. They eat crabs (fiddlers, blues, or greens—red drum love crabs), menhaden (another favorite), shrimp (always a good choice), silversides, finger mullet, mummichogs, striped killifish, clams, sticklebacks, alewives, gobies, herring, eels, and seemingly nearly anything else they can catch.

Flyfishing: Tactics, Techniques, and Tackle

The vast majority of red drum flyfishing takes place on flats, whether flooded spartina flats or flats without spartina adjacent to spartina marshes, such as those found in sounds and along the banks of wide rivers. The most exciting style of flyfishing on the flats is sightcasting to reds, which is much like bonefishing on flats in the Keys, Belize, the Yucatan, Cuba, and the Bahamas.

Move stealthily (wading or poling) along the flat, looking for "nervous" water (a patch of water that is shimmering or wiggling differently than the water surrounding it, indicating feeding reds below); bulges in the surface ("pushes" created by the shoulders of the redfish as it forages along the bottom); swirls; and even the tail of a red poking out of the water in the shallows. Once you spot a fish or a school, watch to see where it goes, what it is doing, and how it is acting (calm or skittish), all of which determine how to approach and cast to the fish.

Warning: When you see a school of redfish, assume that there are others nearby that you do not see. Many redfish scatter because a flyfisher startles some that he doesn't see. When one redfish in a school is frightened, it does not discuss options

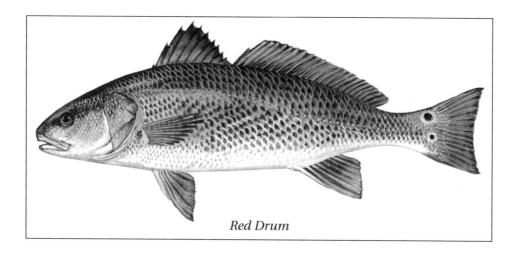

Red Drum

with its friends. It departs rapidly and takes all its friends with it. Once that school is blown out, it is useless to chase it right away and cast into it. Just start looking for another school or pull back and wait a while for the school to settle down into a feeding pattern again. This could easily take 30 minutes, probably longer.

Once in position, try to get the fly in front of the redfish by a few feet. If there is a school there, look for the lead fish. If you line the school in water a couple of feet deep, they may or may not blow out. If they don't, start stripping.

The pickup can be felt in most cases, although sometimes the guide on the poling platform will see the drum eat the fly and you won't feel a thing. If he says strip, then strip. When you feel pressure, tighten up and strip strike the fish. Oh yeah—hanging on at this point is advisable.

When a single red is feeding in spartina, it might change directions often and quickly. If you present the fly and the red doesn't see it and turns away, don't pick it up immediately to cast again. Let it sit there for a moment to see if the red turns back around. If it does, strip.

A leader of 10 or more feet is good in thin water situations, such as flooded spartina flats. A nervous drum that sees or feels a fly line may get scared and flee.

Working a flat beside a river channel or the Atlantic Intracoastal Waterway is another way to flyfish for reds, but they are more difficult to find, and this often this necessitates blind casting. Still, a sinking line with a short leader (3 feet) and a 2/0 maroon and gold Clouser can come up with redfish, especially when working the spartina bank hard and watching for swirls up ahead or scattering baitfish.

On falling tides, watch for redfish moving out of the shallows and into channels. Look for those pushes.

The Outer Banks are home to reds 365 days a year somewhere or another. You can find very large schools of oftentimes huge bull reds chasing baitfish in and out of the surf. You can cast to them from the beach with a stripping basket or from a boat just outside the surf zone. It helps to have someone above you who can see the school and its path. Under the right conditions, fly casting to such trophy reds with a 12-weight rod can be incredibly exciting.

My favorite redfish rod is a fast 8-weight that is 9 feet long. Sage's 890 RPL+ shines as a drum rod for me—I use this rod more than any other for redfish on the flats. Two other excellent choices are L.L. Bean's GQS and Scott's SCS908/3.

Line capacity isn't all that important for a redfish reel, with 200 yards of 20-pound backing being plenty in the vast majority of situations. However, the reel needs a good drag because a drum is going to make repeated runs.

I have been using spoon flies since they showed up, and one model of these is better than the others—Jon Cave's size 2 Wobbler. Jon is a well-known guide and fly-fishing writer from Florida who has many decades of experience flyfishing for redfish all over the Southeast, Florida, and the Gulf Coast. This fly of his is super for reds.

Light Tackle: Tactics, Techniques, and Tackle

Reds are caught with light tackle in several ways, including soaking a piece of cut bait—menhaden, mullet, pinfish—on the bottom of an inlet, river, or in the surf; sightcasting lures to reds either in schools or individually on flats, or using small spinnerbaits, such as Beetle Spins, to blind cast around stumps and spartina edges; and casting a crab body in front of a school of reds on a flat.

Tactics for approaching and presenting to redfish are the same as when fly casting: be quiet (something heavy dropped in the boat near a redfish will make it run off), keep a low profile if possible, don't make unnecessary movements with the rod, and watch for reds that you didn't see at first so you don't spook them.

Spinning rods for reds average about 7 feet with medium-fast actions. I like St. Croix's Model PS70MF2.

You must have a very good drag on the reel you select, and you will need some line capacity to spare. Daiwa's Model SS2600 is perfect for red drum, even ones that weigh 35 pounds.

For lures, a wobbling gold spoon is a splendid offering. I recommend a Dardevle in brass. Soft plastics work well, too. Try Berkley's Power Jerk Shad and Mister Twister's Tri-Alive Sassy Shad. The best color overall is a pearly shade.

Seasons

Red drum can be found in Southeast coastal waters year-round, although some folks think they leave for the winter. I assure you that they don't. Some may move to a different ecosystem, such as from a river into the surf or even offshore, but most stick around home. In fact, you can catch reds on flooded spartina flats 365 days a year in the Carolinas and Georgia. You just have to look for them.

BLACK DRUM

Black drum aren't caught nearly as often as red drum along the Southeast coast, because fishermen don't usually target them unless they happen to see one while looking for some other fish.

Habitat

Black drum live mostly in the same places as red drum—bays, jetties, sounds, inlets, surf zones, rivers, and on flooded spartina flats. They are where you find them, as the saying goes, and can grow to huge proportions.

Still, if there were one type of structure I would say is more likely to hold a black drum, that would be a rock jetty or a rocky or otherwise hard stretch of bottom between two rock jetties. The Fort Macon rock jetty at Beaufort Inlet is a good black drum spot. Piers also hold them.

Prey

Again, their prey is similar to red drum: crabs, mullet, mummichogs, silversides, menhaden, pinfish, clams, croakers, shrimp, and so on. Black drum are good scroungers and make do with what they find.

Flyfishing: Tactics, Techniques, and Tackle

Use red drum gear—that's the best advice I can give you. However, I do recommend that you keep a big-bore rod rigged and ready if you are in an area known to attract large black drum. A 12-weight isn't too much. Flies that hug the bottom are best, with a Clouser being perfect.

Black Drum

Light Tackle: Tactics, Techniques, and Tackle

Cut bait is used most often, but a live shrimp is good, too, maybe even better. I have had good luck with finger mullet right on the bottom or a chunk of adult white mullet. If the current is running hard, you might need a pyramid sinker to keep bait on the bottom and in place. Black drum sometimes hit jigs, too, particularly a smelly jig that has been coated with menhaden oil. Fish a jig fairly slowly.

Black drum tend to mouth a piece of cut bait, so don't set the hook as soon as you feel something. Give the drum a chance to get it all the way into its mouth, then set the hook hard.

Use red drum spinning gear for black drum.

Seasons

Mostly spring through fall, with spring being the best. Spring black drum migrations are well known, but no one, at least to my knowledge, really knows where they spend the winter in large numbers. Many spawn in Chesapeake Bay and Delaware Bay.

SPOTTED SEATROUT

I caught my first spotted seatrout in 1973 beside the north jetty at the mouth of the Banana River at Cape Canaveral. Pulling the fish out of the net, I admired its silvery sides and black spots and took note of the two canine teeth buried in my left index finger. Up until that moment I had intended to release the fish, but its assault on my finger caused me to have a change of heart. That evening I rolled the fish in cornmeal and ate it. I have liked spotted seatrout ever since.

Also known as a speck, speckled trout, speckled seatrout, or simply trout, this fish is common throughout the Southeast coast and is sought by many flyfishers and light-tackle anglers. Its popularity is based upon its willingness to take a fly, lure, or live bait, good fighting ability, beauty, and healthy populations. There seem to be quite a few around, generally speaking, which doesn't necessarily mean that you can go out and catch as many as you like any time you want. In fact, that is another likable quality of the spotted seatrout—it is quite predictable but can also be maddeningly elusive, especially when conditions seem perfect for catching them. For example, an excellent speck hole can be found just north of the swing bridge over the Atlantic Intracoastal Waterway behind North Carolina's Onslow Beach. Starting in late October, specks begin to frequent this spot and are available into December in good numbers. But sometimes, although you may have caught 20 of them in the very same spot under the same conditions the day before, they just don't want to play along. Like I said—maddening.

Habitat

Spotted seatrout are found in many types of habitat. You can find them in deep holes far up creeks and rivers; on shallow flats; in spartina marshes; in the surf; along dropoffs; in tidal rips at the ends of small islands; in sloughs and canals; hanging around jetties; and near pilings, to name just some likely places.

Spotted Seatrout

One of the keys to being a successful speck hunter is to get to know the local populations to learn where they go and when (specks are seasonally nomadic). This is best done by keeping your eyes peeled and questioning the comparatively few speck enthusiasts who are willing to share the location of a good hole. (Spotted seatrout command legions of loyal followers who are notoriously tightlipped about the best trout holes in their area.)

Prey

Spotted seatrout are roamers that eat what they find. The one thing that doesn't especially interest them, comparatively speaking, is cut bait, although every now and then someone catches a speck on a piece of shrimp or menhaden on the bottom. Specks are hunters rather than scavengers, preferring above all else a fat live shrimp. But they eat much more than shrimp. The list includes finger mullet, silversides, anchovies, sardines, crabs, lizardfish, menhaden, striped killifish, mummichogs, herring, sticklebacks, and needlefish—and that's just for starters.

Flyfishing: Tactics, Techniques, and Tackle

Flyfishing tactics and techniques for spotted seatrout revolve around knowing where fish are likely to be and then working the area well during times that are most likely to be productive with flies that have worked before. Sound familiar? Yes, these are the same principles used for every other species of game fish. But there is a difference: Specks are more predictable than some other species and live in more types of habitat than many other species. This makes them more vulnerable to a fly.

Tactics that work most often are those that exploit the seatrout's five favorite types of habitat: creeks and rivers lined with spartina grass—if they abut flats, all the better; backwaters lined with spartina; confluences; rock jetties; and holes in surf zones, rivers, and creeks.

More trout are caught in creeks and rivers than any other type of habitat, so focus primarily on this type of hangout. A floating line is best used for most of these situations with a baitfish imitation, some of the best of which are Clousers, Deceivers, Peterson's Silversides, Spoon flies, and pencil poppers. The edges of spartina banks (where grass stops and the flat or dropoff begins), seams where current runs around small points, and depressions or dropoffs in the creek or river are good spots to probe. The best time to do so is when the tide is running strong (I haven't seen a marked difference in preference for a rising or falling tide in every instance). Edges and seams are often best worked with Deceivers, Spoon flies, and Silversides, whereas holes and dropoffs, where trout may be holding deeper, require a Clouser or similar fly that is meant to sink and hug the bottom (in particularly deep holes, a sinktip or full-sinking line might be needed to get the fly down and keep it there).

Spartina edges must be covered thoroughly—watch for signs of feeding trout, namely scattering baitfish, to be successful more often. Fan-cast to make retrieves parallel to the bank or nearly so; this covers the prime strike zone, which starts right at the bank and extends out about 6 feet or so. When baitfish are really being torn up, a pencil popper can be a great fly because it mimics a wounded baitfish thrashing on the surface.

Backwaters lined with spartina tend to be very shallow, and trout become spooky in such water. These locations are also more likely to have fiddler crabs in them due to the margin of safety found in flooded grass as well as access to exposed mudflats at low tide that are rich in the food that crabs need. This is a good place to try a Jack's Fighting Crab (yes, a permit fly). Remember that in thin water, nervous trout often require a long cast and soft presentation—line a trout and it's out of there.

Confluences—where a creek joins a river or larger creek—are natural attractions for fish because of the additional forage found there. Baitfish and shrimp patterns are best, and keep in mind that there may be a depression at the confluence, so think about a sinktip to work it.

Rock jetties hold many game fish, trout included. Trout tend to hold deep along the sides of jetties, so use a full-sinking line to get at them. Clousers and Gotchas will get down to the bottom and tend to stay there if stripped slowly with an occasional quick and short strip, which indicates a startled baitfish or shrimp. Also try a shrimp pattern (Bramblett's Swimming Shrimp is a solid choice) on a very short leader (2 feet). Visibility in the water is often poor around jetties because it is a high-energy zone, and the slower retrieve with a fly that has some Mylar, Flashabou, or Krystal Flash tied into it can bring impressive results. And if you don't mind getting hung up from time to time, use a crab pattern right up amid the washed-up rocks between the bottom and about a foot from the surface. Trout work this zone for crabs and tend to hit quickly when they see one lest they miss their chance. A sinktip can come in handy for this.

Now we come to the holes in surf zones, rivers, and creeks. Surf zone depressions can be fished two ways: from the beach with a stripping basket attached to the waist and from a boat just outside the surf zone. Trout that don't migrate into deep holes in rivers and creeks move into these surf holes in the winter and can be found packed in there, too. It can be cold and windy—you can almost count on getting wet from spray and crashing waves—but some very big specks live in such holes. A fast (400 to 500 grain) sinking line and a heavy fly, such as a Super Clouser or Gotcha with extra heavy lead eyes, are needed to work these holes correctly.

*Spotted seatrout will enter protected waters, such as
the marina at Calico Jack's on Harkers Island, North Carolina,
to feed around the pilings.*

Deep holes in rivers and creeks also hold big trout come winter. Use the same line and flies that work for holes in the surf. The best holes are those adjacent to flats with dark bottoms, where water warmed by the afternoon sun attracts baitfish. Such holes can be found by slowly motoring up a creek or river with a depth finder running. Record the holes with GPS (Global Positioning System) coordinates or mark them on a map or use both methods.

A medium-fast or fast 8-weight rod, 8½ to 9½ feet long, makes for a good speck rod. St. Croix's Legend Ultra and Sage's RPLXi are very good speck rods.

Fly reels for trout need not be expensive—a fabulous disc drag and a reel with 300 yards of backing capacity aren't necessary. Still, a reel that can handle a drum if one shows up while casting for specks is necessary, as this does happen fairly often.

Light Tackle: Tactics, Techniques, and Tackle

Creeks and rivers lined with spartina certainly represent the classic spotted seatrout habitat, and most anglers after specks in these places use light spinning tackle. Two types of lures are most commonly used to work the structure of these places: soft plastic jigs (usually curltails) and MirrOlures. The jigs are bottom probers, and the MirrOlures, depending on the model, can work the entire water column or surface.

The soft plastic jigs I have found to be most productive—and which are most durable against the teeth of the trout—are Mister Twisters and Kalin's. I have also found that curltail jigs with single tails, as opposed to double tails and split double tails, produce many more trout. Berkley's Power Bait Series of jigs are also good, but they are not as durable. Another jig that has really gotten a lot of attention by speck anglers is the Fin-S Fish. (This bait is produced by Lunker City and requires lead belly weights—not lead heads—designed specifically for them to act right.) In silver phantom, this narrow-bodied jig with the small forked tail can be fantastic.

I normally start off with a 2-inch or 3-inch Mister Twister in chartreuse, chartreuse with black core, neon chartreuse flake, or chartreuse with silver metal flake. My standard lead head is bright orange, but I also carry red, yellow, and white. If I decide to go with a Kalin's, I tie on one that is green/silver laser, watermelon, chartreuse shad, or Tennessee shad.

Presentations of these jigs vary from angler to angler, but in my experience, a short hopping motion is best. The strike most often comes on the drop. If you do not have a rod with a very sensitive tip, keep a tight line during the drop. If the rod tip is sensitive, a little slack is allowable but a moment's hesitation can result in a missed strike.

MirrOlures have been popular trout lures for longer than I can remember, although I do recall receiving my first MirrOlure at the age of eight. One of the best-known trout guides along the Southeast coast is Captain Joe Shute, and no one knows more about MirrOlures and how to use them than Joe.

The three models of MirrOlures Joe uses most often are the 52MR, TT, and 5M. The Model 52MR is the workhorse, and Joe recommends five distinct color patterns: 18 (green with white sides), 26 (red back, white bottom, silver sides), 21 (black back with silver sides), 704 (pink, white, and yellow), 808 (black back, orange sides, gold bottom).

Backwaters lined with spartina, where water is shallow, can be worked well with the 5M MirrOlure, which is a small floater. Just twitch it along the spartina and across the open water slowly. I have had some luck with a slow, steady retrieve, as well.

Confluences call for jigs and MirrOlures but don't forget Rat-L-Traps. The Rat-L-Trap was designed many years ago by Bill Lewis for bass, but speck anglers discovered that it can come up with some downright huge trout. The standard Rat-L-Trap (½ ounce) is about the right size for most situations. The best color patterns are Smokey Joe, Tennessee shad, chartreuse shiner, electric shad (this pattern can imitate a pinfish), tequila sunrise, and Lake Fork special.

For trout in confluence holes (any hole for that matter) with poor visibility, try a Red Zone Rat-L-Trap, which is a suspending model. The best colors are Tennessee shad, bleeding shiner, sunfish, and chrome with a black back.

Rock jetties are best fished with the 52MR series of MirrOlures and jigs. On the Cape Lookout rock jetty, trout lovers use these two lures more than anything else.

Holes in surf zones are fished most consistently with jigs, often larger-than-normal jigs, such as those between 4 and 6 inches long. A heavier lead head is needed to get the jig out and down there. Weights from ½ ounce to ¾ ounce are commonplace.

Any location with deep water, especially if there is a current running, should be considered for the use of live shrimp. Fished below the traditional popping cork, a live shrimp is one of the most deadly seatrout baits. I would rather fish a shrimp than any other natural bait, bar none. While this entails buying some live shrimp or using a cast net to catch them, the extra effort is well worth it.

The idea behind the popping cork is to attract passing trout via sound. Yanking the cork makes a splashing and popping sound, and trout come to have a look at what is going on. They then see the shrimp and eat it.

When using lures for trout, I prefer a 6- or 6½-foot spinning rod with a fast action. My two favorite such rods are Daiwa's Inshore TD-I661-4FS and Shimano's Stimula S166MHA. Both of these rods are rated for line between 8- and 17-pound test. The Daiwa can handle lures between 3/8 and 3/4 ounces, whereas the Shimano can deal with lures between 3/16 and 3/4 ounces. Both rods are 6½ feet long.

When fishing live shrimp with a popping cork, something like a Cabela's Pro Guide Model S662, which is a medium-fast 6½-foot rod, is just right.

Seasons

Spotted seatrout in the Carolinas and Georgia make regional migrations in late fall and early spring. In other words, they just relocate to different water that isn't far away. In summer trout can be found anywhere, but the banks of spartina-lined islands in sounds are always a good choice. Come fall, trout begin moving and school up on their way to deep holes in rivers, creeks, and surf. Spring finds them on the move again to places where they will spread out for the summer.

FLOUNDER

Flounder are a popular game fish because they are found in locations that are often easy to reach, fight fairly well, aren't especially snooty when it comes to eating, and taste good. I am always pleased when I find a flounder on my line.

Habitat

Flatties are found in rivers (often in brackish water), creeks, inlets, sloughs, surf zones, and near jetties. They are frequently encountered in the Atlantic Intracoastal Waterway along flat shelves abutting spartina grass, and can be caught in less than 6 inches of water.

Prey

Baitfish—flounder love baitfish, with striped killifish (alligator minnows), finger mullet, juvenile menhaden, mummichogs, and silversides making up most of their diet along the Southeast coast. However, they do eat shrimp if they have the chance.

Flyfishing: Tactics, Techniques, and Tackle

Generally speaking, my recommendations for spotted seatrout work for flounder, since they inhabit the same waters and eat many of the same things. In fact,

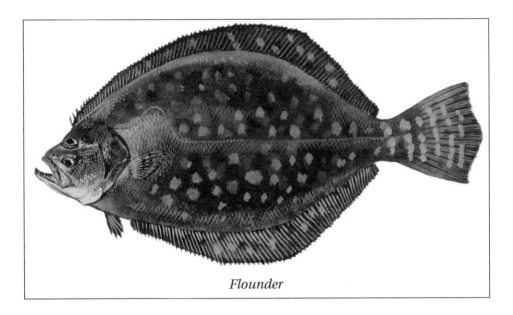

Flounder

many flounder are caught by flyfishers who are looking for trout. So the same rod, reel, lines, and flies used for specks work well for flounder as well.

Light Tackle: Tactics, Techniques, and Tackle

Whereas the tackle is identical to that used for specks, tactics and techniques can vary. For example, in quiet sloughs with but one entrance and exit (backwaters) and a flat, muddy or sandy bottom, live alligator minnows can wreak havoc on big slabs. A simple rig consists of sliding a ¼ to ½ ounce egg sinker onto a line and then tying on a small ball-bearing swivel (size 1 or 2), below which goes 18 inches of 8- or 10-pound test copolymer line. Then tie on a 1/0 bronze octopus hook and run it up through both lips of the alligator minnow. Cast it out and very slowly crawl it along the bottom (about as slowly as possible). This rig and technique is one of the best I have ever used for big flounder.

Seasons

Flounder are around all the time. In winter they move into deeper water, but during warm afternoons move up onto dark-bottomed flats, which hold the heat of the sun, to hunt. Specks do the same thing, of course.

GREAT BARRACUDA

The hit man of the high seas, the great barracuda is many a fish's worst nightmare. Armed to the gills with a monstrous array of teeth, this supreme predator is as fearsome as the tigerfish of the Zambezi and muskellunge of Minnesota and Wisconsin. The cuda has one primary mission in life: kill things—suddenly and graphically—and eat them.

Great Barracuda

Habitat

This seagoing gargoyle skulks around wrecks, rocks, reefs, and other structure. It lives wherever it wants: inshore, near-shore, and offshore. It attacks in 100 feet of water miles out to sea and within spitting distance as you reel in a Spanish mackerel. The great barracuda is the Terminator of the Atlantic Ocean.

Prey

Barracuda prey on any fish available—I won't bother with a long list. Suffice it to say that the barracuda will eat baitfish and game fish so long as it isn't quite as big as the barracuda itself. And it will certainly push the envelope on that account, as well. I have seen barracuda instantly cut a big amberjack in half with one murderous bite.

Flyfishing: Tactics, Techniques, and Tackle

The best way to get a shot at a barracuda in the Carolinas and Georgia is to chum it up off the bottom structure it hides around and then show it something it wants. Run a chum line as usual and watch for a long, narrow fish to appear nearby. Sometimes a barracuda ghosts into the chum slick, other times it explodes onto the scene with horrific force and attitude.

Use a Judas stick to swat the surface while someone else tosses a few chunks of bait and a livey or two into the slick. Use a teaser (a livey on a heavy spinning rod that is allowed to dance around the surface and is then pulled away as the cuda attacks), which seriously irritates the barracuda. Once you have it good and mad, put a large fly in front of it and strip it away quickly. However, don't put the fly too close to the barracuda because this might scare it or make it suspicious. Instead, cast several yards in front of or beside the barracuda and then start stripping fast to make the barracuda think something is trying to get away.

When the barracuda eats the fly, do not set the hook instantly. Instead, wait until the weight of the fish can be felt and then strip strike. Hang on tight! The cuda is going to absolutely lose its mind. It will run like a train, jump like a tarpon, charge the boat, swear out loud, and pull a gun on you—Yowza!

Use a 10-weight false albacore rod for medium-sized barracuda and a 12-weight tarpon rod for bigger models. The reel has got to be great, with lots of capacity and a first-rate drag. Use an albie or tarpon reel, too. A wire shock tippet between 12 (absolute minimum) and 24 inches long is a must.

Light Tackle: Tactics, Techniques, and Tackle

Use the same methods as for flyfishing to get them up and then make them eat. For a rod, use a tarpon spinning rig, and the tarpon reel that goes with it will work for these killers, too.

Tube lures (made of surgical tubing) and assorted crankbaits that are very durable and have stainless steel hooks are needed. Elongated crankbaits seem to work quite well—try a Magnum Rapala.

Live bait is great fun when fishing for barracuda; use a tandem 3-and-1 live-bait rig. This is a stainless steel hook that runs through the bait's lips with a wire leader running back to just behind the bait's dorsal fin. Attached to the wire at that end is a stainless steel treble hook. The size of these hooks will depend on bait size. Experiment, but do not go too large. When in doubt, go smaller.

Seasons

Barracuda seek water temperatures that are subtropical to tropical and can be found anytime the water is in the mid-70s or above. This generally means late spring into autumn.

WEAKFISH OR GRAY TROUT

Commercial overfishing has depleted stocks of these game fish, so they will not be discussed here. To do so would be to encourage more pressure being put on these interesting game fish. Of the Southeast's waters, North Carolina has the "largest" population, but that term is very relative. No government agencies or individuals seem especially concerned with the plight of the gray trout at the moment.

Weakfish or Gray Trout

Spadefish

SPADEFISH

This lovely fish is seldom targeted by anglers, at least when compared to species such as king mackerel, grouper, and spotted seatrout. However, they are available and fun to catch.

Habitat

Near-shore rocks and wrecks are their primary habitat. They can live in large communities on a single wreck, such as some of those found off Bogue Banks.

Prey

Cannonball or blueball jellyfish are a sure favorite, but spadefish also eat shrimp, small crustaceans, and small baitfish.

Flyfishing: Tactics, Techniques, and Tackle

The best way to get at spadefish is to find a near-shore wreck on a nice day (calm water and good visibility without too much of a current running) and suspend a cannonball jellyfish below the boat on a piece of heavy mono. Below the jellyfish on another piece of line tie a few ounces of weight. Lower the jellyfish down to the wreck and every minute or so bring it up slowly a few feet. Watch for spades eating it (they can come out of nowhere and in large schools).

When jellyfish and swarming spadefish are about 15 feet below the surface, start tossing chunks of another jellyfish and shrimp in and let them sink down. Entice the spades up a bit more and then cast a small shrimp imitation in with the real stuff. Watch for a spadefish to come for it and then set the hook when you see it inhale the fly.

Use an 8- or 9-weight red drum rod and the reel that goes with it. A sinktip or sinking line can help get the fly down faster.

Light Tackle: Tactics, Techniques, and Tackle

Read the chumming tactics above to get spades to come up hungry. Red drum spinning tackle is fine and use small hooks—try a 1/0 O'Shaughnessy.

Seasons

Summer is the best time of year to seek this feisty, very pretty, and strong game fish. When the weather is supposed to be really nice and you don't feel like making a long run in the boat, try spadefish. Catch one and you will be hooked forever.

TRIPLETAIL

While this fish isn't chased very often, there are a few anglers who have discovered the tripletail's merits as a game fish. Many of these fish are passed over by anglers in boats who have no idea the fish is even there. That's too bad, because this is a valiant, albeit strange-looking, game fish that is a true fighter.

Habitat

Tripletail live anywhere from the mouths of inlets to well offshore. They hide in surface structure like sargassum, branches and even under cardboard boxes and pallets that have found their way into the water. They are game fish of temperate and subtropical waters.

Flyfishing: Tactics, Techniques, and Tackle

This is easy—look at every piece of surface structure you come across. Watch for this sly, brownish fish hanging right beside the structure pretending to be part of it. They can be hard to see at first, but once you get used to spotting them, they are yours. When you see one, present a shrimp or baitfish imitation—not too big a one —near it and strip the fly in slowly as if the fly isn't scared at the moment. The tripletail will slowly break away from the structure and drift over to the fly. When it gets close enough, it will pounce.

Go with a stout rod, with a 10-weight being the minimum. These are very strong fish that are best controlled with a pretty heavy rod. (Tripletail can weigh more than 50 pounds and sometimes their size, when viewed in the water, can be deceiving.

Tripletail

What looks like maybe a 12- to 15-pound tripletail might weigh 25 pounds or more.) Although you won't need all that much capacity, the reel needs a sound drag.

Light Tackle: Tactics, Techniques, and Tackle

Tossing small jigs, such as a 1/8 ounce marabou jig, at suspended tripletail will work, as will 2-inch to 3½-inch floating Rapalas. I have even caught tripletail on small flatfish. However, a live shrimp is probably the best thing you can toss at a tripletail. They adore shrimp and will get more aggressive with them than jigs and crankbaits. You do not need a popping cork—just toss the shrimp near the structure and watch the tripletail come and get it.

For a rod, I prefer a fairly stout 6- to 7-foot stick that can turn the fish when it tries to bolt back to its lair. Fenwick's HMX Series Model HMXS70H is a 7-foot 1-piece rod that can handle up to 20-pound test and is good as a tripletail rod. Penn's 6500SS reel is a good match.

Seasons

Spring through fall on the Southeast coast, then tripletails start heading out to the Gulf Stream or venture south for the winter.

Crevalle Jack

CREVALLE JACK

I wish I could say that no one knows about the great crevalle jack fishing in Charleston Harbor—the best such spot in the region—but the truth is that the word has gotten out, and now more and more folks are heading for Charleston in the summer, fly rods in hand. It is people like me, of course, who spread the word, and I have nothing good to say about such people. They think only of the happiness of others and shouldn't—despicable.

Habitat

Jacks are wanderers. They roam about looking for baitfish to terrorize, and they do a fine job of it. Places to begin your search include harbors, inlets, rivers, canals, and channels. Do they go elsewhere? Yes, but these five locations are where they are most likely to be found.

Flyfishing: Tactics, Techniques, and Tackle

Jacks are most often found in one of two ways: they are seen feeding on baitfish, which are terrified at the sight of a jack, or they are seen tailing in open water.

This is not technical flyfishing. If you see birds working hard, have a look; jacks may be crashing a school of bait. Even without the birds, jacks can be found feeding because baitfish are jumping all over to escape the very sharp and pointy teeth of the maniacal jacks. Just get a Deceiver or other baitfish pattern in there that looks something like the baitfish being chased to quickly get into a jack. Use a shock tippet of at least 20-pound test, probably more. (I have had jacks go through 16-pound test as though it wasn't even there.) Strip very quickly and make the retrieve erratic. Try a big, light-colored popper with a dark back, too. If you see the jack coming, do not panic and strip strike before he eats it.

Charleston Harbor is good for sightcasting to schooling jacks on the surface. See the fishing in South Carolina section for the scoop.

Small jacks need an 8-weight or so. The big guys require that you upgrade to as much as an 11-weight, although you can certainly get away with a 9- or 10-weight if you know how to use it.

Light Tackle: Tactics, Techniques, and Tackle

Once you have found them as described in the flyfishing section above, get poppers out. Any popper that pushes a lot of water and splashes a lot will get their attention. Go fairly big but not too big—experiment. Keep the popper chugging straight away from the school with steady jerks. Do not stop it for any reason—the jack will know something is wrong since its prey wouldn't stop and wait to be eaten.

If you have live bait, toss it right into the fracas. If the action suddenly stops, and this happens all the time, leave the bait right there. The jacks may not have left but only moved a short distance away, and they often come back within minutes.

Seasons

Crevalle jack are fish of summer in these parts. North Carolina does not have any consistent fishing for them, but they do show up here and there from time to time, usually unexpectedly. Charleston Harbor is your best bet for consistent jack action in the region. Inlets along the Georgia coast also produce good catches.

LADYFISH

Little cousin to the mighty tarpon, the ladyfish has been called the poor man's tarpon. It is a wonderfully acrobatic jumper that is always a lot of fun to catch. I have been catching them since the early 1970s and always look for them if I suspect they are around. I encourage you to do the same.

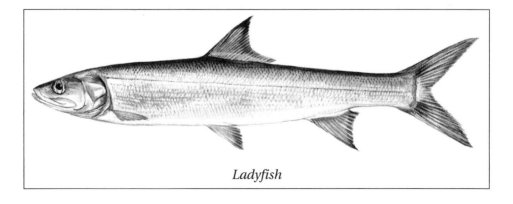

Ladyfish

Habitat

Ladyfish are fond of jetties, rivers and creeks, harbors, bays, flats, sounds, and inlets. They frequently travel in schools, so when found, there are probably more nearby.

Ladyfish are found throughout the region, although infrequently north of South Carolina. However, several years ago I was in a tackle shop in Swansboro, North Carolina, when I overheard (I was eavesdropping, actually) two anglers telling the store owner that they had caught several "baby tarpon" way up the White Oak River around Stella. The store owner just grunted (his standard response to almost anything). Baby tarpon? Way up the White Oak? Suspicious. I am quite sure that what those two characters had discovered was a school of ladyfish rather than a pod of baby tarpon, because tarpon under 40 pounds in North Carolina are very rare, and tarpon of any size that far up the White Oak are rarer still.

Prey

Ladyfish love shrimp and baitfish, with silversides, finger mullet, and menhaden being three important species of the latter.

Flyfishing and Light Tackle: Tactics, Techniques, and Tackle

Ladyfish are usually caught as incidentals by people flyfishing for trout, and for the most part, the very same flyfishing tactics, techniques and tackle can be used for them. One thing that ladyfish don't do is get into deep holes in the winter. If the water gets too cold, they either head south or go find a power plant that is generating warmer water.

Seasons

Once the water warms up into at least the middle 70s, the ladyfish arrive. They stay into fall until water temperatures drop back down, then move to Florida for the winter.

FALSE ALBACORE

I have no way of estimating how much money has been brought into North Carolina since the word got out that false albacore—a.k.a. fat Alberts, little tunny, little tuna, and albies—are incredible game fish in every way except taste. Suffice it to say that there are many guides, motels, marinas, and tackle shops that are very happy indeed with the false albacore fishery, most notably the run that takes place at Cape Lookout during the fall.

Members of the mackerel and tuna family, false albacore are speedsters that hunt their prey by suddenly surprising them and then catching them in a burst of speed. They are sometimes mistaken for bonito and skipjack tuna.

Habitat

Fat Alberts are found from inlets and capes to many miles offshore. They are constantly on the move and chase baitfish regardless of where baitfish try to hide, even

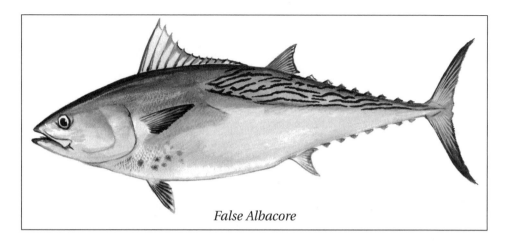

False Albacore

through flooded spartina grass flats. Areas with high concentrations of moving forage seem to draw them the most, with inlets and capes being prime spots.

Prey

The false albacore's diet consists largely of baitfish including, among others, herring, sardines, anchovies, mullet, menhaden, and silversides. They will also eat shrimp and squid.

Flyfishing: Tactics, Techniques, and Tackle

Nothing very technical is needed to fish false albacore. After finding their favorite locations, cast flies at them as they break the surface while chasing bait— that's about it. Also, cast in the blind; the albies might be just beneath the surface.

The fly can make a difference, however. Although albies take a wide variety of baitfish imitations, they sometimes get picky about size and color, and even the pattern itself. For example, on a false albacore outing with Tom Earnhardt, I was getting albies to follow my fly, a 3/0 green and white Deceiver, but they would refuse it at the last second. Tom told me to tie on a small chartreuse-and-white Clouser and throw it amid the next mob of deranged albacore that came by tearing up the surface. I did so and instantly stuck one of them. The lesson is that if you know the false albacore are seeing the fly but are refusing it, switch flies. Tom says that one of the most common mistakes flyfishers make with albies is that they use too big a fly.

The rod (and you) should be able to cast good distances into the wind. False albacore often only appear for a few seconds on the surface before they vanish, only to reappear 100 feet away. You must be able to get the fly to them immediately. And the rod has to have a lot of backbone to lift the fish quickly. I like a Sage RPLXi 9- or 10-weight, 9-foot rod for this.

The reel needs to have a reliable drag that doesn't skip. False albacore make repeated surges and will certainly test your drag. However, line capacity isn't as critical, with 200 yards of 20-pound backing being more than enough.

Cape Lookout is outstanding habitat for false albacore. The flyfishers on this Conch 27, and thousands more like them, all know this and descend on the region from late October through November.

Light Tackle: Tactics, Techniques, and Tackle

As is the case with flyfishing tactics, it's not necessary to be a marine biologist to quickly figure out what a false albacore will take and how to present it. Crankbaits are most popular, with Rapalas and Rat-L-Traps being commonly seen. Just get the lure in front of the feeding albies and start reeling fairly fast, twitching the rod tip while reeling. When the fat Albert hits, strike it with a quick side twist, which should produce a hookup. Be prepared for a fast first run and several more runs after that.

I seldom use spinning gear for false albacore because I enjoy catching them on a fly rod so much, but when the wind is really howling I use a spinning rod. I like a somewhat fast action on a 7- to 7½-foot rod that can cast long distances, but it also has to be a rod that has the lifting power for an albie circling below the boat toward the end of the fight. St. Croix's PS70MF2 is just right for this. This 2-piece rod is rated for line up to 12-pound test and for throwing lures that weigh up to 5/8 ounce. (St. Croix rods are very popular in the upper Midwest as musky, northern pike, and walleye rods.)

A good reel for false albacore will hold a couple hundred yards of 12- or 15-pound test line, such as Super Silver Thread. (An excellent line, Super Silver Thread is the only copolymer line I use nowadays. And no—they do not sponsor me and I do not get free line from them. It's just good line.)

Seasons

Although false albacore can appear at any time of the year along the Southeast coast, autumn is consistently the best time. If you can take the chill, albies sometimes hang out in good numbers off North Carolina well into January.

BLUEFISH

I caught my first bluefish back in 1973 in Maine's St. George River and have pursued them ever since. They aren't sophisticated and they aren't known for spectacular jumps, but they make up for these shortcomings by being vicious, gluttonous, and oftentimes available. These are three qualities I like—in a game fish at least.

Habitat

Inshore and near-shore waters including rivers and creeks, inlets, sounds, bays, flats, sloughs, cuts, canals, around jetties, in the surf, around piers, and in backwaters.

Prey

It might be easier to list forage species that bluefish do not eat. The truth is that they are willing and able to eat a great many things, such as any baitfish and small game fish that gets in front of them. On this extensive menu are sardines, anchovies, menhaden, cigar minnows, striped killifish, mummichogs, sticklebacks, silversides, herring, needlefish, gobies, mullet, Spanish mackerel, croakers, whiting, flounder, pinfish, seatrout, and weakfish. Blues also eat crabs, squid, and shrimp.

Flyfishing: Tactics, Techniques, and Tackle

Once blues are located by watching for feeding frenzies or other feeding activity, or by prospecting around rips, in channels, and around structure, show them a Deceiver or Clouser. If they see it and it's moving, they are likely to eat it. The size of the fly depends on the size of the average blue in the vicinity. For instance, if you're after big winter blues found along the Outer Banks, go with the largest Deceiver or Clouser (try a Super Clouser) available. Smaller blues like a bit smaller fly, although there are many instances of very small blues pouncing on flies as big as they are.

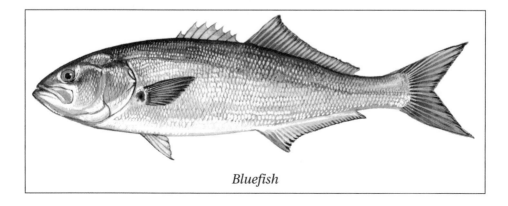

Bluefish

There is no single rod that can handle all bluefish properly. Whereas an 8-weight will do for many small blues (called "snappers") in an estuary, such a rod would be all but useless against 20-pound blues in the winter surf. A nice rod for small blues is Scott's Heliply Series Model HP 888/3, which is an 8-foot 8-inch, 3-piece 8-weight. Blues in the 8- to 12-pound range would need something like a Sage Model 1090-4 RPL+ (a 4-piece 9-foot 10-weight). Truly big blues demand an 11- or 12-weight, such as Winston's Model 9012-5, which is a 5-piece, 9-foot 12-weight.

Small blues don't need a special reel. But blues big enough to fool with a drag should be handled with a solid reel and good drag.

A shock tippet of 15-pound mono is needed for small blues and a 20-pound wire tippet for big ones.

Light Tackle: Tactics, Techniques, and Tackle

The tactics in the flyfishing section used to find blues can be used for light tackle, too, of course. But what of tackle? Think two lures: curltail jigs and Got-Cha plugs. These two lures will take 90 percent of small blues. Outside inlets where larger blues often patrol, use diving crankbaits like Magnum Rapalas. During a feeding frenzy of large blues, a Zara Spook walked through the fray can bring murderous results very quickly.

One thing about those curltail jigs for small blues: The little toothy buggers tend to bite off the tail of the jig and miss the hook, which can drive you nuts. To stop them from doing this, attach a short stinger hook to the upper hook. This almost always does the trick.

Rods and reels for the small guys? Use speck tackle. For the big guys, use false albacore tackle.

Seasons

Spring all the way through autumn sees many blues in Southeast waters. Come winter they move offshore or head south to Florida.

DOLPHIN

This bluewater game fish is one of the most beautiful in the sea and is very well suited for both fly gear and light tackle. These are most often caught when small—less than 5 pounds—but larger fish in the 30- and 40-pound range are caught frequently as well.

Habitat

Subtropical and tropical by nature, dolphins are found offshore over structure and amid sargassum. They are attracted to anything that floats and almost never venture into near-shore waters.

Prey

Flyingfish are their favorite, but they will also eat cigar minnows, various baitfish like juvenile filefish and triggerfish, squid, menhaden, mullet, small crabs (dislodged from sargassum), and other forage.

Dolphin

Flyfishing: Tactics, Techniques, and Tackle

Probe sargassum (whether large mats, broken mats, or small pieces) with a small Clouser or Deceiver. Toss a few pieces of chum around mats to see if any dolphin appear. With fly rods at the ready, trolling around sargassum or other surface structure to see if any dolphin are in the area is a good way to get started. When one is hooked, it is allowed to stay on the line and remain in the water. This draws other dolphin to it. Once the hooked dolphin is within casting range, the flies are sent out. The dolphin's willingness to stay very close to a hooked comrade is responsible for many catches.

An 8- or 9-weight rod, fast to medium-fast action, is all that's needed. I like the standard 9-foot rod, with a Scott Eclipse 8-weight being my all-time favorite dolphin rod.

The reel should have a good drag, not so much for the average dolphin but in case something else with a lot more power shows up, such as a wahoo or even a sailfish, or a giant bull dolphin piling into the fracas. Something like an Orvis Odyssey III is right, or perhaps a Scientific Anglers System 2 (not an especially expensive reel but one I use all the time and which has yet to have fail me).

I've found that a handful of flies in yellow, chartreuse, and white are the most productive. Go with smallish Clousers (2/0) and Deceivers (2/0 or 3/0) for the fastest action. Poppers can also be very effective; I keep a selection close at hand at all times when looking for dolphin. You don't often need a much larger selection because an average dolphin isn't all that smart and likes to eat.

To try these fun game fish in North Carolina, give Captain Joe Shute a call. He now runs regular trips for flyfishers interested in catching dolphin on the fly. He is listed in the North Carolina fishing section under guides.

A decent male dolphin caught during a king mackerel tournament out of Swansboro, North Carolina. Dolphin are often in the same offshore areas as kings.

Light-Tackle: Tactics, Techniques, and Tackle

Dolphin are often anxious to hit chunks of bait, live baitfish, jigs (yellow, chartreuse, and white are best, but green, brown, and gray can work, too), and crankbaits. I often use my seatrout jigs for dolphin.

Having surface structure such as sargassum, forage in the area, and water temperatures in the upper 70s at a minimum are three factors crucial to finding dolphin that are ready to eat.

Seasons

Think warm—these are subtropical and tropical fish requiring warm water to be happy. Offshore in the Gulf Stream, they can be found nearly year-round, but they won't leave the Gulf Stream until the surrounding water warms up. The mid-80s surely aren't too warm for dolphin.

The fastest dolphin action runs from May through September, although some great October catches are reported if the surface temps stay up there.

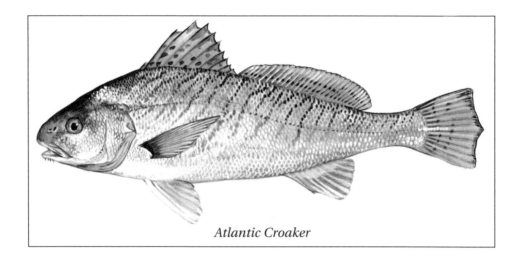

Atlantic Croaker

ATLANTIC CROAKER

This amusing game fish doesn't get enough respect, which is a shame, because croakers can salvage a bad day and are good game fish for beginners to learn on. Nearly everything about the lowly croaker is simple.

Habitat

Croakers can be found in rivers and creeks, inlets, and around piers, and they are attracted to structure and holes.

Prey

Croakers eat crustaceans, marine worms, and whatever small baitfish they can catch.

Flyfishing: Tactics, Techniques, and Tackle

Not much to it, really. Flies with the ability to sink fast and stay close to or on the bottom are best. Small Clousers and shrimp patterns work well. Menhaden oil applied to the fly will catch even more. A sinktip of full-sinking line is most useful.

Rod weight? No more than a 7-weight for sure, with a 6-weight being even better in most cases. St. Croix's Imperial Model IF8667 is perfect. This is an 8-foot 6-inch, 2-piece moderate-action rod for 6- and 7-weight lines. The reel can be low end. No drag is needed and very little capacity is needed.

Light Tackle: Tactics, Techniques, and Tackle

No technical stuff here, either. I have caught innumerable croakers using one technique: throwing a marabou jig into a hole near a buoy or bridge. I use either a white or pink jig and soak it with menhaden oil and then attach a squid trailer, which is a 1-inch long, ¼ inch wide strip of squid body. Hopped along the bottom, this rig is unbeatable.

I use an ultralight spinning rod for croakers. Cabela's 5-foot, 1-piece, moderate-action, Pro Guide Model S501 is one of my favorites. For a reel I use a Shimano Sidestab Model SI-1000RB or a Daiwa Regal Model S1500iA. Both of these reels are inexpensive and are all that is needed for croakers, but they can also handle a speck if one shows up. Go no heavier than 6-pound test Super Silver Thread.

Seasons

Croakers are always around, but spring into fall is best.

SPANISH MACKEREL

Spanish mackerel are caught most often by pier anglers and spincasters in boats working inlets and areas just outside the surf zone. They are good fighters, although not great, and are quite abundant much of the time. Pretty, too.

Constantly on the run, these little speedsters are like miniature kings and can weigh 10 pounds or so. When you see one, there are more in the vicinity.

Habitat

Spanish mackerel are inshore and near-shore game fish that show up suddenly and vanish just as suddenly, so you have to be ready for them. Look around the lower (wider and deeper) ends of rivers, bays, sounds, inlets, and from the back of the surf zone out a few miles but within sight of land.

Prey

These mackerel eat mostly baitfish, with menhaden and mullet being favorites, but shrimp are also on the menu.

Flyfishing: Tactics, Techniques, and Tackle

To locate these fish, watch for birds working a school of baitfish that are being eaten up by a pack of marauding Spanish. Also be on the lookout for jumping Spanish, although this doesn't always mean that they are feeding—they may just be cavorting and racing to get somewhere.

After determining the direction Spanish mackerel are moving and how fast, get in front of them but off to one side. Start casting well before sighting them because they are probably moving faster than they appear. They need to see the fly either right in front of them or just off to one side and in front of them. Spanish don't like to turn around and mill about eating bait that has been wounded; they leave it for the next Spanish most of the time.

Spanish Mackerel

Flies are easy—use Deceivers (2/0 to 3/0) in green and white, all white, or blue and white. Strip fast and erratically. When one hits, just hold on and it will usually hook itself. At the most, give it a quick strip strike.

I don't like to go any heavier than an 8-weight rod that is 9 feet or 9 feet 6 inches long with a moderately fast action. Fly Logic's FLO+ 908/3 is a very good Spanish rod.

The reel should be good but it need not be stupendous insofar as drag and capacity go.

Light Tackle: Tactics, Techniques, and Tackle

When a working school of Spanish is in sight, get to within casting distance but just barely (a school can be easily spooked). Use a Got-Cha plug with gold hooks and whip it out in front of them, then start cranking fast and snapping the rod tip. I know of few Spanish who turn their nose up at this approach.

Spoons are good too, with the Clark spoon being very popular. This lure is usually trolled with a feather duster in front of it. When a school is in sight, get in front of it a few hundred feet and start letting out line. Cut across the path of the school so that the spoon is dragged right in front of them. Do not go too slowly because Spanish are used to bait running from them. And don't get too close to the school when getting past them—they will scatter and sound.

Inside inlets, try trolling at a fairly fast pace with a curltail jig. Grays, greens, browns, and silvers all work. I don't think the color of the lead head makes all that much difference most of the time.

Seasons

Spanish mackerel show up in spring between early and late March and sometimes early April. Once they arrive, they stay into fall, sometimes late in the fall. They then move south to Florida.

KING MACKEREL

King mackerel generate more money and general excitement than any other game fish species along the Southeast coast. Huge tournaments are held from spring through fall, and there can be so many boats on the water, it looks like some kind of amphibious invasion.

There is good reason for the popularity of the king mackerel (aka king and king-fish): their numbers are high; they can be hard to find; fight vigorously; grow very large; are found inshore, near-shore, and offshore; hit very hard; and taste great. Big kings get the nickname "smoker" because they take the line so fast, it appears that the drag is smoking.

They are notorious for insane leaps many feet above the surface, especially right after they feel the hook sink in. They will attempt to empty the reel of line. Add the fact that in a tournament like the annual Hardy's, a winner can walk away with a truck full of money (tens of thousands of dollars).

Habitat

Kings are found from the surf zone (they are frequently caught by pier anglers who use special two-rod rigs to float live bait off the end of the pier) to inlets to channels inside inlets to just outside of inlets to far offshore (into the Gulf Stream). They roam the open seas and hang out over bottom structure within view of the beach. The only place they won't go, it seems, is up a river.

Kings are found from the surface to more than 100 feet deep. It all depends on where food is available and the water temperature.

Prey

Boy, they eat a lot of everything, including menhaden, cigar minnows, ribbon-fish, pinfish, juvenile fish of various species, smaller game fish (Spanish mackerel, etc.), shrimp, flyingfish, mullet, and a host of other things. King mackerel are great opportunists.

Flyfishing: Tactics, Techniques, and Tackle

Flyfishing for kings really began to get established in the Keys. Today, very few flyfishers target kings, I believe, because they just don't know how to do it correctly. The key is the chum slick.

A menhaden or other good chum slick, run back over structure where kings are holding, can bring fish up to investigate. Once they are seen in the slick, a few livies are tossed in along with a few larger chunks of bait. This fires the kings up and gets them thinking about food. When they get riled, put a Lefty's Deceiver, Cockroach, Clouser, Blanton's Sar-Mul-Mac, pencil popper, Tabory's Sea Rat, or similar baitfish imitation right into the slick and start stripping it vigorously to mimic a baitfish trying to flee.

Warning: Be ready to strip strike the king when it hits, have a good grip on the rod, and have the drag set right. A king is going to bolt at a very high rate of speed and

King Mackerel

maybe jump wildly and repeatedly. Be ready to bow to the king every time it leaves the water, and be ready for sudden runs even when it seems tired and is close to the boat. Never trust a king mackerel.

The rod should be at least a 9-weight, 9-foot fast-action rod that has backbone to set the hook hard. A 10-weight isn't too heavy.

As for the reel, think drag and capacity. The king is absolutely going to try out the drag and is going to run long distances, as I said, especially on the first run. Two hundred yards of 20-pound backing is the minimum.

Use a shock tippet of at least 12 inches of 50-pound test; kings have serious teeth and a mouthful of them at that. Remember, however, that the International Game Fish Association (IGFA) says that the maximum length of a shock tippet is 12 inches when submitting for a record.

Light Tackle: Tactics, Techniques, and Tackle

Because kings have such a diverse diet, many types of lures and baits work, as do various presentations of them. For example, a dead cigar minnow tossed over some bottom structure 130 feet down and allowed to drift near the surface can be fantastic if other fish, such as grouper and snapper, are feeding below. This works best if another boat is nearby and its anglers are fishing the bottom (look for party boats).

Large spoons should be tried, such as Clarks, Krocodiles, Doctors, Mepps Syclops, Dardevles, and Crippled Herrings. Add a feather duster a few feet in front of the spoon to sweeten the pot.

Cast and trolled crankbaits are also an option, with silver or gold finishes and dark backs being most productive in my experience. I have found that longer, thinner crankbaits seem to take more kings than shorter, fatter models. Some worth trying are the Countdown Rapalas, jointed Rapalas, jointed Countdown Rapalas, Husky Jerk Rapalas, Smithwick Rattlin' Rogues, Yo-Zuri Crystal Minnows (expensive but quite good), and Deep Thundersticks.

To ward off rust and corrosion, I recommend replacing the standard hooks that come on these lures with stainless steel hooks of the same size.

*A duster is useful
for trolled bait
and some lures.*

When kings have come all the way up and are feeding aggressively in a chum slick on the surface, try some surface jerkbaits. Kings hit these things viciously. Go with Zara Spooks ("walking the dog" with a Zara Spook in a king feeding frenzy can be murder), Skitterpops (especially in silver blue), and Dalton Specials. I am convinced that the size of the splash these surface plugs make is important. The more splash, the more hits.

Large yellow, white, or chartreuse bucktail jigs with soft plastic curltail trailers are also good—the larger the better. I sometimes run a flasher 6 feet in front of the jig to draw more attention. The jig can also have a set of small treble hooks with 30-pound wire between them run back down the length of a ribbonfish, with the jig at the head of the ribbonfish.

This large king is probably a "money" fish, meaning it could win some money in a tournament. Is killing such large fish—the ones with the best genes—damaging the king population?

Feather dusters at the head of cigar minnows are a good way to draw kings, as are slow-trolled live menhaden. I suspect that more trophy kings are taken by this latter method than any other.

The downrigger is a critical piece of gear when after kings. One never knows at what depth the kings are going to be holding, and trolling some of these aforementioned baits and lures at various depths is a great way to find kings. A set of downriggers worked with assorted baits and lures at various depths, when worked over structure in water that is in the king's comfort zone (temperatures about the mid-70s to the mid-80s, depending on who you ask), is one of the very best ways to locate cruising kings.

Spinning rods that are between 6 and 7½ feet long are the norm, fast to medium-fast action. Get a good reel with a drag that will not burn up.

Seasons

Technically speaking, there really isn't a season for kings along the Southeast coast. They are always there, but you have to find them. Some move offshore during the winter and stay in the warmer Gulf Stream and start heading out when the water gets and stays in the 60s.

April is probably the month when most kings begin moving inshore. They hang around close to land until November or so, when they relocate for the colder months.

A Word on King Mackerel Tournaments

I mentioned king mackerel tournaments earlier. These events are fun and a pile of money can be made by winning or placing well, but the jury is still out on what effect these tournaments have on king populations. They are not like bass tournaments, where bass are kept in live wells and released after weighing. The vast majority of king mackerel tournaments are catch-and-kill because kings can't be kept alive in live wells. (Besides, how are you even going to get a 50-pound king into a live well?) With so much pressure from tournaments and recreational anglers on these fish, populations need to be monitored. As responsible sportsmen, the last thing we want to be accused of is knowingly harvesting king mackerel to such a degree that populations fall off dramatically.

The Southern Kingfish Association is the organization most tightly associated with tournaments. We must call on them to work even more closely with responsible fisheries management agencies to insure we do not damage king mackerel populations.

WAHOO

The speedy, powerful, and beautiful wahoo is slowly but surely becoming more and more of a target for flyfishers and light-tackle anglers, although the vast majority are still caught by bluewater anglers trolling with heavy gear for marlin, sailfish, tuna, and dolphin.

Habitat

Wahoo are found well offshore, usually many miles. The Gulf Stream is a favored haunt. Wahoo are subtropical and tropical game fish, which means that they prefer water to be in the high 70s or above.

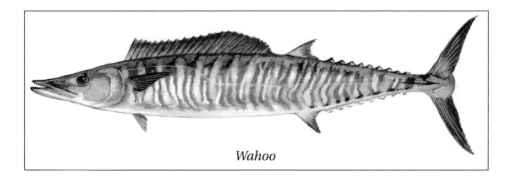

Wahoo

I wasn't exactly looking for this wahoo when it hit, but I didn't mind it showing up. Photo by Ken Wiles.

Prey

One of the most important wahoo forage items is the flyingfish. Find them and there might well be wahoo around. Bottom structure that produces upwelling currents, which carry nutrients and bait to the surface, can be important in finding wahoo. Also look for sargassum that holds baitfish (put on a diver's mask and actually look under the sargassum for baitfish). Wahoo also eat squid.

Flyfishing: Tactics, Techniques, and Tackle

Use dolphin tactics, especially with chum, and be ready to cast instantly when one comes into the chum slick. These guys are very fast and will show up and depart in a second.

Go with a large fly akin to a 4/0 Deceiver, Sardina, Bunker, Sar-Mul-Mac, or Abel Anchovy. Use a heavy shock tippet (30-pound test is light) because wahoo have nasty teeth.

Rods have to be 12-weights and up for serious wahoo fishing. Go with a fast action in a 9- or 10-footer.

Don't skimp on a reel—Penn's 4G and Orvis' Vortex 11/12 are very good for wahoo. Both these reels have the drags and capacities to handle wahoo.

Light Tackle: Tactics, Techniques, and Tackle

Now that we've covered how to find wahoo and hook up with one (don't forget to try live bait once a wahoo is seen in the slick), let's get right into tackle.

A 6½- to 7½-foot fast rod, such as a Fenwick GPLS70H-2 (a 7-foot, 2-piece fast rod rated to 20-pound test) is correct for wahoo. Match the reel to it with something like Penn's 7500SS.

Be ready for a wahoo's first screaming run and then the next few screaming runs. Wahoo tend to make sudden changes in direction, so watch it.

Seasons

Although many wahoo are caught in the summer, winter can be the fastest action of the year, especially out near and in the Gulf Stream. These are subtropical and tropical fish, so warm water is demanded—70s and above.

YELLOWFIN TUNA

Bringing in a yellowfin can be like reeling up a safe—no exaggeration. Yellowfin are being sought by more anglers with fly and light tackle, so here is some info for getting started in the right direction.

Habitat

These tuna are found offshore in blue water most of the time. They do come in occasionally, but most often they are well outside the inlet. When they do come in, however, it can get crazy.

Prey

Tuna eat all manner of schooling baitfish and squid. Flyingfish are important, as are small bonito, skipjack tuna, mackerel, and the like.

Flyfishing: Tactics, Techniques, and Tackle

Watch for yellowfins busting bait on the surface or chum them up. When they come in, get the fly out there. If one misses it—and this happens all the time—leave the fly in and keep stripping. Another might be along any second.

Yellowfin are fast, unbelievably strong fish that grow to huge proportions. Never underestimate how quickly they can appear and eat a fly, then run like mad and

Yellowfin Tuna

sound. A yellowfin will fight a long time unless the right tackle is used and put to the fish every time there's a chance.

The same flies used for wahoo will work for yellowfin, but a 14-weight is necessary to lift the bugger from the depths, where it likes to dive after the initial runs. It then becomes a test of wills. The best yellowfin rod I have used is an Orvis Trident 8614-3. This rod can lift a car out of the Mariana Trench. Fix a Vortex 13/14 to it and go fishing.

Light Tackle: Tactics, Techniques, and Tackle

Toss a live menhaden or mullet into the feeding frenzy and watch the fireworks, or troll a balao (ballyhoo) in a known yellowfin area until something tries to tear you out of the boat.

Yellowfin tackle is possibly the stoutest light tackle a fisherman might use, but it is needed to control the fish. I use a Penn PG-5870 rod, which is a 1-piece rated to 25-pound test. I use a Penn 7500SS with it.

Seasons

March and April see yellowfin arrive west of the Gulf Stream, but they can be found all winter in the Gulf Stream. They stay around well into autumn.

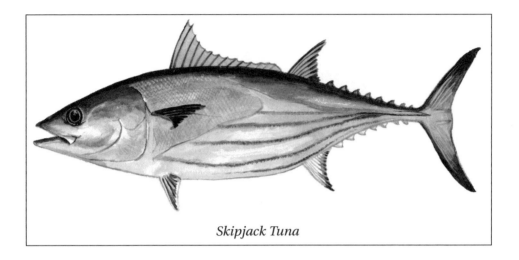

Skipjack Tuna

SKIPJACK TUNA

Almost always caught incidentally out in the Gulf Stream or close to it, skipjack tuna are very much like false albacore. Use the same tackle, including flies, for small ones, but those in the 20-pound range require a heavier rod, such as a 12-weight or even a 13-weight.

Skipjacks can be found in the Gulf Stream off the Carolinas and Georgia all the time, but they are a hit-or-miss game fish.

SHEEPSHEAD

The clever, strong, and pugnacious sheepshead is very popular among light-tackle anglers who have discovered their many notable qualities, but flyfishers have yet to catch on. I hope to change that.

Habitat

A game fish of inshore structure such as pier or dock pilings and rock piles, this species of porgy is a crafty bugger. They can often be spotted working pilings if the water is clear, and even if they aren't visible, they might very well be there. Rivers and inlets with piers on old pilings (covered with barnacles and other forms of sea life) and oyster-encrusted rocks in spartina openings and channels attract and hold sheepshead.

Sheepshead

Prey

Sheepshead eat crustaceans mostly, with crabs being their favorite and shrimp their second favorite. However, they will eat small baitfish if they seem easy to catch and are right near their structure.

Flyfishing: Tactics, Techniques, and Tackle

On flats covered with flooded spartina and in situations where it's possible to cast at pilings so that the fly gets very close to structure, sheepshead can become vulnerable to a flyfisher's approaches. I especially like stalking sheepshead on the flats, but caution and stealth are needed because sheepshead are nervous—one look at your mug and they'll run for it.

Sheepshead work structure by circling it. Once a sheepshead is spotted, watch it for a few minutes to see how it's moving around structure. Get ready to cast when a sheepshead moves to the back side of the structure so that the structure is between you and it. Cast just before you think the sheepshead is going to reappear.

Crab and shrimp patterns are best. Jack's Fighting Crab is a top choice, with Del's Merkin, the McCrab, and the Flexo Crab being good choices, too. For shrimp patterns try a Borski's Fur Shrimp or a Bramblett's Swimming Shrimp. The crab and shrimp imitations should be size 2 or 4.

For tackle, use spotted seatrout gear. When using a sinktip or full-sinking line while blind casting to structure, make sure the leader is very short (no more than 30 inches). Pay attention because strikes can be very soft. If there's any hesitation, strip strike and be ready to pull the sheepshead away from the structure so it doesn't wrap the leader around it and break it off.

Light Tackle: Tactics, Techniques, and Tackle

Dropping live fiddler crabs and pieces of shrimp down beside pilings from bridges, piers, and docks is the way most anglers catch sheepshead—it's simple, but it works. To increase the odds, catch a bunch of fiddlers at low tide (just throw a thin-mesh cast net over them; sneak up on them through the spartina so they don't see you and scatter) and put them in a large pickle jar. At a fishing location, fill the jar with water, put the lid on, and tie some very heavy mono around the lid. Now drop the jar into the water right beside the structure. Let it sink and tie it off.

Sheepshead will see all the fiddlers swimming around inside the jar and come for a look. They usually just hang out right around the jar gawking at all the goodies. Now drop a live fiddler in attached to a small stainless steel hook. It won't take long at all in most cases for a sheepshead to come over and eat it.

A sensitive tip on the spinning rod is needed as well as your best trout rod. When there's a change in the bait's position or a very light tug, set the hook. The old adage used by experienced sheepshead anglers is to set the hook two seconds or so before the strike is felt.

Seasons

Spring through fall.

GREATER AMBERJACK

The amberjack is primarily a fish of offshore bottom structure, although it wanders inshore from time to time for whatever reason. They are strong fighters that can really get anglers worked up and aggressive. To demonstrate this fact, read the sidebar, "Striking Oil on the *Continental Shelf*," which is a true story that first appeared in print in the June/July 1998 issue of *The Sportfishing Report*.

Habitat

Amberjack prefer to hang out above offshore bottom structure close to the bottom, but they are certainly not glued there. They will readily leave the bottom and come all the way to the surface if it seems to be in their best interest, i.e., there appears to be a lot of feeding going on up there and they want to get in on the action. In summer they sometimes wander in to piers and give some poor guy using a light spinning rod an awful scare—and a huge thrill.

Prey

If it's there and swimming around and they think they can swallow it, amberjacks will eat it. They are aggressive gluttons.

Flyfishing: Tactics, Techniques, and Tackle

Chum them up. Because they like to hang around the bottom, it will be difficult to get the chum down there. Amberjacks, once they get the scent, will start up the line feeding along the way. When they're in sight, start whacking the water with a gaff or

Greater Amberjack

something (the "Judas stick" technique). This sound can be heard by feeding jacks and will usually keep them coming up to see what is happening.

Now throw the fly in and start stripping. Avoid the urge to set the hook hard and fast because this often results in a missed fish. Let the fish eat it and turn down again, then hang on and lift the rod when pressure is felt. This should do the trick, since amberjacks are not dainty eaters. When they see something they want, they just go get it.

I don't go with anything lighter than a 9-weight rod that has good lifting power (amberjack like to slug it out much like a tuna does by heading straight down). I like a rod between 8 feet 6 inches and 9 feet in length, with two good choices being R.L. Winston's Model 9010-5 (a 9-foot 10-weight, 5-piece rod that I trust when lifting) and Thomas & Thomas' Model HS910S-4 (a 9-foot 10-weight, 4-piece). However, these rod weights are for smaller amberjack. Larger jacks require a 12-weight at a minimum, and a 14-weight isn't too heavy. In fact, Capt. Joe Shute uses 14-weight rods all the time for the big amberjacks he chums up offshore. I like R.L. Winston's Model 9012-5 for a 9-foot 12-weight, and Sage's Model 1489-3 RPLXi for an 8-foot 9-inch 14-weight.

A reel with a smooth drag and lots of capacity—for when the amberjack sounds —is required.

As for flies, I am not convinced that hungry amberjacks have a definite color, size, or pattern preference. Try something generic like a 3/0 gold and maroon Clouser.

Light Tackle: Tactics, Techniques, and Tackle

A whole squid or cigar minnow fished close to the bottom is a favorite bait, but amberjacks also hit pieces of cut bait and squid. They are notorious for hitting small snappers and spottail pinfish that are being hauled up, too.

A good amberjack rod is about 6 feet long with a powerful butt for lifting, such as a Fenwick Model HMXS60MH, which is a 6-foot 1-piece rod rated for line up to 20-pound test. Attached to it is a reel that sports a reliable drag and plenty of capacity, because the jack is going to regain a purchase near the bottom after it is hooked. An Ahab 16A or 20A works well.

Striking Oil
on the *Continental Shelf*

The art and science of head (party) boat fishing is something comparatively few anglers ever really get a good grasp of . You can always tell the pros. They're the guys who show up at the dock at least two hours before the office even opens, this to make sure they are first or nearly first in line so that they can stake out the coveted stern position before the next guy gets to it. They will have their own rods (two for sure; a bottom rod for grouper, snapper, and triggerfish, and a surface rod for dolphin and kings) and will be toting a weathered tackle box crammed with specialized bottom rigs and secret gadgets. Their cooler will be filled with soft drinks, beer, cigar minnows, and perhaps a frozen mackerel or two. They'll be wearing footwear—often rubber boots or old sneakers—that they have found to be practical on deck over the years, along with a couple of large rags, a fillet knife, and pliers, the latter two items in a holster attached to their belt. They move about the boat with ease and familiarity and know the mates by name.

The novices you can identify, too. They arrive 20 minutes before the boat sails and are carrying nothing but their wallet.

I fall into the pro category, of course, and I know all the tricks of the trade, usually coming home with at least one fish that comes close to taking the day's big-fish pot and sometimes taking home the money. But I recall the day aboard the *Continental Shelf* out of Morehead City that I was shown how a real pro operates. I was sworn to secrecy not to reveal the master's name, but his initials are John Nuckolls.

John and I arrived early and secured our positions along the stern at the starboard corner. I had the corner itself and John was on my left as you face aft. We tied our rods to the rail, which safely established a buffer zone for elbow and maneuvering room. We were confident that we would, as usual, do very well indeed.

Pizza Cannon, the captain, anchored the boat over a wreck and sounded the horn to lower your baits. John and I were ready and our baits hit bottom first. Instantly we both felt tugs and we set the hooks, rods bending nicely. Four triggers were hauled up. We dropped them down again right away and again nailed four fish, this time two triggers and two vermilion snapper. This went on for about an hour with John and I slaying the fish like nobody's business, the chunks of cut squid and cigar minnows we were using being of great interest to what appeared to be every fish on the bottom. The other anglers were doing only so so. We began to get bad looks from them.

John and I were spraying our bait with menhaden oil—Captain Joe Shute's menhaden oil, in fact—which is the best anywhere. Yes, we were cheating and cheating damn well, thank you, and therein lies a tale.

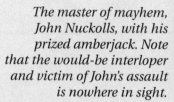

The master of mayhem, John Nuckolls, with his prized amberjack. Note that the would-be interloper and victim of John's assault is nowhere in sight.

After the first hour we noticed that the anglers to John's left were beginning to encroach on us, cleverly moving closer and closer to us in a brazen attempt to get near the lucky spots on the rail that we obviously had. The fellow right beside John, a chubby, pasty looking kid of perhaps 20 years, was really getting aggressive and actually rubbed elbows with John on two occasions before the master stopped him cold.

I saw the dark look on John's battle-scared (well, at least truck-crash scared) face and knew that trouble was afoot. Reaching into his pocket, I saw him remove the spray bottle of menhaden oil; however, John's bait was still on bottom. Uh-oh.

A fish hit John's bait and he set the hook, then tucked the rod under his left arm, the menhaden oil cocked and ready for employment in his right hand, which was hanging at his side. With the rod bending under his left arm, the kid tried to make his move as John took a step to his right to pull the fish away from the other lines. The kid also stepped to the right, thinking he had just gained a foot or so of lucky rail. John fired instantly.

Stepping back from the rail two steps, John pointed the bottle into the air and pushed the plunger, the oil perfectly catching the light breeze and sailing right into the unsuspecting kid's face, who was apparently inhaling at the very moment the oil passed by. The effect was immediate and stunning.

"Erckkkkk. Erckkkkkkkk. Akkkkkk," the foolish encroacher croaked, his face twisted in a grotesque mask of green revulsion. His rod fell to the deck and a stream of puke shot from his mouth, much like that scene from *The Exorcist*. He vanished forward to complete his incessant retching, which lasted for some while.

Strangely, no one claimed his spot and John and I were left in peace to catch great hoards of fish. In fact, a few anglers along the stern rail actually moved to the side rail.

Novice and other anglers who think it smart to encroach on the pros, beware: the man you are standing beside might be armed, and he might be willing to defend his section of rail with a hideous weapon deserving of being banned by the Geneva Conventions.

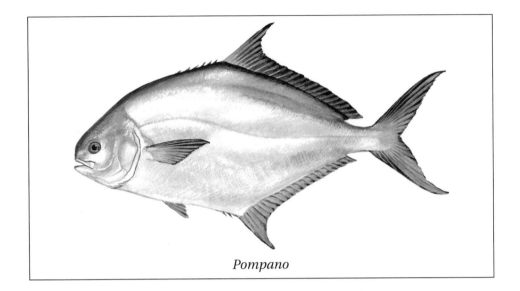

Pompano

Seasons

Amberjacks can be found offshore throughout the year and inshore from time to time around piers during the warmer months.

POMPANO

Pompano are small panfish-like fish of the inner surf zone. They eat sand fleas. I suppose you could go catch some with a sand flea fly, but I don't know of any, so you are going to have to tie it yourself. Use a stripping basket and a sinking line, maybe a 6-weight. A 9-foot rod with a moderate fast action should suffice. Look for pompano spring through fall.

ATLANTIC BONITO

Like the now popular autumn run of false albacore, these members of the mackerel and tuna family are now being pursued by more anglers, especially flyfishers. Soon they may be as popular as the bonito runs along the coast of Southern California.

Habitat

Bonito are fish of the open ocean and only occasionally come near shore. They are fast fish that never stop to rest, chasing baitfish everywhere they go. They always travel in schools and can attain weights of 10 pounds or so. In the Gulf Stream they can be thick.

Atlantic Bonito

Prey

Menhaden, Spanish sardines, and anchovies are three important forage fish for bonito, but bonito will take any baitfish it finds, including flyingfish. Shrimp don't seem to be all that important to the bonito, although they will eat them if the opportunity presents itself.

Flyfishing: Tactics, Techniques, and Tackle

Finding bonito can be done by several methods: watching for birds working a school of baitfish being attacked by bonito; watching for frothy water that could indicate bonito feeding; looking for jumping bonito as they race along the surface; listening for other anglers talking on their radios about the bonito they've found and then getting them to tell you where they are (maybe they will, maybe they won't); staying in areas offshore, even out to the Gulf Stream, where bonito have been lately.

Bonito can be very much like dolphin in that they follow and stay near a bonito that is hooked. Therefore, a good way to get them to come close enough to the boat for a cast is to troll until you hit one. Once hooked, fly rods are brought into action. Note, however, that bonito may not stick around the boat watching their hapless friend as long as dolphins do.

Once located, bonito feed much like false albacore, eating Clousers and the like. One popular fly is the Bonito Bunny in sizes 2 and 4. This all-white fly imitates a silvery baitfish. Pencil poppers and Skipping Bugs work as well (size 2 is best).

A fast 9-weight 9-foot rod is needed a lot of the time to deliver flies in the offshore breeze. The Scott Tactical Series is a solid choice. Orvis' 4-piece Trident TL 909-4 is also a decent bonito rod (the 2-piece is too slow).

The reel has to have at least 200 yards of backing capacity and needs a good drag. Bonito run and run fast, just like their cousins. Go with a false albacore reel.

Light Tackle: Tactics, Techniques, and Tackle

I'll keep this easy: use false albacore tackle with the same techniques. I haven't found any significant difference in tactics or techniques being needed, nor tackle.

Seasons

Off Georgia and southernmost South Carolina, bonito show up in March. Between there and the Virginia border they arrive in April. Remember, however, that fish are not always predictable and sometimes they are earlier or later than the previous year. Keep your eyes and ears open.

Forage Species

There are 23 marine forage species eaten by game fish along the Southeast coast. Fortunately, it's not necessary be an expert in the natural history of each and how it relates to every species of game fish in the region to be a successful flyfisher or light-tackle angler.

What a fisherman needs to know is what forage species live in the specific ecosystem to be fished at a particular time. In other words:

- what species live in a certain inlet, sound, river, bay, etc., and when they are available;
- what species of game fish are likely to be in the vicinity at a particular time and what they eat (some game fish will only eat certain forage species, whereas others will eat anything and everything they can find);
- how to identify each forage species;
- how to imitate a forage species successfully.

The first three points will be covered in this section. The fourth point is covered in the individual game fish tactics, techniques, and tackle sections of this chapter, and in the chapters covering each state.

Discussions of each forage species are intentionally brief to avoid unnecessary information. What follows is the information you need to be successful in most situations, rather than needless details and microdata.

Common Squid

One of the most important near-shore (spring into very early fall) and offshore forage species, the common squid is a favorite of tuna, amberjack, wahoo, and dolphin. It is less common along the Georgia coast because squid prefer cooler water.

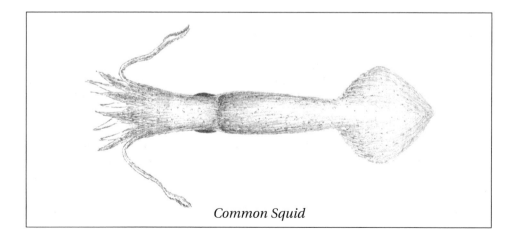

Common Squid

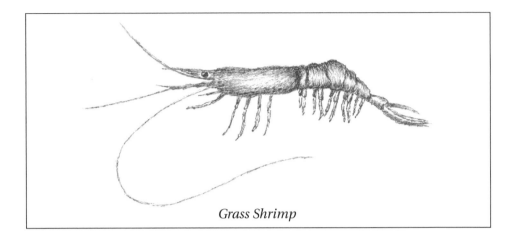

Grass Shrimp

The trouble with imitating a squid with a fly is its ability to change colors depending on mood—alarm, fright, relaxed, feeding, happy, calm—so fast that you can hardly see it happen. Still, go with a light cinnamon brownish color. The best-known squid fly is called a Sea-Arrow. Dan Blanton, who also created the Sar-Mul-Mac, was instrumental in this fly's development. I asked him about this fly's development, and he told me that it is one of the best squid imitations he has ever used or seen used.

Grass Shrimp

Estuaries, bays, sounds, and flooded spartina flats are home to the grass shrimp, one of the most important forage species to spotted seatrout, red drum, black drum, stripers, and flounder. They average an inch or two and are able to change color, like the mummichog, to blend in with their surroundings. They can be almost clear, white, gray, brown, and shades between all these.

They inhabit the waters of the Southeast coast all year. To imitate one, try a 1/0 Bramblett's Swimming Shrimp. Grass shrimp are extremely common, although you may seldom see them unless you are looking for them.

White Swimming Shrimp

This is the big shrimp you find in many bait shops. They grow to 8 inches in length and are found just outside the surf zone and in to estuaries and bays and inlets. These are burrowing shrimp, so you will find more of them where the bottom is soft.

Cape Fear seems to be a rough dividing line for migrating populations, i.e., white swimming shrimp north of Cape Fear move south in the autumn and return in the spring. From just below Cape Fear, they seem to go nowhere and are extremely abundant in estuaries from about Myrtle Beach on south.

A 3/0 white Rattle Rouser can mimic one.

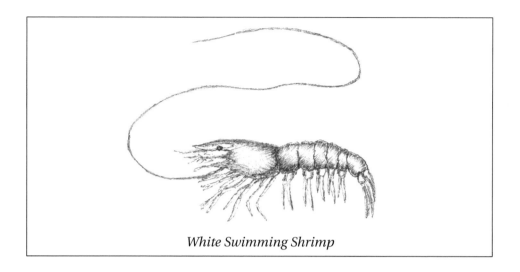

White Swimming Shrimp

Blue Crab

This is the famous swimming crab. Although called the blue crab, this inhabitant of all littorals in the region can be gray or even greenish blue. It prefers some vegetation and is mostly found in vegetation, but they are sometimes found on soft bottoms without any vegetation whatsoever. In winter, blue crabs often try to find deeper water, but they seldom venture very far from the littorals.

Janssen's Floating Crab is as good an imitation as you can get, but go with a 2/0 in this region rather than traditional smaller patterns.

Blue Crab

Green Crab

Green Crab

Found only in the extreme northern range covered in this book, the green crab is more likely to stick very close to shoreline structure, such as rocks and pilings. The striped bass is its primary predator. Although it can swim, it doesn't do so very well and likes to stick to bottom structure where it can quickly hide. They are found in this structure all year.

A McCrab is a reasonable imitation.

Fiddler Crab

Fiddlers are creatures of the radically changing world of marshes, estuaries, and creeks with soft bottoms, especially mud since they are burrowers. Red drum root around in the mud to suck them out of their holes and expend considerable energy doing so. Spotted seatrout, black drum, and sheepshead also eat them. They live in the intertidal zone throughout the year and are often quite small, an inch or so across the carapace, often less.

Carl Richards of *Emergers* fame designed the Red-Jointed Fiddler to mimic this creature.

Fiddler Crab

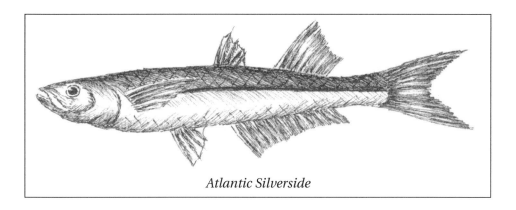

Atlantic Silverside

Atlantic Silverside

This very important baitfish is found throughout the range covered in this book, inhabiting estuaries, rivers, creeks, sloughs, sounds, and bays. It is a light olive green on the back with silver sides and a thin, dark stripe running down the sides. The maximum length is 6 inches or so.

Bluefish, false albacore, spotted seatrout, flounder, stripers, Spanish mackerel, and other game fish find it tasty. They are often seen scattering across the surface as game fish attack them. Schools of these are sometimes confused with menhaden, which also dimple the surface. Silversides are abundant throughout the year.

Popovics' Surf Candy Spearing imitates this species quite well, as does a Bar Fly.

Alewife

Found from South Carolina's mid-coast at about Winyah Bay and north, but being most common from about Swansboro, North Carolina (lowermost Bogue Inlet), northward, this large schooling baitfish is the target of bluefish, stripers, false

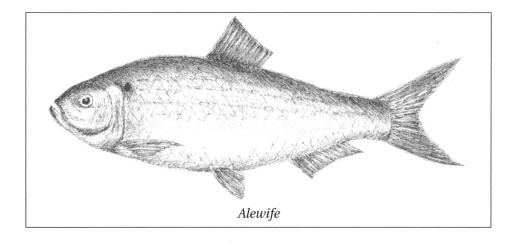

Alewife

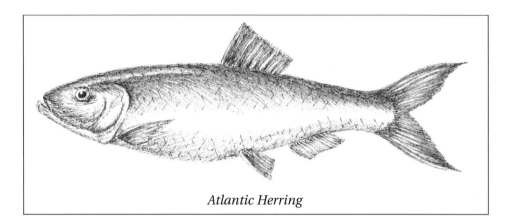

Atlantic Herring

albacore, redfish, king mackerel, and other predators. They can attain a length of 12 inches and have an olive-gray back with silvery or gold sides. Near-shore and inshore waters are its prime hangouts, with rivers, bays, and sounds being especially important. Although they can be found in these waters much of the year, autumn is best because juveniles move down rivers to the ocean at this time.

To imitate this baitfish, use something like a Baby Bunker.

Atlantic Herring

Not all that important in this region because it is infrequently found (Cape Hatteras is about its southernmost range), the Atlantic herring does show up in large bays, in the surf, and in other fairly expansive inshore and near-shore waters. Seldom getting any more than 8 inches long, it has silver or bright gray sides with a dark back of blue or green-blue. Winter is their season along the Southeast coast.

Abel's Anchovy is a good imitation, as is a Lefty's Deceiver with white sides and a blue back.

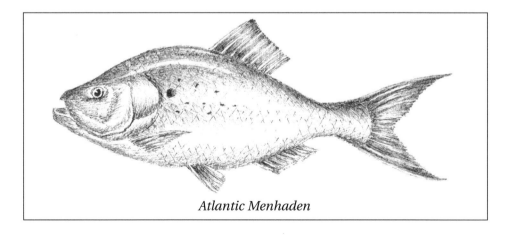

Atlantic Menhaden

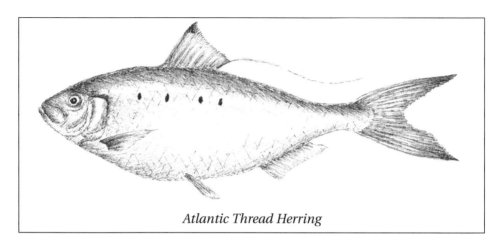

Atlantic Thread Herring

Atlantic Menhaden

Perhaps the most important overall baitfish along the coast of the Carolinas and Georgia, the Atlantic menhaden is preyed on by everything from yellowfin tuna to flounder. It winters and spawns offshore from about Bogue Banks north to the Outer Banks of Hatteras.

Nine inches is about the longest length a menhaden reaches. They are a shade of brown, green, gray, blue, or a combination of these colors on the back, with somewhat golden sides that sometimes appear almost yellow. Rivers, creeks, bays, estuaries, and other inshore and near-shore waters are home to the Atlantic menhaden. When juveniles leave their estuary rearing areas in late summer through fall, game fish feed especially heavily on them.

Try a Baby Bunker or Bucktail Menhaden to imitate this species.

Atlantic Thread Herring

Growing to a foot long, these baitfish are an important forage fish for flounder, seatrout, drum, and other game fish that hunt in protected bays and harbors. It is most often blueish-green along the back with silvery sides and a line of dark spots below the dorsal fin. It gets its "thread" description from the long, threadlike last ray of the dorsal fin.

Thread herring can be found throughout the year in this region but can become scarce in colder months. The Sar-Mul-Mac (Dan Blanton's excellent and versatile creation) is a good imitation.

Code Goby

Found in bays, sloughs, rivers, inlets, and on flats, the code goby is eaten by redfish, black drum, spotted seatrout, and other inshore predators. Growing to a length of only 2 inches, it is not an especially important forage species because it does not

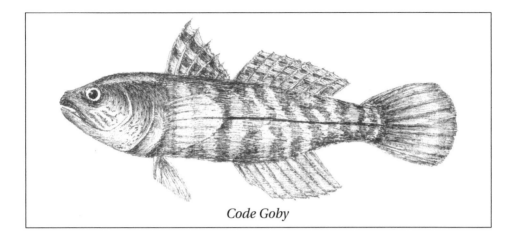

Code Goby

school up in the way menhaden do and is not found in huge numbers like mullet and silversides.

Code goby like bottoms with rough structure. They are greenish with mottled stripes and are most abundant from late spring into early fall. A dark green 2/0 Clouser is a fair imitation.

Mummichog

This 5-inch baitfish prefers vegetation to hide in, such as spartina, and ventures into water only inches deep, much like its cousin, the striped killifish. Estuaries, harbors, creeks, rivers, and marshes are favorite abodes. It can be found in coastal Southeast waters all year.

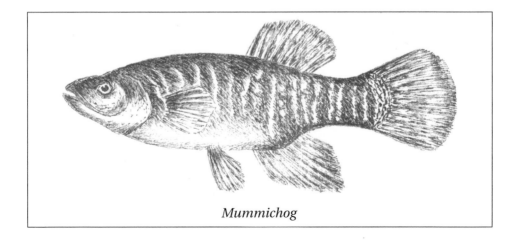

Mummichog

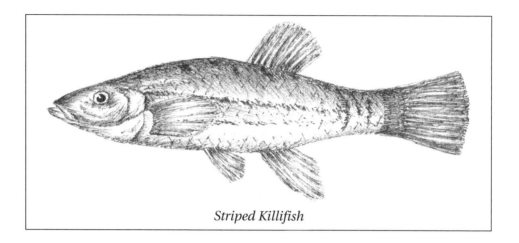

Striped Killifish

Dark green in color with a yellowish belly, the male's coloring becomes sharper during spawning. Mummichogs also have the annoying ability to change their color to better match their microenvironment. This ability has clear implications for the flyfisher, as it requires determining what color to imitate in each place that is fished.

A 2/0 Deceiver with a green body and yellowish belly can do the trick.

Striped Killifish

This is a common baitfish of shallow, often sandy, inlets, bays, estuaries, and sometimes surf zones. Greenish-brown to dark green along the back, it fades to a tannish-white on the sides with a varying number of black stripes. It is found along the coastal Southeast throughout the year.

Although they can grow to lengths of 7 inches, I have found that in this region 4 or 5 inches is much more likely. They can be difficult to see, even in very thin water, because of their coloration, which blends in with the bottom. Flounder, spotted seatrout, and red drum are three of the striped killifish's most common predators.

To imitate the striped killifish, tie some peacock herl into the middle of a tan and white 2/0 Clouser.

American Sand Lance

This elongated fish is common only from about Cape Hatteras northward. Found moving in schools (loose and compact) during the day and night, it is most important as a forage species for striped bass, at least along the Outer Banks. It grows to a maximum length of about 7 inches and comes in assorted colors including brownish, olive, grayish, and sort of a blue-green. It has silver sides and a white belly. Ecosystems include estuaries, protected bays, and other inshore waters with mud or sand bottoms. Late fall and winter are when they are most abundant.

American Sand Lance

Fly imitations include Lou Tabory's Sand Eel, Bob Popovics' Surf Candy, and Dave Whitlock's Sand Eel. Note that these three highly regarded fly tiers all chose to tie versions of this fish, which indicates its importance.

American Eel

This slimy fish of many an American boy's childhood memories is especially important to striped bass. It is found throughout the Southeast range covered here.

These eels grow to a maximum length of around 18 inches, but only those specimens of perhaps 8 inches or less are imitated by flies. Elvers are of great importance, not only to stripers but also bluefish. Most eels are brownish-green or olive in color and inhabit inshore waters, ascending rivers. Look for them spring through fall.

One of the better eel imitations is Whitlock's Eelworm.

Common Halfbeak

Averaging 8 or 9 inches as an adult, the common halfbeak is a surface-dwelling baitfish found in bigger sounds and bays and the open ocean. It is occasionally

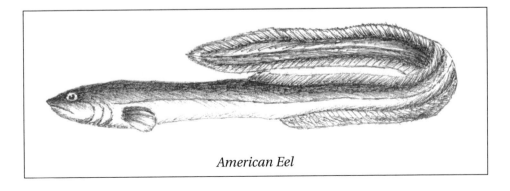

American Eel

Common Halfbeak

mistaken for a flyingfish because of the way it leaps from the water to escape predators. Dark above and silvery below, it is a fast swimmer.

Wahoo, tuna, sailfish, and king mackerel are the common halfbeak's main predators. They can be found in warmer waters (the Gulf Stream) throughout the year. I didn't know a true imitation of one existed until Lefty Kreh showed me how he ties his Lefty's Ballyhoo one day—use a 3/0.

Balao

Quite similar in appearance to its cousin, the common halfbeak, the balao grows a few inches longer and has a darker back. It is found most often offshore. If you want to tie a fly to mimic one, just tie a large Lefty's Ballyhoo (4/0).

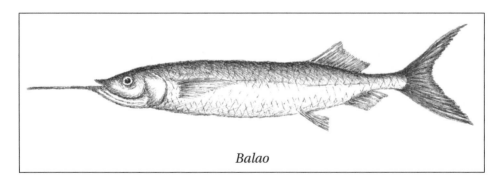

Balao

Atlantic Needlefish

A very common sight in bays, estuaries, rivers, harbors, and offshore, this narrow and long needlefish earns its name. Olive or blue along the back with a pearl belly and silver sides, it can grow to 2 feet long but is usually seen in smaller versions.

Needlefish don't mind cold water and can be found along the Southeast coast in every season. I have seen them get hit by king mackerel, houndfish (a bigger cousin), and large Spanish mackerel, and I suspect a false albacore or bonito would attack them, too. I have never fished an imitation of one—never felt the need to,

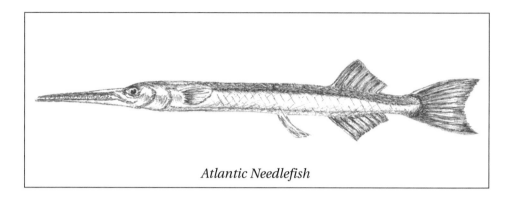

Atlantic Needlefish

frankly—but I am told that a FisHair Needlefish is the way to go if you simply must try one out.

Bay Anchovy

A very common and widely distributed baitfish along the Southeast coast, the 4-inch bay anchovy is somewhat tan along the back with silvery or pearl sides and head. It is found in nearly all types of water, but it is most often found in estuaries. The bay anchovy travels a long way up rivers and creeks—well into fresh water. It

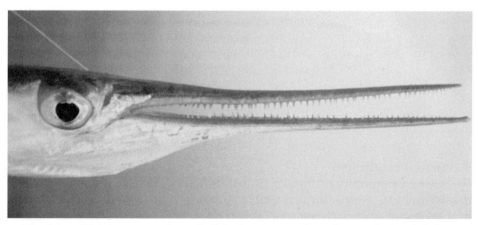

The houndfish is a type of needlefish that is occasionally caught by flyfishers and light-tackle anglers in near-shore waters. Flyfishing author Tom Earnhardt has been experimenting of late with these toothy fish on the fly. I have caught them as well and must say that they fight better than I expected, although I would never admit to having caught one in public.

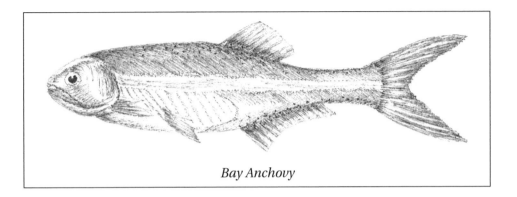

Bay Anchovy

inhabits Southeastern coastal waters year-round. Just about every game fish in the region eats it.

A 2/0 tan and white Clouser is the best imitation.

Threespine Stickleback

You need only consider this baitfish if you are on the Outer Banks above Cape Hatteras or in Pamlico Sound northward, and then not very often. The reason is that the threespine stickleback is not a favorite forage species of any game fish because the little bugger can "lock" its spines straight up, making it very difficult to swallow. Only very hungry game fish with large mouths and throats and with no options for lunch consider this baitfish.

You can find these fish milling about in small schools along spartina banks, in rivers and creeks, in bays and sounds, and occasionally in the surf or just outside it. During winter they migrate offshore, returning in spring.

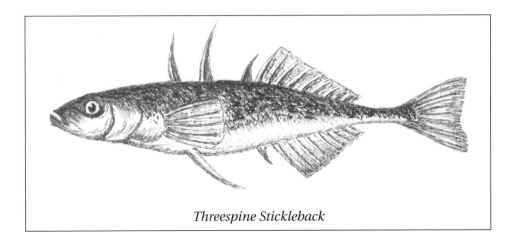

Threespine Stickleback

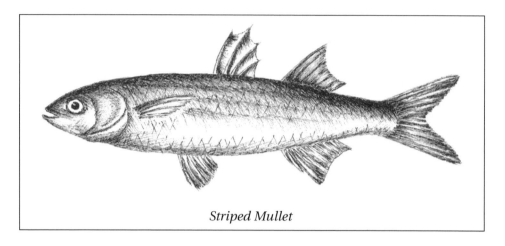

Striped Mullet

The threespine stickleback is dark gray-blue-black along the back with a white belly. I doubt that it's necessary to carry a fly that imitates this fish. If you simply must try one, go with a dark Clouser with a light belly, about 2/0.

Striped Mullet

Definitely one of the most significant baitfish in the waters covered here, the striped mullet—juveniles are called finger mullet—is eaten by a long list of game fish, including tarpon, red drum, black drum, Spanish and king mackerel, cobia, spotted seatrout, flounder, bluefish, striped bass, and more. They live inshore and

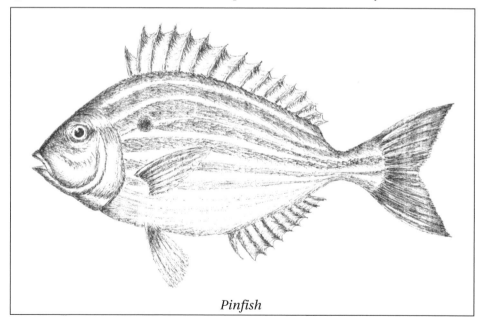

Pinfish

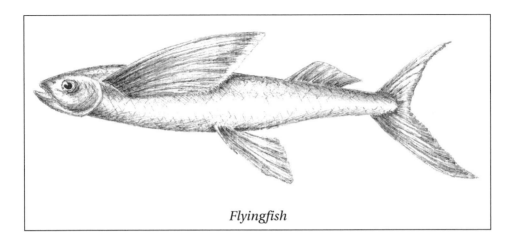

Flyingfish

near-shore in all types of littoral ecosystems and are a common sight jumping clear of the water as adults, apparently for no reason. The finger mullet do not jump for fun but can be seen scattering when attacked.

With an olive back and silver sides, it is easily mimicked with a Deceiver tied with the same colors. For finger mullet, tie a 2/0 or maybe a 3/0. Adults can easily grow to 28 inches, perhaps more.

Pinfish

Found in many inshore situations—rivers, creeks, around piers and docks, inlets, rock piles, wrecks, debris-covered bottoms, etc.—and also near-shore and even offshore in fairly deep water, the ubiquitous pinfish has saved many a day's fishing. Although pinfish can grow to lengths well beyond 12 inches, they are much more commonly found around 5 inches.

With a dark back and sides covered with faint horizontal yellow and greenish-blue stripes, the pinfish is taken by spotted seatrout, drum, kings, Spanish, flounder, and most other game fish in the region. I am unaware of any good imitations of pinfish that are tied specifically with the pinfish in mind, but a small Baby Bunker will often suffice.

Flyingfish

The strange and wondrous flyingfish is often seen skimming the waves—flying —in blue water or at the edge of green water. Dolphin, tuna, wahoo, and king mackerel are its main predators. Flyingfish are subtropical by nature and must have warm water. They appear in the northern end of this zone in late spring and stay into the middle of autumn or so. As reported by McClane, flyingfish really do fly rather than skim the water's surface and then glide.

I know of no fly tied to really imitate a flyingfish.

North Carolina Coast

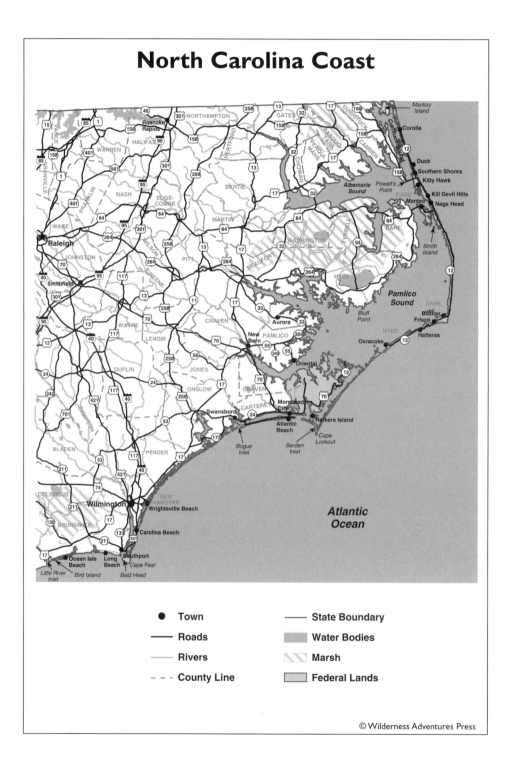

Mackay Island

Corolla

Duck
Southern Shores
Kitty Hawk
Kill Devil Hills
Manteo — Nags Head

Albemarle Sound
Powell's Point

Smith Island

Pamlico Sound

Bluff Point
Buxton
Frisco
Hatteras
Ocracoke

Aurora

New Bern — PAMLICO

Oriental

Morehead City
Swansboro
Atlantic Beach
Harkers Island
Cape Lookout

Bogue Inlet
Barden Inlet

Raleigh

Smithfield

Wilmington
Wrightsville Beach
Carolina Beach

Ocean Isle Beach
Long Beach
Southport
Cape Fear
Little River Inlet
Bird Island
Bald Head

Atlantic Ocean

● Town	— State Boundary
— Roads	▨ Water Bodies
— Rivers	▨ Marsh
- - - County Line	▨ Federal Lands

© Wilderness Adventures Press

North Carolina

The coast of North Carolina has more water than anyone could thoroughly fish in a lifetime. The littorals are an intricate maze with seemingly countless creeks, cuts, sloughs, canals, rivers, bays, and sounds, every one of which holds game fish. For information on current regulations, contact the North Carolina Department of Environment and Natural Resources, Division of Marine Fisheries Headquarters, 3441 Arendell Street, Morehead City, NC 28557 or phone: 252-726-7021.

I debated for some time before settling on how to start this chapter and section of this book, because North Carolina's coast is so complex. I first looked at doing all the rivers and then all the sounds and so on, but in the end I decided to proceed from north to south, a plan I used for South Carolina and Georgia, as well.

Getting There

Coastal North Carolina isn't easily accessible—there is no major interstate along the coast, and no large airports are nearby. If all routes seem circuitous, they are. But a little planning and wise use of your time will get you there.

By Road

The major coastal highway along the mainland is US 17. While it isn't a fast road, it does suffice. Interstate 95 runs through eastern North Carolina and several access routes are available from it.

Currituck Sound: US 158, which goes to Kill Devil Hills, is accessible from I-95 at Roanoke Rapids and from US 17 at Elizabeth City.

Albemarle Sound: US 64, which runs along the south side of Albermarle Sound and connects with US 158 just south of Kill Devil Hills, is accessible from I-95 just west of Rocky Mount and US 17 just east of Everetts.

Pamlico Sound: US 264, which provides access to the north side of Pamlico Sound, is accessible from I-95 east of Wilson and from US 17 at Washington. To reach the central part of the sound, take SR 33 (runs parallel to the Pamlico River) from US 17 just south of Washington, and SR 55 from New Bern (located on US 17). From New Bern, US 70 heads southwest to the coastal towns of Morehead City and Beaufort.

Jacksonville (on New River): Take SR 24 from I-95 at Fayetteville to US 258, which is just northwest of Jacksonville, and head south. From I-40 at Burgaw, take SR 53 to Jacksonville.

Wilmington: From the north, take I-40 from I-95 at Benson; from the west, take US 74 and 76 from I-95 just south of Lumberton; US 17 runs north and south through Wilmington.

By Air

Norfolk, Virginia, is served by commercial airlines. This coastal city isn't very far north of the Currituck region and the northern Outer Banks.

*A typical red drum that fell
for a shrimp imitation.*

Raleigh-Durham International Airport offers easy access to Interstates 95, 85, and 40 and other US highways.

The next commercial airport to the south is Beaufort-Morehead City Airport, which gives you very fast access to Beaufort Inlet and Cape Lookout.

Jacksonville has commercial service, as well. However, this isn't a major jumping-off point for sportfishing along the coast. Beaufort-Morehead City is better.

New Hanover County Airport services Wilmington. Commercial service is available by commuter flights, just like the ones listed above.

Myrtle Beach International Airport has commercial jet service and is a short drive from the North Carolina coast.

By Water

The Atlantic Intracoastal Waterway is the route of choice, of course. This waterway is well maintained, and hundreds of thousands of vessels of all sizes use it annually—your tax dollars at work.

Game Fish Species

The species listed below are the game fish of North Carolina's littorals and near-shore waters. Some species I have intentionally left out because they are incidentals (white grunts, saltwater catfish, juvenile grouper, etc.). Others, such as bluefin tuna,

The author took this speck right up against the bank in about a foot of water.
Photo by Rick Pelow.

shouldn't be attempted on light tackle or a fly by anyone other than the most experienced professionals.

The fact of the matter is that bluefin tuna are too big and too strong to take on
light tackle unless you plan to kill the fish and eat it yourself or, with the proper per-
mits, sell it. Participation in this late fall and winter fishery off the Outer Banks has
exploded. With this increased pressure, the bluefin run is now beginning to show
signs of stress. More and more anglers are showing up with tackle that is too light for
these tuna. With a top class reel and the right line, you can beat a bluefin on your bass
rod, but the fish is going to die even if you release it at the end of the fight.

The following North Carolina game fish are what fishermen can usually target
with fly rods and light tackle:

- Amberjack
- Black drum
- Bluefish
- Bonito
- Cobia
- Crevalle jack
- Croaker
- Dolphin
- False albacore
- Gray Trout
- King mackerel
- Pompano
- Red drum
- Sheepshead
- Spanish mackerel
- Spotted seatrout
- Striped bass
- Tarpon
- Tripletail
- Yellowfin tuna

Currituck Sound

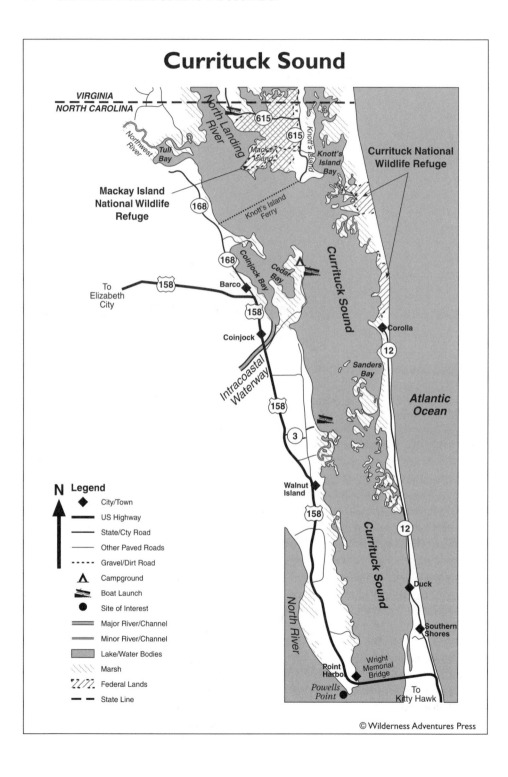

© Wilderness Adventures Press

CURRITUCK SOUND

This northernmost inshore water of North Carolina offers some outstanding angling opportunities to both the fly caster and light-tackle angler. There's a tremendous amount of water available, with many niches and nuances that take a very long time to learn completely, if ever. The jagged back edge of the Outer Banks, numerous islands and sloughs, and indentations of all shapes and sizes, plus creeks, rivers, and sloughs, add up to a great piece of water.

Currituck Sound lies between Mackay Island (home of the lovely Mackay Island National Wildlife Refuge) to the north and the Wright Memorial Bridge (named after North Carolina's beloved Wright Brothers, of course), which spans the lowermost sound between Point Harbor and Kitty Hawk. Two rivers that deserve a fisherman's

This seatrout was fooled in a sound and went for a green jig.

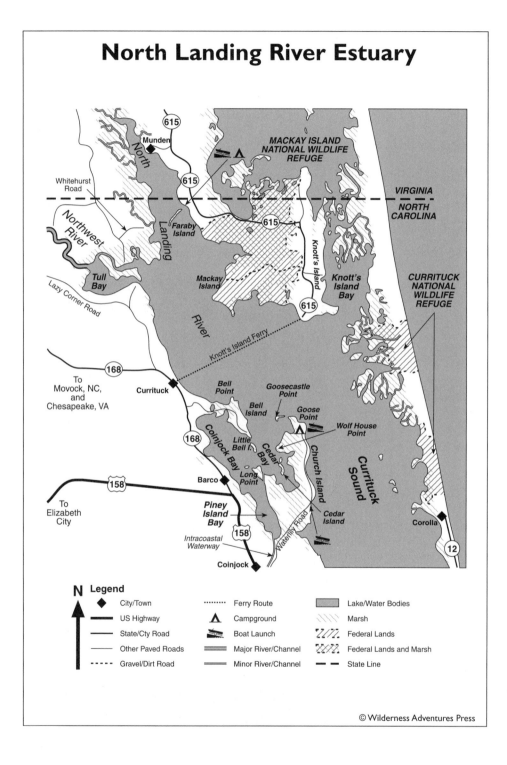

North Landing River Estuary

Britta Newman holds a young flounder that was enticed by a soft jig.

interest are the broad North Landing River that filters down from Virginia's Blackwater area and the much narrower Northwest River, which comes out of Virginia's end of the Great Dismal Swamp (a cute name that is most fitting, I assure you, unless you are a mosquito or an alligator).

North Landing River Estuary

Access to the North Landing River region isn't necessarily easy. Due to the type of land on the river's banks, there are no highways leading to it from the west. To launch a boat on the upper estuary, you have to come in on SR 615 from Virginia, unless you happen to be on Mackay Island. The southern end of the North Landing estuary is accessible from a boat launch located at Goose Point, south across the sound from Mackay Island. The boat launch can be reached from the south via US 158, just south of Coinjock. Turn onto Waterlily Road from US 158 and head north.

Croakers aren't especially smart, which is helpful.

Once you get on the water, there is some decent fishing, and I can almost guarantee that you will be the only flyfisher out there, if solitude is what you want.

Because the North Landing River is part of the massive ecosystem of sounds, marshes, rivers, creeks, islands, beaches, and inlets that make up the Outer Banks, flyfishers and light-tackle lovers will find all the game fish traditionally found around the Outer Banks, a list that includes the popular puppy drum, flounder, Spanish mackerel, striped bass, spotted seatrout, gray trout, bluefish, and croakers, to name just a handful.

Of all these game fish, the Spanish mackerel is a catch that frequently surprises anglers unfamiliar with these waters because they associate mackerel with the ocean, not as inshore fish, especially in a river. But the truth is that Spanish mackerel are common in these parts. Arriving in the spring from points south, they invade the North Landing to hunt for baitfish that swarm in these waters until late autumn. True

Lures such as these jigs, MirrOlures, and Got-Cha plugs,
take seatrout as well as Spanish mackerel.

to form, you find Spanish where you find them. In other words, they roam around looking for meals such as menhaden and finger mullet. Spanish mackerel do not usually inhabit waters surrounding shoreline structure to the degree specks and drum do, preferring channels with deeper water where they can maneuver quickly to get out of harm's way by the likes of such birds of prey as ospreys.

In the main channel of the North Landing River, try an old Down East Maine trick with a fly rod: troll a streamer fly in the wake at a fairly brisk clip. An intermediate or sinking line is the best way to use this technique—work the fly in gentle pulls and twitches to give it a fleeting motion. When a Spanish sees a fly that is moving right along, appearing to be a baitfish fleeing from something, the feisty little mackerel has a habit of just slamming into the fly without much forethought.

Light spinning tackle is perfect for the hardware specialist using this trick. A soft-body curltail jig in green or chartreuse trolled in the same manner can be very productive, as can Got-Cha plugs and silver spoons.

There is nothing at all different in the way you go after seatrout, gray trout, and puppy drum in the North Landing than how it is done in any other region of the Carolinas. A 7- or 8-weight 9-foot, fast action is the choice here. The traditional

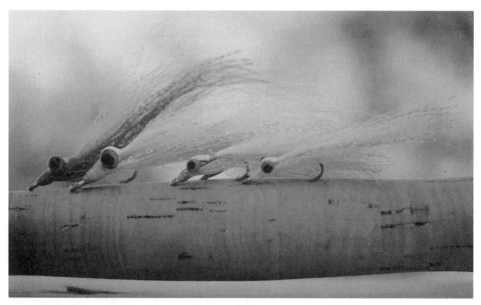

The Clouser Deep Minnow is one of the most versatile flies in existence.

assortment of Clousers, Deceivers, Bend Backs, Crazy Charlies (yes, a bonefish pattern), and crab patterns, such as Merkins and Jack Samson Fighting Crabs (permit patterns), are probably all that is needed. Flats behind points, bays, and cuts as well as points with current running over them are prime targets, as are oyster rocks and dropoffs. In the winter, use a fast-sinking line with a Clouser on a short leader (3 or 4 feet max) to search deep holes in the river, particularly those that border flats having a dark bottom. The short leader is very important because the fly must be kept on the bottom to dredge these recalcitrant specks out of their grottos, while a long leader allows the fly to rise too far up from the bottom. And don't forget to use a *fast-sinking* line, which gets the fly down to the bottom and doesn't have as much trouble with a heavy current trying to pull the line laterally. Teeny makes some of the best sinking lines, as does Orvis (try the Orvis Depth Charge).

For light tackle, sinking MirrOlures, assorted jigs (try the old walleye trick of tipping a bare jig with a small baitfish, such as a finger mullet), large live shrimp fished below popping corks, live finger mullet, and crankbaits, such as Rapalas, Rebels, Rat-L-Traps, and other crankbaits with action that mimics baitfish can all do the job.

Specific areas in which to focus for specks, drum, and gray trout include the creek mouths east and south of Whitehurst Road (opposite Faraby Island); the creeks of Mackay Island; Coinjock Bay (Little Bell Island, Goosecastle Point, Cedar Island, Long Point, Bell Point, the south tip of Bell Island, Wolf House Point, Cedar Bay, and the bars and shoals of Piney Island Bay).

Crankbaits should always accompany jigs.

Stripers come and go through this region, just as they do throughout their range. You have to watch for them if you are unfamiliar with the river. Look for birds diving and distant splashes indicating stripers hitting a shoal of baitfish. Keep an eye on other boats, as well.

Flyfishers find that Deceivers, Clousers, and Crazy Charlies are three flies that can usually be depended upon for stripers, but Dahlberg Divers, pencil and typical bass poppers, bucktails, and streamers that imitate sand eels are also productive. For the spinning guys, bucktail jigs, crankbaits, and surface plugs are often worthwhile. A crankbait, such as a floating Rapala, pulled very slowly and steadily along the surface can be murder (this tactic imitates a wounded or oxygen-starved baitfish).

Croakers are almost never targeted by flyfishers, which is a shame since they are fun little fish on a light fly rod (like a 6-weight). As is the case with all inshore saltwaters in the Carolinas, croakers are where you find them, which might be anywhere. However, channel markers and docks are good places to start. Small Crazy Charlies and custom-made flies created from a thin (⅛ inch) strip of bunny fur with lead eyes riles the croakers up, especially if the fly is soaked in squid juice. Use a sinking line to get right down to the bottom and a very short leader (no more than 3 feet).

Croakers targeted by spin fishermen are easily caught using small marabou jigs tipped with a thin strip of squid. Use ultralight tackle for the most fun. A 5½-foot medium action rod with a small reel filled with 4-pound test is just right.

Lefty's Deceivers and Clouser Deep Minnows are the two most important flies for coastal North Carolina.

Bluefish are very common around North Landing River, but don't expect the big bruisers found in the surf of the Outer Banks. These are the little "snapper" blues, weighing from about a pound to maybe two pounds. Like their big brothers, these juvenile bluefish are vicious, voracious, and not to be taken lightly when it comes to your fingers. Even a snapper blue of one pound can shred a finger in a heartbeat with its pointy, very sharp teeth.

You'll likely need only two flies for these guys: Deceivers and Clousers (2/0 is the size, although 1/0 will take them, too). Still, if you want to have some real fun, a 7-weight rod throwing pencil poppers can be a real treat. Snapper blues remind me in more ways than one of the bigeye trevally found on the Golfo Dulce along Costa Rica's Pacific Coast.

Blues move around a lot. Anywhere you find a rip or some small baitfish, toss a fly in. Don't expect birds to give away these little guys' position, however, because these blues don't do anywhere near the damage that adult fish do to a school of baitfish. Small jigs are best on light tackle, but it's best to have plenty because blues bite off a lot of jig tails. Go light with a fast 6-foot rod loaded with 6-pound test. Use a mono shock leader of about 15-pound test rather than the wire required for the large blues.

Fred Kluge with a young bluefish that tried to eat a green curltail jig with a red head.

Northwest River

The Northwest River is very different from its big brother, the North Landing. It is really little more than a wide creek dumping into Tull Bay. The name of the game on this river is puppy drum, specks, and flounder.

To gain access to the Northwest River via boat, the quickest way is to use the launch off SR 615 on the east side of the North Landing River estuary off Mackay Island. Otherwise, the ramp at Goose Point on Church Island is good. If using a canoe, any of the arms and creeks feeding the river, such as in the Northwest River Marsh Game Lands region around Panther Landing, will all provide access. And speaking of the game lands, a lot of duck hunting goes on up here, so when fishing at first light, be on the lookout for decoy spreads.

The flies and tactics recommended for the North Landing River apply here, as well.

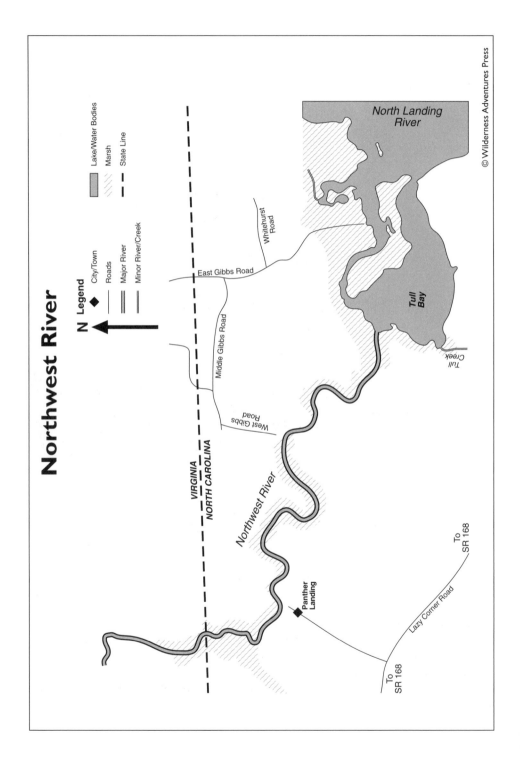

Northwest River

N **Legend**

◆ City/Town
— Roads
— Major River
═ Minor River/Creek

▨ Lake/Water Bodies
▨ Marsh
- - - State Line

North Landing River

Whitehurst Road

East Gibbs Road

Middle Gibbs Road

West Gibbs Road

Tull Bay

Tull Creek

Northwest River

VIRGINIA
NORTH CAROLINA

Panther Landing

Lazy Corner Road

To SR 168

To SR 168

© Wilderness Adventures Press

Currituck Sound Backside

Keeping one's bearings is easier when fishing the backside of Currituck's barrier island. Days could be spent just getting to know the northern end between Deal Island on the north and Luark Hill on the south. This area encompasses:

- Knott's Island Channel
- Knott's Island Bay
- part of the Currituck National Wildlife Refuge
- Swan Island
- Johnson Island
- South Channel
- Raymond Island
- Oak Pond
- and a slew of little indentations with no names

I can't say that any one of these areas is necessarily always better than the rest, because the truth is that the fish hold locally. They orient on structure and other anomalies and follow baitfish and other forage, such as shrimp and crabs, causing things to change fairly regularly.

Sheepshead, a type of porgy, are sly eaters, but they can be fooled with crab patterns and, to a lesser degree, shrimp patterns.

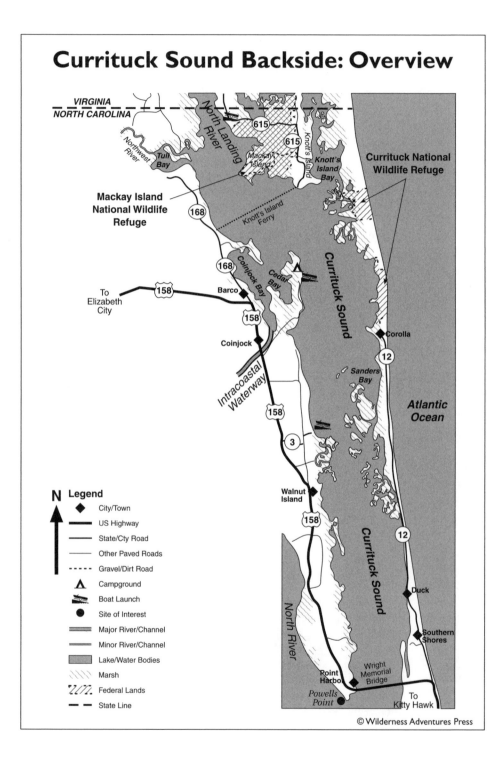

Currituck Sound Backside: Overview

VIRGINIA
NORTH CAROLINA

North Landing River

Northwest River

Tull Bay

615

615

Mackay Island

Knott's Island

Knott's Island Bay

Currituck National Wildlife Refuge

Mackay Island National Wildlife Refuge

168

Knott's Island Ferry

168

Coinjock Bay

Cedar Bay

Currituck Sound

To Elizabeth City

158

Barco

158

Corolla

Coinjock

12

Sanders Bay

Intracoastal Waterway

158

Atlantic Ocean

3

Walnut Island

158

Currituck Sound

12

Duck

North River

Southern Shores

Point Harbor

Wright Memorial Bridge

To Kitty Hawk

Powells Point

N Legend

◆ City/Town
━━ US Highway
── State/Cty Road
─ Other Paved Roads
---- Gravel/Dirt Road
⚠ Campground
🛥 Boat Launch
● Site of Interest
▬ Major River/Channel
▬ Minor River/Channel
▨ Lake/Water Bodies
▨ Marsh
▨ Federal Lands
— — State Line

© Wilderness Adventures Press

Currituck Sound Backside
Knott's Island to Luark Hill

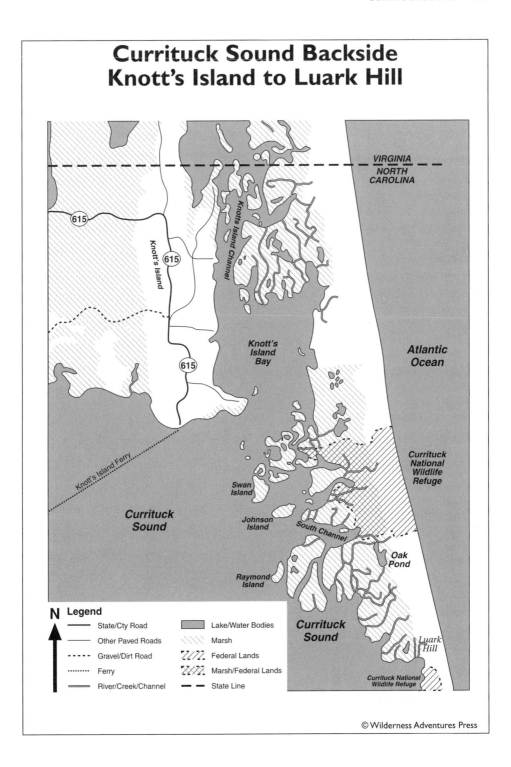

VIRGINIA
NORTH
CAROLINA

615

Knott's Island

615

Knotts Island Channel

615

Knott's
Island
Bay

Atlantic
Ocean

Knott's Island Ferry

Currituck
National
Wildlife
Refuge

Swan
Island

Currituck
Sound

Johnson
Island

South Channel

Oak
Pond

Raymond
Island

Currituck
Sound

Luark
Hill

Currituck National
Wildlife Refuge

N

Legend

——	State/Cty Road	
——	Other Paved Roads	
- - - -	Gravel/Dirt Road	
·········	Ferry	
═══	River/Creek/Channel	

Lake/Water Bodies

Marsh

Federal Lands

Marsh/Federal Lands

State Line

© Wilderness Adventures Press

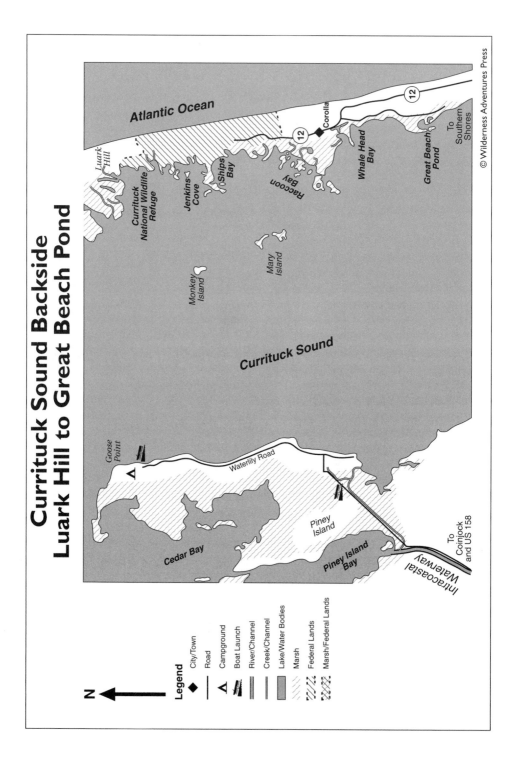

Currituck Sound Backside
Luark Hill to Great Beach Pond

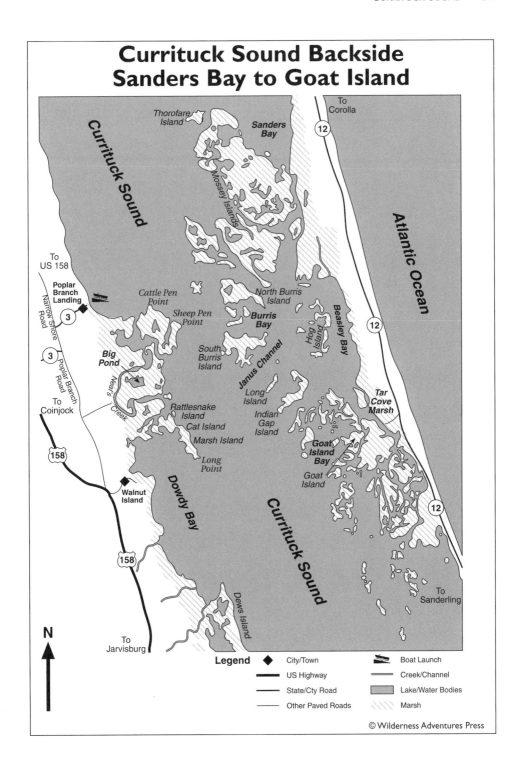

Currituck Sound Backside
Sanders Bay to Goat Island

To Corolla

Thorofare Island

Sanders Bay

Currituck Sound

Mossey Islands

Atlantic Ocean

To US 158

Poplar Branch Landing

Narrow Shore Road

Cattle Pen Point

Sheep Pen Point

North Burris Island

Burris Bay

Beasley Bay

Hog Island

Poplar Branch Road

Big Pond

South Burris Island

Janus Channel

Neal's Creek

To Coinjock

Rattlesnake Island

Long Island

Tar Cove Marsh

Cat Island

Indian Gap Island

Marsh Island

Goat Island Bay

Long Point

Goat Island

Walnut Island

Dowdy Bay

Currituck Sound

Dews Island

To Sanderling

N

To Jarvisburg

Legend

◆ City/Town

▰ Boat Launch

▬ US Highway

═ Creek/Channel

— State/Cty Road

▒ Lake/Water Bodies

— Other Paved Roads

▨ Marsh

© Wilderness Adventures Press

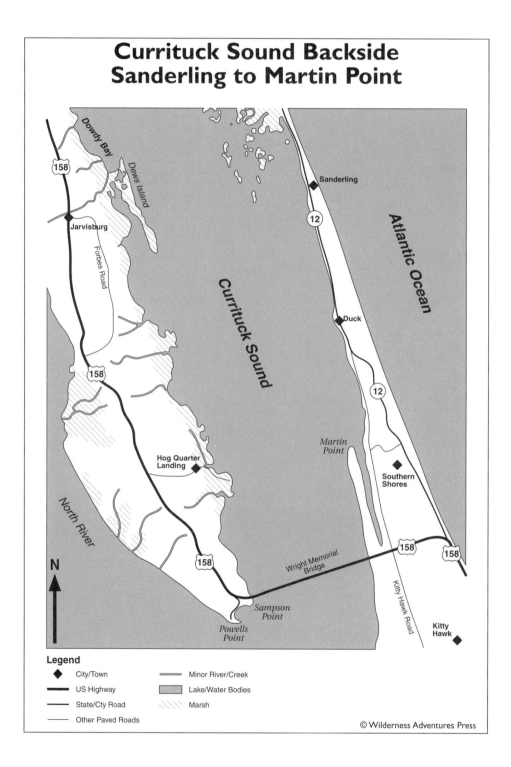

Currituck Sound Backside
Sanderling to Martin Point

Dowdy Bay

158

Dews Island

Jarvisburg

Forbes Road

Sanderling

12

Atlantic Ocean

Currituck Sound

158

Duck

12

Martin Point

Hog Quarter Landing

Southern Shores

North River

158

Wright Memorial Bridge

158

158

N

Kitty Hawk Road

Sampson Point

Powells Point

Kitty Hawk

Legend

◆ City/Town

▬ US Highway

━ State/Cty Road

─ Other Paved Roads

▬ Minor River/Creek

Lake/Water Bodies

Marsh

© Wilderness Adventures Press

From just south of Luark Hill down to about the Wright Memorial Bridge there are many, many opportunities for specks, flounder, and redfish (look hard for the latter—they tend to be more shy than specks and flounder). To work this area from north to south, start by heading down the shore, working slowly and covering the water and structure thoroughly. Don't automatically rule out one area over another because game fish may be searching for things that a fisherman can't see, such as an oyster rock, a wreck, or a hole.

Starting at the little nubs of land above Jenkins Cove, work:

- Monkey Island (out in the sound)
- Ships Bay
- Mary Island (also out in the sound but worth the effort because of the specks there)
- Raccoon Bay
- the spartina around Corolla
- Whale Head Bay (flounder)
- Great Beach Pond (really just a cove)
- Sanders Bay and the entire complex of islands, channels, and ponds that lie between Thorofare Island and North Burris Island (the Mossey Islands)
- the islands, channels, and ponds south of the Mossey Islands (Burris Bay, South Burris Island, Janus Channel, Hog Island, Beasley Bay, Long Island, Indian Gap Island, Goat Island, Goat Island Bay, Tar Cove Marsh, etc.)

On the western side of Currituck Sound are some good areas for specks, flounder, drum, croaker, blues, and even Spanish mackerel. These include:

- the ponds, islands, and other features between Poplar Branch Landing and Walnut Island (such as Neal's Creek, Cattle Pen Point, Sheep Pen Point, Big Pond, Rattlesnake Island (never seen one there), Cat Island, Marsh Island, and Long Point, etc.
- Dowdy Bay
- and Dews Island

From Sanderling on down to about Martin Point of the Outer Banks, I have never had all that much luck except for flounder from time to time. I think this is because there isn't a great deal of structure in this area. On the other hand, the western shore of the sound in this area does hold specks, blues, and other regional game fish. Hog Quarter Landing is good, and the sheepshead fishing around the Wright Memorial Bridge can be very good, indeed.

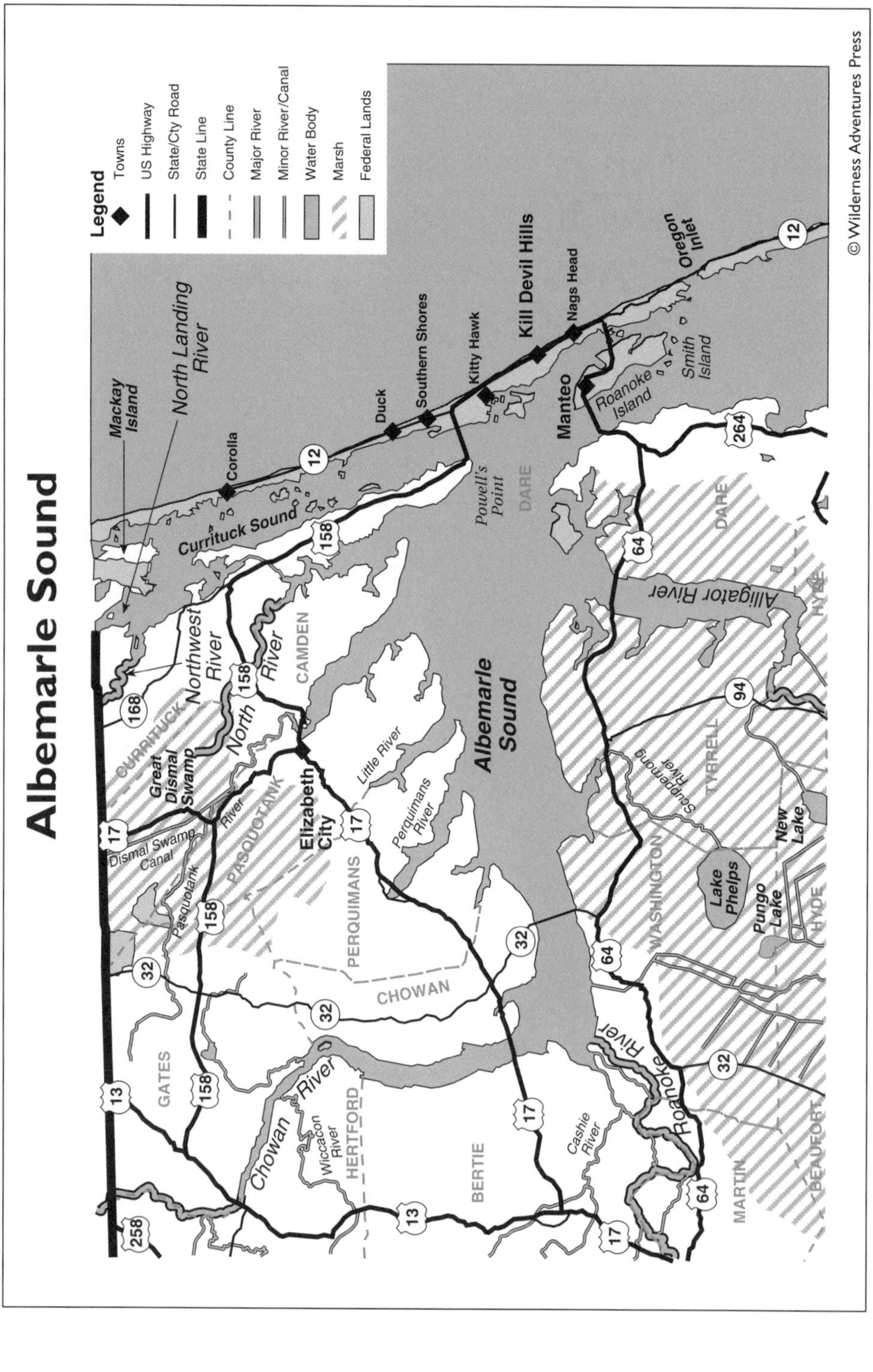

Albemarle Sound

© Wilderness Adventures Press

Legend

◆ Towns
US Highway
State/City Road
State Line
County Line
Major River
Minor River/Canal
Water Body
Marsh
Federal Lands

Mackay Island

North Landing River

Kill Devil Hills

Nags Head

Oregon Inlet

12

Corolla

Duck

Southern Shores

Kitty Hawk

Manteo

Roanoke Island

Smith Island

12

Currituck Sound

Powell's Point

DARE

264

DARE

158

64

Alligator River

HYDE

Northwest River

CAMDEN

Albemarle Sound

168

CURRITUCK

Great Dismal Swamp

North River

158

Little River

94

Scuppernong River

TYRRELL

New Lake

17

Dismal Swamp Canal

River

PASQUOTANK

Elizabeth City

17

Perquimans River

WASHINGTON

Lake Phelps

Pungo Lake

HYDE

Pasquotank

158

PERQUIMANS

32

64

32

GATES

158

CHOWAN

32

Roanoke River

32

BEAUFORT

13

Chowan River

Wiccacon River

HERTFORD

BERTIE

17

Cashie River

MARTIN

258

13

17

64

ALBEMARLE SOUND

With more water than Currituck Sound to the north but much less than sprawling Pamlico Sound to the south, Albemarle is a sound filled with lore, legend, and tradition. Its many rivers, bays, creeks, coves, and other features attract a great many game fish, from tarpon to croakers and everything in between. It is nearly as easy to become confused or even lost on this water as it is on Pamlico Sound, so pay attention to charts, landmarks, and markers. Remember: When in doubt, put ashore and simply ask someone where the hell you are.

Pasquotank River

The Pasquotank River changes from a weedy creek to a good-sized river by the time it hits Albemarle Sound. We need only concern ourselves with that stretch of the river starting at Elizabeth City. Standard flatty and speck tactics will work around the creek mouths, which are the draw on the Pasquotank, including:

A Clouser was used to convince this speck.

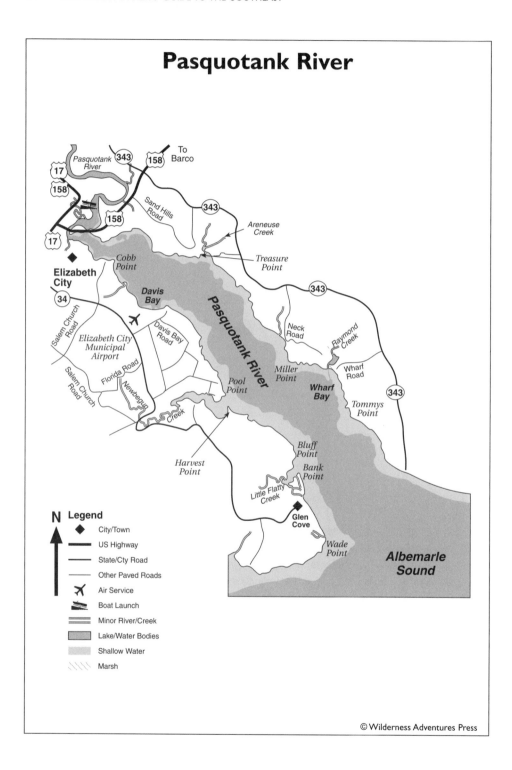

Little River

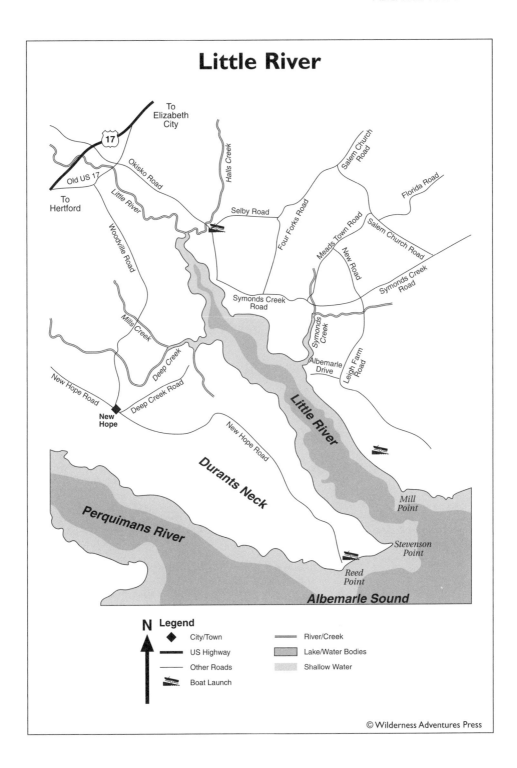

To
Elizabeth
City

17

Old US 17

Okisko Road

Little River

To
Hertford

Woodville Road

Halls Creek

Salem Church Road

Florida Road

Selby Road

Four Forks Road

Meads Town Road

Salem Church Road

New Road

Symonds Creek Road

Mills Creek

Symonds Creek
Road

Deep Creek

Symonds
Creek

Albemarle
Drive

Leigh Farm Road

New Hope Road

Deep Creek Road

New
Hope

New Hope Road

Little River

Mill
Point

Durants Neck

Stevenson
Point

Perquimans River

Reed
Point

Albemarle Sound

N Legend

◆ City/Town

River/Creek

US Highway

Lake/Water Bodies

Other Roads

Shallow Water

Boat Launch

© Wilderness Adventures Press

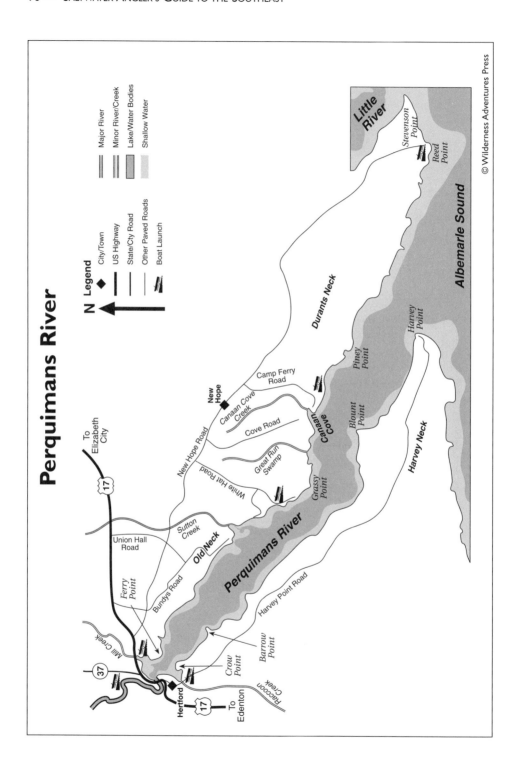

Perquimans River

Soft jigs soaked in menhaden oil can drive flatties crazy.

- Little Flatty between Blank Point and Bluff Point
- Newbegun between Harvest Point and Pool Point
- Raymond in Wharf Bay
- Areneuse at Treasure Point

Little River

The Little River's creeks and creek mouths, as is the case with all the rivers of Albemarle, are a natural game fish hangout; try:

- Deep Creek and where Mills Creek enters Deep Creek
- Halls Creek (there is a launch ramp off Okisko Road right on Halls Creek)
- Symonds Creek

Perquimans River

Also born in the Great Dismal Swamp, the Perquimans River has fairly easy access off US 17 between Elizabeth City and Hertford on Woodland Church Road (if heading south) to New Hope Road, and then onto the aptly named Boat Ramp Road. Heading north out of Hertford, take New Hope Road off the US 17 bypass to Boat Ramp Road. Check these waters:

- Sutton Creek on Old Neck
- Raccoon Creek within the town of Hertford

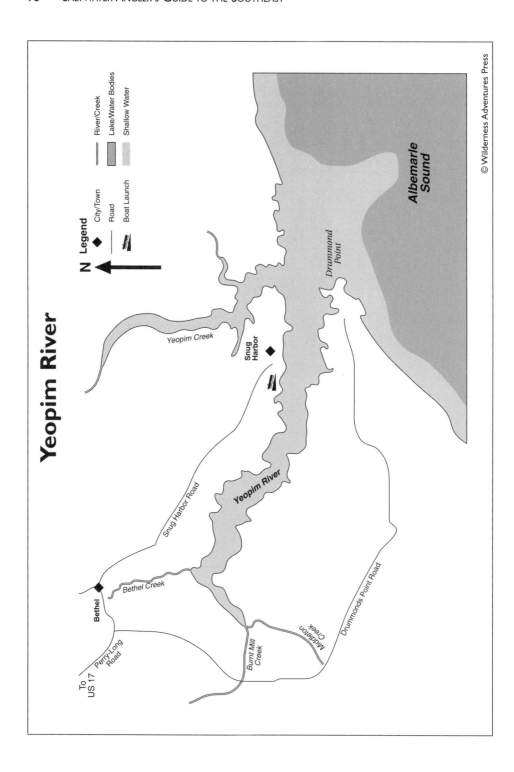

Yeopim River

Albemarle Sound

Drummond Point

Yeopim Creek

Snug Harbor

Yeopim River

Snug Harbor Road

Bethel

Bethel Creek

Burnt Mill Creek

Middleton Creek

Drummonds Point Road

Perry-Long Road

To US 17

© Wilderness Adventures Press

N

Legend

City/Town
Road
Boat Launch

River/Creek
Lake/Water Bodies
Shallow Water

Weighing a striped bass, or "rockfish," prior to release.

- Mill Creek across from town
- the likely looking water between Great Run Swamp and Canaan Cove Creek on Durants Neck

Yeopim River

One of the more narrow rivers of the region, the Yeopim River begins just below Snug Harbor and meanders up toward US 17. This river has plenty of nooks and crannies ready for exploring. Creeks on this river include:

- Middleton
- Burnt Mill
- Yeopim (the largest creek, which is right across from Drummond Point at the mouth of the river)

Chowan River

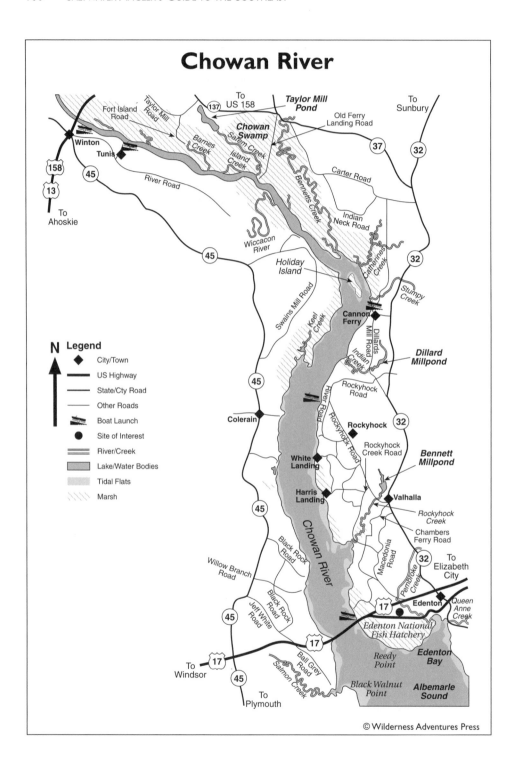

Legend

- City/Town
- US Highway
- State/Cty Road
- Other Roads
- Boat Launch
- Site of Interest
- River/Creek
- Lake/Water Bodies
- Tidal Flats
- Marsh

© Wilderness Adventures Press

Chowan River

The Chowan River begins between Black Walnut Point and Reedy Point at the western end of Albemarle Sound. There is a launch ramp right near the Edenton National Fish Hatchery (take a tour). After launching, head straight south-southwest to Salmon Creek, which is a run of three and a half miles. Other good creek mouths to hit are:

- Rockyhock
- Keel (at Cow Island, which isn't an island, of course)
- Indian
- Stumpy (just above the launch ramp at Cannon Ferry)
- Catherine
- Bennetts (good seatrout water)
- Sarem (in the Chowan Swamp, Sarem comes out of Taylor Mill Pond; there is a ramp at the end of Old Ferry Landing Road)
- Barnes

There are two additional ramps upriver. One is below Winton on Tunis Road, the other in Winton off US Route 13.

Cashie River

The Cashie River is really part of the intricate wetlands associated with Batchelor Bay. It empties into Batchelor Bay at Goodmans Island. Flounder, specks, and stripers are found here. The lower ramp on the river is at Sans Souci, with the upper being at Windsor where the river is quite narrow. Fish can be found all up and down this pretty river, but the following deserve special attention:

- Grennell Creek
- Broad Creek
- the Thoroughfare at Devils Elbow, which links the Roanoke to Cashie
- the outside bends of the many twists and turns on the river

Middle River

The Middle River links the Cashie with the Roanoke, forming Huff Island (really just a swamp) and cuts straight across Batchelor Bay Game Land. It offers the usual specks and flounder, for the most part. During the season, take a shotgun and hunt marsh hens (rails) when the bite is off.

This can just barely be called a river—it's really just a cut between Goodmans Island and Rice Island linking Batchelor Bay to the Roanoke.

Roanoke River

Now we're really getting somewhere. The Roanoke River has become the striped bass river from hell and has been written about in national flyfishing magazines and has been featured in syndicated angling television programs, which means you aren't going to be alone on the Roanoke anymore.

Sometime in the early 1990s, stripers began returning to the lovely Roanoke River in large numbers after their populations started to recover from commercial

Cashie, Middle, and Roanoke River Systems

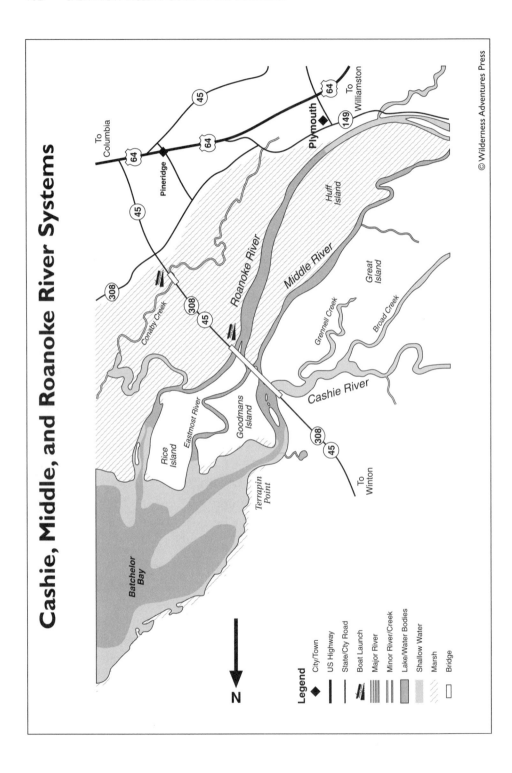

To Columbia

To Williamston

Plymouth

Pineridge

Huff Island

Roanoke River

Middle River

Great Island

Grennell Creek

Broad Creek

Conaby Creek

Cashie River

To Winton

Eastmost River

Rice Island

Goodmans Island

Terrapin Point

Batchelor Bay

© Wilderness Adventures Press

N

Legend
- City/Town
- US Highway
- State/Cty Road
- Boat Launch
- Major River
- Minor River/Creek
- Lake/Water Bodies
- Shallow Water
- Marsh
- Bridge

Large flounder have gotten smart and usually require specialized tricks and tactics.

and recreational overfishing as well as habitat destruction and degradation on Chesapeake Bay, the primary spawning grounds of Atlantic stripers, where 9 out of 10 stripers are hatched and reared. The river is long, twisting, and lined with wetlands. It even has its own national wildlife refuge. There is very little development along the Roanoke, which helps a great deal to preserve this amazing bounty of wonderful game fish.

One of the keys to the Roanoke's success in attracting stripers en masse are the millions of baitfish (mullet, menhaden, and so on) that swarm into the river. These aren't the giants caught off New England's rocky promontories or in the surf along the Outer Banks, but they are good fish that hit with typical striped vigor and fight like demons. They absolutely love flies.

Roanoke River

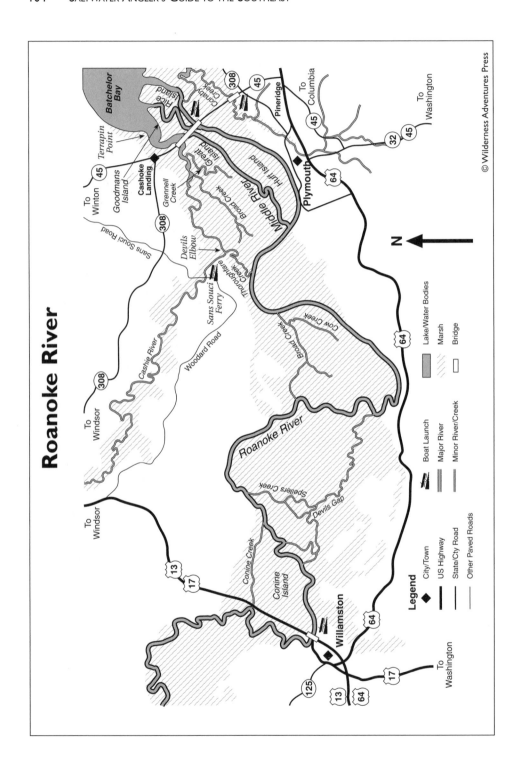

© Wilderness Adventures Press

Legend

◆ City/Town

— US Highway

| | State/Cty Road

— Other Paved Roads

Boat Launch

Major River

Minor River/Creek

Lake/Water Bodies

Marsh

Bridge

Instead of just bringing a floating line, bring a sinking line and don't be afraid to use it. Master flyfisher and caster Lefty Kreh, in Sycamore Island Books' *Gray Ghosts and Lefty's Deceiver: Flyfishing Wisdom from the Masters*, writes about the importance of flyfishers using sinking lines more often and learning how to cast them correctly (efficiently casting a sinking line involves no repeated false casting and open loops rather than tight loops). The Roanoke River's striper fishing is the perfect place for a sinking line because stripers frequently refuse to come to the surface, demanding that the fly be brought down to their level.

All the traditional striper flies produce on the Roanoke, but one of my favorites is Curcione's Sardina, the creation of a deranged man forced to live in Southern California where he actually gets paid to teach deviant behavior. (It's true—Nick Curcione is a college professor who teaches wannabe lawyers and head shrinkers how to recognize psychopaths.)

Crankbaits that imitate baitfish also work, but it's important to have the entire water column covered; diving plugs and surface plugs are needed to handle various conditions.

Roanoake River access is easily accomplished by launching above Plymouth off SR 308, or in Williamston off the SR 17 bypass.

What's a good day on the Roanoke? Knowledgeable flyfishers, such as Tom Earnhardt (one of the southeast's best known anglers), can catch and release nearly 100 in a day. Really! Such numbers are why the Roanoke has been drawing anglers away from the Northeast's famous striper waters, such as those around Nantucket and Maine's Kennebec River.

Water levels play an important role at times within this river system. In 1999, with a generally dry winter and spring, water levels were very low, and municipalities were forced to draw down Lake Gaston above the river. As of this writing stripers have gathered in the sound and are staging below the river's mouth, but the water level may prevent them from moving up in numbers.

Crankbaits, spoons, poppers, and streamers are favorites of guides working the river. Rapalas (Skitter Pops, Jointed, Countdowns, Husky Jerks, Ristos, Shad Raps, and Original Floaters), Rat-L-Traps (the suspending models with factory-applied scent are promising), Zara Spooks, soft plastic jerk baits (Super Floozies, Slug-Gos, and Power Jerk Shads), and flies such as brown and gold Clouser Deep Minnows, Lefty's Deceivers in green and white, red and white, yellow and green, and yellow and gray, and pencil poppers are usually very productive. Take sinktip lines and full-sinking lines for the times when stripers go into deep water and don't want to come up.

Scuppernong River

This is a short river that flows into Bull Bay near the town of Columbia. A ramp is located across from Columbia off US 64, which links the Outer Banks at Hatteras with Rocky Mount and beyond into the heart of North Carolina. Specks, flounder, croakers, and striped bass are found in the Scuppernong.

Scuppernong River

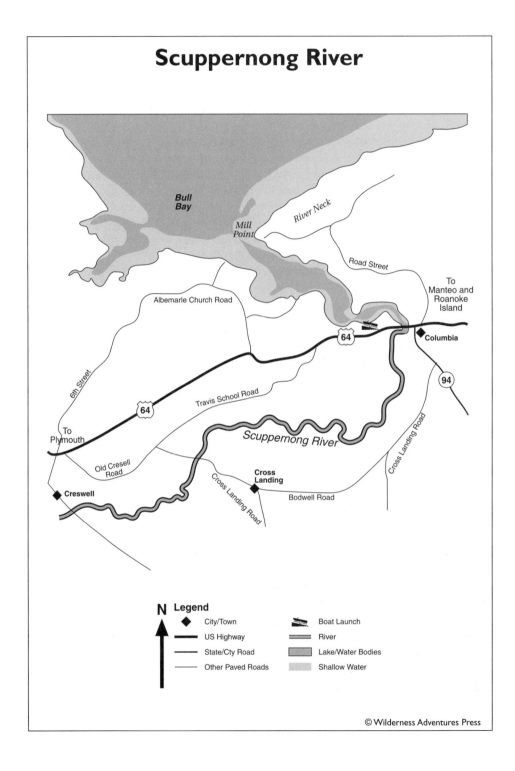

Bull Bay

River Neck

Mill Point

Road Street

To Manteo and Roanoke Island

Albemarle Church Road

64

Columbia

6th Street

94

Travis School Road

64

Cross Landing Road

To Plymouth

Scuppernong River

Old Cresell Road

Cross Landing

Cross Landing Road

Bodwell Road

Creswell

N Legend

- ◆ City/Town
- ▬ US Highway
- — State/Cty Road
- — Other Paved Roads
- Boat Launch
- River
- Lake/Water Bodies
- Shallow Water

© Wilderness Adventures Press

Alligator River

Whereas there are some alligators in the Alligator River, the same can be said of most coastal rivers in North Carolina. The Alligator begins between Sound Point on Durant Island and Long Shoal Point on Goat Neck and is nearly 4 miles wide at this point. It stays wide all the way to about Newport News Point, where the gradual narrowing suddenly increases.

There are three launch ramps along the Alligator. One is located off US 64 at East Lake Landing (remember, East Lake isn't a lake), one is at Frying Pan Landing off Frying Pan Road in the Pocosin Lakes National Wildlife Refuge, and the third is at Gum Neck Landing down on Buck Island, which, of course, isn't an island.

For puppy drum, specks, and flounder try the following:

- the Frying Pan (the entrance to this Frying Pan—remember, there are two Frying Pans—is between Orange Point and Catfish Point)
- the Frying Pan (East Lake north of Long Point)
- Second Creek south of the U.S. Route 64 bridge
- Grapevine Bay at Grapevine Landing
- the narrows around Cherry Ridge Landing

The Alligator River National Wildlife Refuge consists of a large point of land between the Alligator River and Croatan Sound. I have found the best fishing to be from about East Lake Landing around the tip and down to the Roanoke Marsh. Names to remember as potential hot spots include:

- Northeast Prong of South Lake
- Hooker Gut of South Lake
- Tom Mann Creek (northeast side of Durant Island)
- Caroon Point
- Redstone Point
- Mann's Harbor
- Fleetwood Point
- Spencer Creek
- Callaghan Creek

The above-mentioned locations represent a lot of water, enough so that it would take a few weeks to really cover them all.

Oregon Inlet

Moving out across the interior sounds to the Outer Banks, a visiting angler finds Nags Head at the north end of Roanoke Sound and Oregon Inlet at the south end, home to some of the best offshore fishing in the United States and also the hub of one of the finest inshore fisheries in the three-state region. Spencer Marchant, one of North Carolina's most innovative fly tiers and saltwater anglers, has this to say about the area, "Everyone knows about the 1,000-pound blue marlin and the packs of white marlin (offshore), but when you get on the causeway and there's that great marsh across from Pirate's Cove and then all of that backcountry as you ride south on Highway 12, you know that you are in a special place for light tackle inshore fishing."

Alligator River

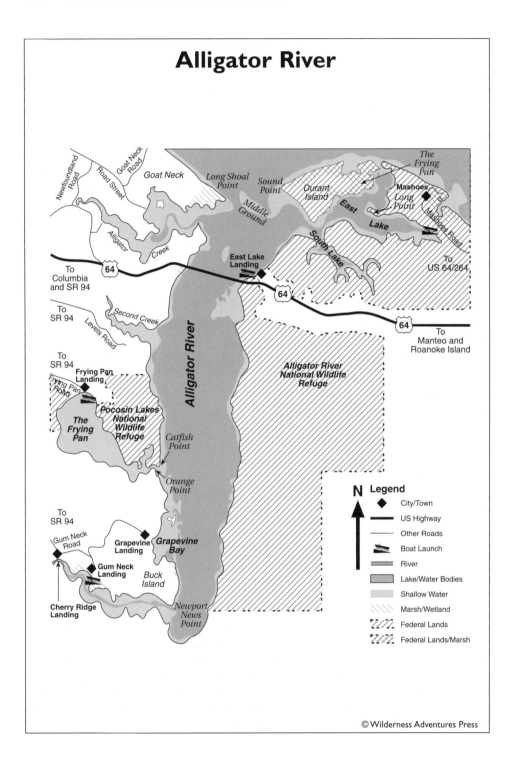

N **Legend**

◆ City/Town

━━ US Highway

── Other Roads

🚤 Boat Launch

═══ River

�\ Lake/Water Bodies

▒ Shallow Water

╲╲╲ Marsh/Wetland

⁄⁄⁄ Federal Lands

⁄⁄⁄ Federal Lands/Marsh

© Wilderness Adventures Press

Alligator River National Wildlife Refuge

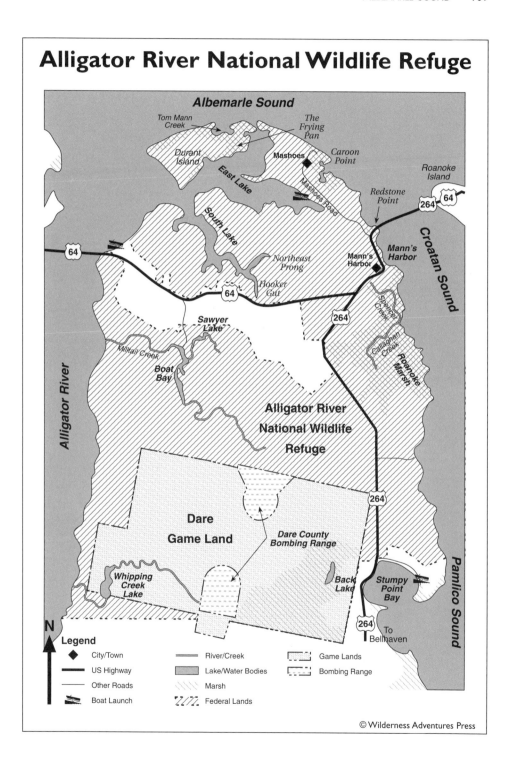

Albemarle Sound

Tom Mann Creek

The Frying Pan

Durant Island

Mashoes

Caroon Point

Roanoke Island

East Lake

Redstone Point

264 64

South Lake

Northeast Prong

Mann's Harbor

Mann's Harbor

Croatan Sound

64

Hooker Gut

64

264

Spencer Creek

Sawyer Lake

Milltail Creek

Callaghen Creek

Roanoke Marsh

Boat Bay

Alligator River

National Wildlife

Refuge

264

Dare

Game Land

Dare County Bombing Range

Whipping Creek Lake

Back Lake

Stumpy Point Bay

Pamlico Sound

264 To Bellhaven

N

Legend

◆ City/Town

━ US Highway

─ Other Roads

Boat Launch

River/Creek

Lake/Water Bodies

Marsh

Federal Lands

Game Lands

Bombing Range

© Wilderness Adventures Press

Oregon Inlet

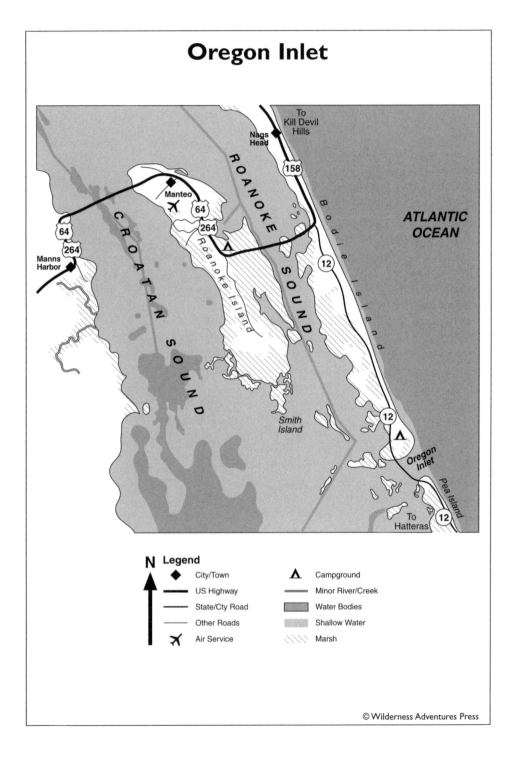

To Kill Devil Hills

Nags Head

158

ROANOKE

Manteo

64

264

CROATAN

SOUND

64

264

Manns Harbor

Roanoke Island

ROANOKE SOUND

Bodie Island

ATLANTIC OCEAN

12

Smith Island

12

Oregon Inlet

Pea Island

To Hatteras

12

N

Legend

◆ City/Town

▬▬ US Highway

▬ State/Cty Road

▬ Other Roads

✈ Air Service

Λ Campground

▬ Minor River/Creek

▨ Water Bodies

▨ Shallow Water

▨ Marsh

© Wilderness Adventures Press

World record class striped bass and red drum inhabit the area, and there is spectacular action for speckled trout, gray trout, and bluefish. Two of North Carolina's best skippers, Captain Brian Horsley and Captain Sarah Gardner have perfected near-shore sight fishing for false albacore, amberjack, and cobia during the summer. I spoke with Brian about the way he hunts fish around Oregon Inlet.

Come spring, Brian looks for two primary species of game fish around the inlet: stripers and redfish. The stripers around Oregon Inlet in the spring are mainly schoolies that can be found chasing the myriad baitfish in the water at this time of year around marshy points, sloughs, and the many shoals behind the inlet. These young stripers ("rockfish" to a lot of folks along the North Carolina coast, you will recall) move quickly from place to place, so watch for signs of them feeding, such as birds wheeling and diving into the water. Crankbaits that imitate wounded baitfish and flies like the Lefty's Deceiver will bring strikes—often plenty of them because these are inexperienced stripers. Spring reds can produce some of the fastest action of the year, according to Brian. In the spring of 1999, Brian took 100 reds in three days of flyfishing, with the reds running between 14 and 30 inches, with lots of fish in the 26- to 28-inch range. Traditional bottom flies like the Clouser are often best. He looks for the best action around shoals and on the ledges of sloughs where the drum hunt crabs, baitfish, and shrimp.

Although many anglers think that the heat of summer puts off the bite, the truth is that summer around Oregon Inlet means a lot of fish, for those who know where to look and how to fish them. Brian is known as a speck specialist, and when he wants summertime specks he oftentimes begins by hitting the grassy areas of flats and points in the sounds. He also checks bridge pilings from time to time, although he says "that really isn't my bag." Oregon Inlet's grassy flats can hold tremendous numbers of midsized specks, and a fly rodder with a few Clousers can have a great deal of fun. Light-tackle guys should throw jigs and MirroLures.

However, specks aren't the only thing around the inlet in summer. When a client wants something bigger, Brian goes to the near-shore wrecks for amberjack, which are very powerful fish requiring heavy fly rods to be lifted up and away from the structure of the wreck. For the best control, I recommend a 12-weight rod with a lot of butt. Cobia are also available, mostly just outside the inlet. Buoys and wrecks are good places to look for these unusual, hard-fighting game fish.

Oregon Inlet is extremely well known for its world-class angling in autumn. Over the last few years, guides have seen more and more anglers showing up in the fall, many of them flyfishers. The reason is that North Carolina has been receiving quite a bit of ink in the angling press lately, with several renowned flyfishing writers covering the area.

Autumn is the time of year when the great false albacore runs strike the Tar Heel coast. Oregon Inlet sees large numbers of these brawlers, which hang over the wrecks and also come right inshore. The flyrodder with a small green-and-white Clouser that mimics glass minnows can have the time of his life. No, Oregon Inlet doesn't get the attention from flyrodders and light-tackle buffs that Cape Lookout to the south does, but the advantage of this is that there are far fewer boats loaded with anglers chasing the albies. But fat Alberts aren't the only game in town—big reds come up onto the shoals in the fall, and the giant schools of marauding blues show up as well, with the latter being one of the most exciting events along the coast. The stripers are back, hanging around the marshy points, and the specks have grown quite fat; what Brian calls "quality fish." True, there don't seem to be quite as many around, but the fish are bigger, fatter, and more aggressive.

Winter means stripers around Oregon Inlet, and some real dandies are caught this time of year, too. Check the rips for signs of the line-siders feeding below or even right on the surface, but always check right along the beach on bluebird days.

All in all, Oregon Inlet is classic North Carolina coastal angling, whether you are in love with your fly rods or more into spinning gear.

For anglers travelling without a boat, there is excellent wade-fishing with a fly rod for specks on the eastern end of the Oregon Inlet fishing docks. Anglers with a boat would do well to put in at the Fishing Center and prospect their way toward the Oregon Inlet bridge. There are inumerable sandbars, oyster bars, and marsh creek mouths that are home to specks, drum, and flounder during most months.

The long span of bridge across the inlet supplies a great striper fishery, second only to the bridge from Mann's Harbor to Manteo as a rockfish landmark. Live bait and bucktails are the rule of thumb here with large, dark Deceiver patterns on sinking lines often bringing success to fly anglers. Fall stripers up to 40 pounds can be found crashing bait on the shoals, but a serious word to the wise is in order: be careful. It can be very exciting—the birds up and the fish visibly crashing bait—but it can be extremely dangerous even in good weather. Horsley, who grew up on the Outer Banks and has been flyfishing here since 1973, says, "I will not fish in the shoals any more. It is simply too dangerous."

Keep in mind that this is one of the busiest and best known angling spots along the coast of North Carolina. The huge array of boats can be as diverse as the fishing, and it always pays to keep an eye on the weather. Mother nature can kick up some big waves in this area.

The Outer Banks

The Outer Banks cover quite a long stretch and facilities are numerous though sometimes far apart. There are quite a few chain motels around Nags Head and Kill Devil Hills, such as Comfort Inns, Holiday Inns, Best Westerns, Days Inns, etc. Below are some other choices as well.

ACCOMMODATIONS

Nags Head Beach Motel (Kill Devil Hills), SR 12 / 252-441-0411
Cape Hatteras Bed and Breakfast (Buxton), Old Lighthouse Road / 252-995-6004
Comfort Inn (Buxton), Old Lighthouse Road / Buxton, NC 27920 / 252-995-6100
Lighthouse View Motel (Buxton), SR 12 / 252-995-5680
The Inn at Corolla Light (Corolla), on the Waterfront / 252-453-3340
Atlantic View Motel (Hatteras), SR 12 / 800-986-2330
Beach Haven (Kitty Hawk), SR 12 / 252-261-4785
Three Seasons Inn Bed & Breakfast (Kitty Hawk), SR 12 / 252-261-4791
Elizabethan Inn (Manteo), 814 North Hwy / 252-473-2101
Roanoke Island Inn (Manteo), 305 Fernando Street / 252-473-5511
Nags Head Inn (Nags Head), SR 12 / 252-441-0454
The Vacationer Motel (Nags Head), SR 12 / 252-441-7487
Berkley Manor Bed & Breakfast (Ocracoke), 60 Water Plant Road / 252-928-5911
Harborside Motel (Ocracoke), SR 12 / 252-928-3111

CAMPGROUNDS

Colington Park Campground (Kill Devil Hills),1608 Colington Road / 252-441-6128
Joe and Kay's Campground (Kill Devil Hills), Colington Road / 252-441-5468
Cypress Cove Campground (Manteo), 818 US 64 & 204 / 252-473-5231

RESTAURANTS

Awful Arthur's Oyster Bar (Kill Devil Hills), SR 12 / 252-441-5955 / Good menu in addition to what's served up at the oyster bar, daily specials
Millie's Diner (Kill Devil Hills), SR 12 / 252-480-3463 / A good variety of dishes and interesting place
Steamer's Restaurant & Raw Bar (Corolla), Timbuck II Shopping Center / 252-453-3344 / Beef, seafood, and steamer pots (to go)
Duck News Café (Duck), 1564 Duck Road / 252-261-1549 / Seafood and Italian cuisine
Sonny's (Hatteras), Hatteras Village / 252-986-2922 / Owned by the Quigley family for well over 20 years, this is a good restaurant featuring fresh seafood without the heavy batter / Also do good steaks, prime rib, and chicken
Big Al's Soda Fountain and Grill (Manteo) / 252-473-5570 / Cool off with a treat from Big Al
Hurricane Mo's (Manteo), Nags Head Causeway / 252-473-2266 / A steam bar, raw bar, and fresh seafood lineup are available
George's Junction (Nags Head), 2608 Virginia Dare Trail / 252-441-0606 / Seafood buffet (just start eating)

Kelly's Outer Banks Restaurant & Tavern (Nags Head), Mile Post 10½, 158 Bypass / 252-441-4116 / Beef, seafood, and pasta

Oasis Waterfront Oyster Bar and Seafood Restaurant (Nags Head), Nags Head/Manteo Causeway / 252-441-7721 / A full menu is available along with the raw bar, which offers shellfish, crab legs, and shrimp

Pirate's Cove Restaurant & Raw Bar (Nags Head), Pirate's Cove Marina (Manteo-Nags Head Causeway) / 252-473-2266

Tortugas' Lie (Nags Head), SR 12 / 252-441-7299 / Caribbean style seafood, beef, chicken, and vegetarian cuisine, as well as sushi

Cosmo's Pizzeria (Southern Shores), The Marketplace / 252-261-8388 / Hearty home cooking

AIR SERVICE

Nearest Commercial Airport: Norfolk, Virginia (approximately three hours depending on traffic)

TACKLE AND FLY SHOPS

Whitney's Bait & Tackle (Kill Devil Hills), SR 12 / 252-261-5551

Cape Point Tackle (Buxton), SR 12 / 252-995-3147

Red Drum Tackle Shop (Buxton), SR12 / 252-995-5414

Martyn's Sea & Stream (Durham), 4711 Hope Valley Road, Suite 1J / 919-403-1604 / John and Kathy Martyn own and operate this outstanding tackle shop (including a full line of flyfishing tackle) / John is a keen albacore angler, too, so stop in for a little advice when in the area

Frisco Rod & Gun (Frisco), SR 12 / 252-995-5366 / This shop carries both light tackle and fly tackle

Pelican's Roost (Hatteras), SR 12 / 252-986-2213

T.J.'s Bait & Tackle (Kill Devil Hills), 100 West Clark Street / 252-441-3166

Trade Winds Tackle Shop (Ocracoke), SR 12 / 252-928-5491

Captain Marty's (Kill Devil Hills), 5151 South Croatan Hwy / 252-441-3132

Pirate's Cove Yacht Club & Marina (Nags Head), Manteo/Nags Head Causeway/800-367-4728

MARINAS

Oregon Inlet Fishing Center (Manteo) / 800-272-5199 / Website: www.oregon-inlet.com / E-mail: oregon-inlet@outer-banks.com

Pirate's Cove Yacht Club & Marina (Nags Head), Manteo/Nags Head Causeway / 800-367-4728

Hatteras Landing (Hatteras), 58848 Marina Way / 252-986-2205 or 800-551-8478 / Website: marina@hatteraslanding.com

Teach's Lair Marina (Hatteras), SR 12 / 252-986-2460

FOR MORE INFORMATION

Outer Banks Chamber of Commerce
Ocean Bay Boulevard and Mustian Street
Kill Devil Hills, NC 27948
252-441-8144

Elizabeth City
Population–18,000 • Located on Pasquotank River

ACCOMMODATIONS
Comfort Inn, US Hwy 17 South / 252-338-8900
Holiday Inn, 522 South Hughes Boulevard / 252-338-3951
Whistling Pines Motel, 1151 US Hwy 17 South / 252-335-0817
Travelers Motel, US Hwy 17 North / 252-338-5451

RESTAURANTS
Colonial Restaurant, 418 East ColonialAvenue / 252-335-0212 / Serves southern
   style cuisine / Breakfast, lunch, and dinner
Thumper's Downtown Bar and Grill, 200 North Poindexter Street / 252-333-1775
   / Serves burgers and sandwiches
Mulligan's Waterfront Grille, 400 South Water Street / 252-331-2431 / Seafood,
   beef dishes, and sandwiches / Has a great reputation
Marina Restaurant, Camden Causeway / 252-335-7307

AIR SERVICE
Nearest airport is in Norfolk, Virginia

MARINAS
Pelican Marina, 43 Camden Causeway /^252-335-5108
Riverside Boat Works, 708 Riverside Avenue / 252-335-2118

FOR MORE INFORMATION
Chamber of Commerce
502 East Ehringhaus Street
Elizabeth City, NC 27909
252-335-4365

Some Words on Surf Fishing

Because this isn't a surf-fishing manual, I do not go into great detail on this sport. However, some general advice should be mentioned.

A surf caster focuses on three features of the beach: natural structure and other features in the surf zone that attract baitfish and therefore game fish, such as rocks, holes, wrecks, troughs, rips, points, hooks, and so on; water adjacent to piers; and inlets.

Every major surf-fishing location holds something like the aforementioned structure and other features. Flat stretches of beach having little of these features hold fish only temporarily, i.e., fish that are very transient (moving from one favored feeding location to another).

Traditional surf tackle along the Outer Banks consists of long, heavy rods and huge spinning reels that can toss heavy weight and large chunks of cut bait a long way. I do not consider such tackle to be much fun, although fighting a 45-pound bull red on tackle such as this isn't exactly boring, either. If you want advice on surf casting, read Robert J. Goldstein's *Coastal Fishing in the Carolinas from Surf, Pier, and Jetty* (John F. Blair, Publisher).

Some surf casters have figured out that light spinning tackle can be used on the beach for smaller species of game fish.

Outer Banks Tarpon

Starting in about late June, tarpon show up from Florida. Whereas most North Carolina tarpon are caught in sounds and rivers, there are some spots along the Outer Banks that are well known tarpon hangouts.

Hatteras Inlet, "The Bight," and Diamond Shoals north of the inlet all hold tarpon because of the baitfish that swarm there. Chum slicks with chunks of menhaden or live bait drifted in the slick can be strong medicine for the silver kings, and once in a while a king mackerel angler gets the surprise of a lifetime when a 100-pound tarpon crashes a slow-trolled menhaden.

At the southern end of the Outer Banks lies Cape Lookout. Best known for spotted seatrout and false albacore, tarpon get in and around the shoals and can be taken with standard tarpon techniques.

Bottom rigs can be as specialized for a surf caster as flies and leaders can be for a flyfisher. Here, George Misko readies an offering.

Pamlico Sound

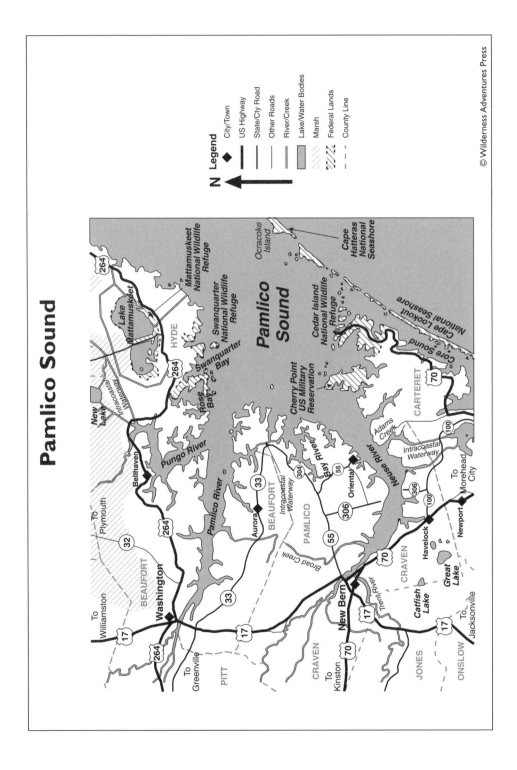

© Wilderness Adventures Press

PAMLICO SOUND

Forget ever fishing all of this water very completely in one lifetime; there is just too much of it. Try as I might, I can't say that I have fished every piece of this water—no one can. Nevertheless, it is a lot of fun trying.

Caution is called for on this stretch of water more than any other inshore water along the Southeast coast because of the broad nature of Pamlico Sound and the way serious waves can build up in a hurry. This is no little salt pond—it's a huge piece of water with a way of sneaking up on if you aren't paying attention to the weather and water.

Some good rules for Pamlico Sound:

- If you don't know where you are, then don't go any farther; determine your location and then move on.

One of North Carolina's top light tackle and flyfishing guides, Captain George Beckwith of Down East Guide Service, admires a good speck taken on Pamlico Sound.

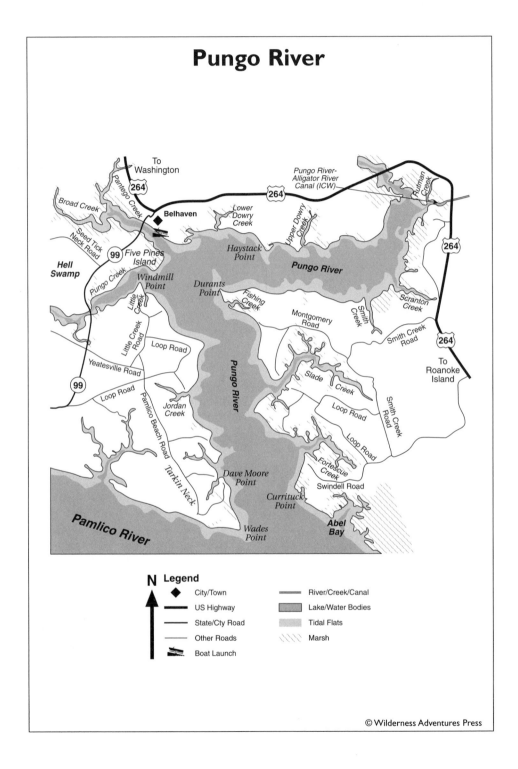

Pungo River

- The wind and waves can build at any time of the day, not just in the afternoon —watch the weather.
- Take water (lots of it), protection, and food with you.

These three rules will keep you in less trouble, I assure you. Follow them.

North Carolina's largest sound, Pamlico sprawls across the map and can produce its own weather systems. It takes a long, long time to learn this sound and its four rivers. Pamlico Sound is extremely important to the health of the coastal ecosystems that make up this historic and fascinating water.

Of the four rivers that help form Pamlico's littorals—the Pungo, Pamlico, Bay, and Neuse—two are especially well known as recreational fisheries: the Pamlico and the Neuse. But to be honest, although there are still game fish to be caught in these rivers, commercial overfishing, destructive netting practices, and agricultural runoff have gotten the attention of national environmental organizations. The fight is on between the pillaging netters and the recreational anglers. The outcome remains to be seen.

Pungo River

This is a fun river with many locations that are seldom seriously fished by recreational anglers. The river opens into Pamlico Sound between Wades Point on Tarkin Neck and Currituck Point. Some definite areas to explore include:

- Fortescue Creek's many arms and sloughs
- the fingers of Slade Creek
- Fishing Creek below Durants Point
- Smith Creek and Scranton Creek bordering the Pungo River Game Lands
- Rutman Creek at the mouth of the Pungo River-Alligator River Canal (this section of the Atlantic Intracoastal Waterway joins the Pungo to the Alligator River at Winn Bay)
- Upper and Lower Dowry Creeks, which bracket Haystack Point (the slough behind Haystack Point should be examined)
- Pantego Creek and Broad Creek near Belhaven above Five Pines Island (which isn't an island)—there's a launch ramp in Belhaven;
- Pungo Creek on Hell Swamp (avoid wandering around in Hell Swamp);
- Little Creek below Windmill Point;
- Jordan Creek;
- the fingers of Tarkin Neck above Dave Moore Point.

Pamlico River

This river is getting a reputation as a tarpon river, but the truth is that tarpon have been coming into the Pamlico for as long as anyone can remember. The silver kings show up in late June or early July most years, and how many show up seems to vary each year. I know of no one who has taken a tarpon in the Pamlico on the fly, although a few years ago a rumor was going around that someone had done it and was keeping it quiet for some reason.

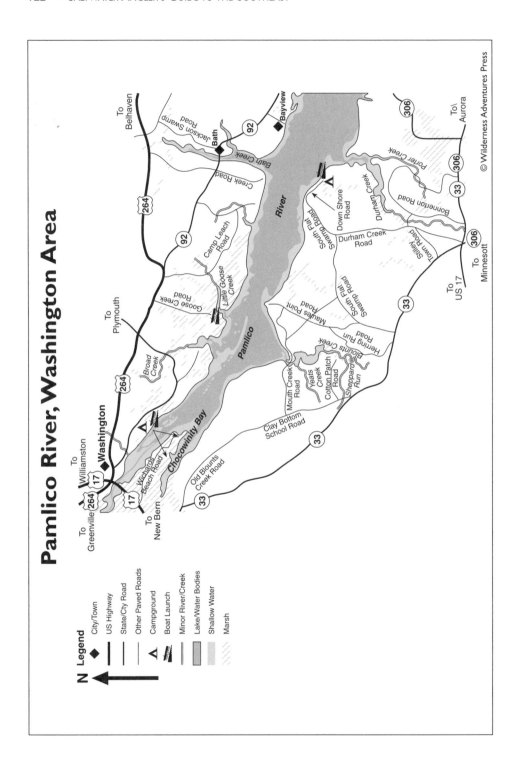

Pamlico River, Washington Area

Pamlico River Mouth

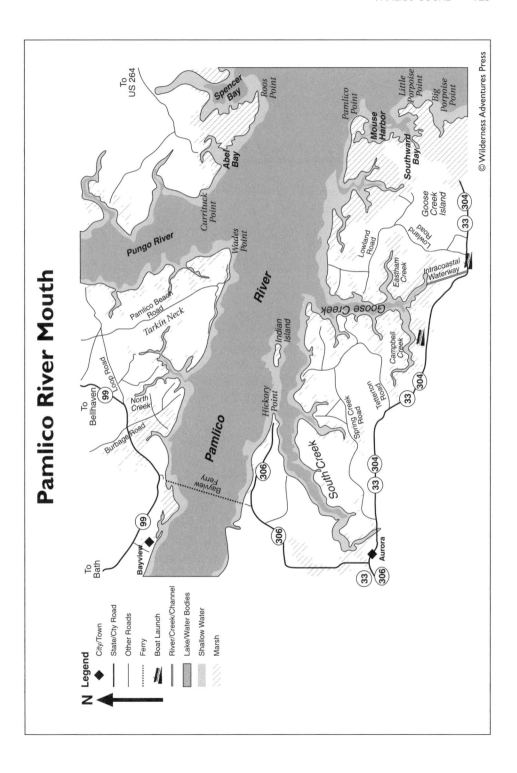

© Wilderness Adventures Press

Legend

N

◆ City/Town
State/Cty Road
Other Roads
Ferry
Boat Launch
River/Creek/Channel
Lake/Water Bodies
Shallow Water
Marsh

To US 264

Spencer Bay
Roos Point
Abel Bay
Currituck Point
Wades Point

Pungo River

Pamlico Beach Road
Tarkin Neck

Loop Road

To Bellhaven

North Creek

Burbage Road

To Bath

Bayview

Bayview Ferry

Pamlico

River

Indian Island

Hickory Point

South Creek

306

306

Spring Creek Road

Teterton Road

33 304

Aurora

33 306

Pamlico Point

Mouse Harbor

Southward Bay

Little Porpoise Point

Big Porpoise Point

Goose Creek Island

Lowland Road

Eastham Creek

Goose Creek

Campbell Creek

Intracoastal Waterway

304

33

304

33

304

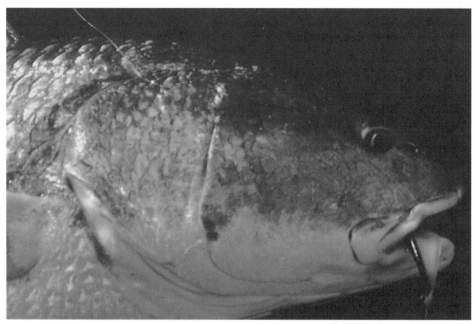

*Big red drum live in Pamlico Sound in huge schools. Jigs account
for many of them, although cut bait is also very popular.
More and more people are also flyfishing for them.*

What makes flyfishing for tarpon so difficult or nearly impossible on this river —
and every other river in North Carolina apparently—is the problem of sight casting
to them. The stained waters of the rivers and sounds don't allow stalking the way the
Florida flats do. But anglers using dead or cut bait on the bottom in a chum slick are
another matter altogether.

I have seen huge numbers of tarpon (big ones that all went in the 100-pound range
and then some) rolling in Pamlico Sound just outside the mouth of the river. They then
head upriver in search of baitfish that are easier to catch within the confines of the
river. The way to find poons is to watch for them rolling (gulping air—tarpon have an
air bladder) on the surface. When you see this happen, it has to be tarpon because
there is no other fish about 6 feet long and made of solid, shiny silver armor.

Once you spot one (often there are more than one, since tarpon travel in pods
quite frequently), move upriver past where the tarpon were spotted and drop anchor.
Begin chumming and set a dead menhaden on the bottom with a circle hook. A
chum slick created by chunks of menhaden, oil, scales, and blood creates a nice
aroma in the water—once tarpon smell it, they come to investigate.

Red drum love crabs above nearly all else, but few North Carolina anglers use them. Florida guides, on the other hand, use them all the time.

A tarpon might keep moving forward after picking up the menhaden, which puts slack in the line. If this happens, reel up fast until the line tightens. Once the tarpon's weight is felt, it's best to lay into it both hard and repeatedly to drive the hook into its bony mouth—and then hang on! The tarpon will become very upset: jumping repeatedly with wild thrashing gyrations; dancing on its tail; sounding; charging the boat; running out all the line it can; trying to jump into the boat (if it does, get out in order to avoid a broken arm or leg); and pulling all sorts of other crazy stunts trying to get that hook out of its mouth. When it jumps, bow to him by pointing the rod straight at him to reduce the strain on the line. When it hits the water, bring the rod back up. Every time it turns one way, flip the rod the other way to put pressure against it. This tires the tarpon out faster and facilitates a safe release.

A stiff spinning rod with a reel capable of holding at least 300 yards of 30-lb. test line, such as Super Silver Thread, is needed. Use a very tough leader with a Bimini twist for added strength.

But there's a lot more than tarpon in the Pamlico. Spotted seatrout, puppy drum (especially around stumps), flounder (on a moving tide, flounder go nuts chasing baitfish moving with the tide), striped bass (nothing like the Roanoke, but still respectable from time to time), croaker, gar (this very brackish river even holds bass and bream), and Spanish mackerel on the lower end.

Dropoffs around creek mouths on the Pamlico River are often very productive spring through fall. Good creeks include:

- Goose Creek (Campbell Creek and Eastham Creek are off Goose, and there are several sloughs that are worthwhile, too)
- North Creek on Tarkin Neck

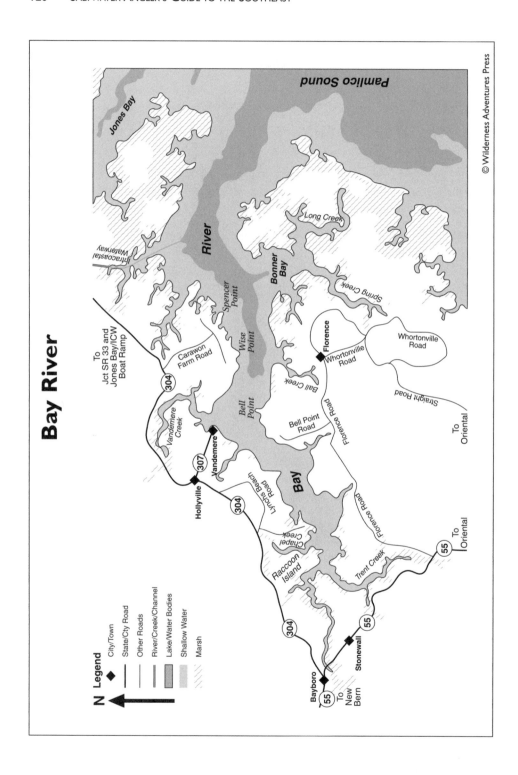

Bay River

- Bath Creek (try going a long way up this creek and also State Reef AR-291, known as Bayview Reef, which is just southeast of the creek's mouth)
- Little Goose Creek (not part of Goose Creek, Little Goose is part of Goose Creek State Park off US 264)
- Broad Creek (just up from Little Goose)
- Blounts Creek (check Sheppard Run and Yeats Creek off Blounts)
- Durham Creek (hit Porter Creek on Durham)
- South Creek (this is a big creek with a lot of flounder and specks)

Launch ramps to use on the Pamlico include: the ramp off Wichards Beach Road on Chocowinity Bay below Washington; Dinah Landing on Little Goose Creek; Down Shore Road above Durham Creek; and in the Goose Creek Game Lands off SR 33.

Most recreational anglers on Pamlico are after specks and flatties. Jigs are the way to go most of the time when using light tackle, and flyfishers use Clousers in chartreuse and white or maroon and gold about 1/0 to 2/0 in size. Make sure you have a sinking line or at least a sinktip to work the holes and dropoffs.

Bay River

Bay River is very jagged, offering numerous creeks, fingers, sloughs, cuts, and other opportunities for speck and flounder lovers, and even some puppy drum. The mouth begins between Sanders Point and Pine Tree Point, running southwest to Stonewall, where it turns south and then southeast to where Trent Creek joins up with it.

There are almost too many good areas to mention along the Bay River, so I'll keep the list to the best of the best. As you might expect, these spots have to do with creeks, dropoffs, and points that form shallow bays behind them. By all means try these:

- Bonner Bay, with Spring Creek and Long Creek running off the south end of the bay
- Ball Creek above Florence
- around Bell Point
- the area around Raccoon Island (don't confuse this island with Raccoon Island farther south where the Neuse River meets the sound)
- Chapel Creek
- the fingers of Wise Point and Spencer Point
- Vandemere Creek, which winds up behind Hollyville toward SR 304

The best way to get a boat up Bay River is to launch at the ramp off SR 304 along the cut of the waterway just above Jones Bay.

Neuse River

The Neuse River has been in the national spotlight lately because of *Pfiesteria* problems. Nevertheless, although puppy drum and speck angling has fallen off, stripers have returned to the river, and more and more are available to catch, although it still seems that fewer than expected anglers seek them.

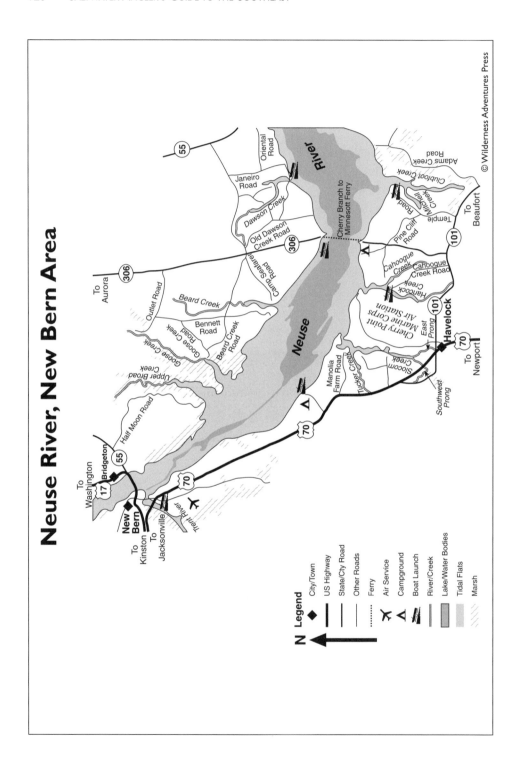

Neuse River, New Bern Area

© Wilderness Adventures Press

Neuse River Mouth

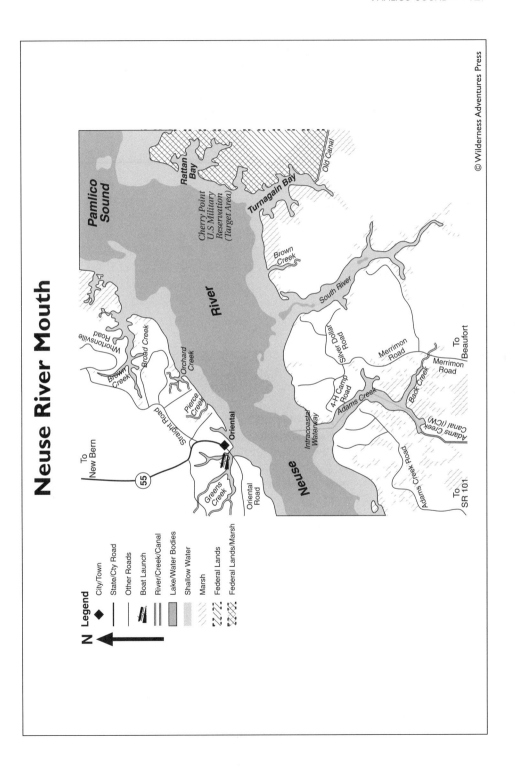

Legend

- ◆ City/Town
- — State/City Road
- Other Roads
- Boat Launch
- River/Creek/Canal
- Lake/Water Bodies
- Shallow Water
- Marsh
- Federal Lands
- Federal Lands/Marsh

N

Pamlico Sound

Rattan Bay

Turnagain Bay

Cherry Point U.S Military Reservation (Target Area)

Brown Creek

South River

River

Old Canal

Whortonsville Road

Broad Creek

Brown Creek

Orchard Creek

Pierce Creek

Straight Road

Oriental

Greens Creek

Oriental Road

To New Bern

55

Neuse

Intracoastal Waterway

Silver Dollar Road

4-H Camp Road

Adams Creek

Merrimon Road

Merrimon Road

Back Creek

Adams Creek Canal (ICW)

Adams Creek Road

To Beaufort

To SR 101

© Wilderness Adventures Press

A brace of Neuse River stripers.

The Neuse is big—its mouth stretching between Point of Marsh on Piney Island and Tonney Hill Point—and offers many possibilities beginning at Rattan Bay and South Bay, which indent the western side of Piney Island. (A word of caution: Don't wander around anywhere on Piney Island because the Marines drop bombs on it.) Below these two bays are Cedar Bay and Turnagain Bay, the latter being linked to Long Bay and the Cedar Island region via Old Canal. There are a lot of puppy drum in this area, some of which are not puppies!

On the north side of the Neuse, try these areas:

- Upper Broad Creek between Roland Point and Creek Point
- Goose Creek (North Carolinians ran out of names for creeks long ago and are now recycling them)
- Beard Creek

Piney Island Area

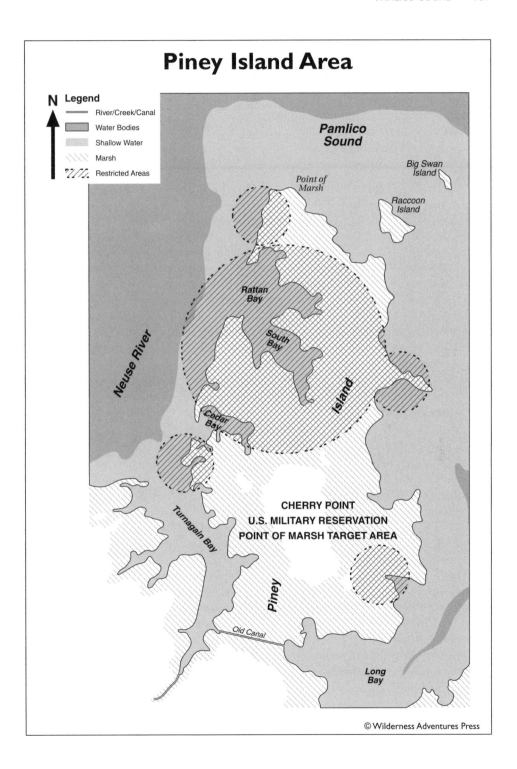

N

Legend
- ─── River/Creek/Canal
- Water Bodies
- Shallow Water
- Marsh
- Restricted Areas

Pamlico Sound

Big Swan Island

Point of Marsh

Raccoon Island

Rattan Bay

Neuse River

South Bay

Island

Cedar Bay

**CHERRY POINT
U.S. MILITARY RESERVATION
POINT OF MARSH TARGET AREA**

Turnagain Bay

Piney

Old Canal

Long Bay

© Wilderness Adventures Press

- two-pronged Dawson Creek
- three-pronged Greens Creek at Oriental, home to the now famous Oriental Rotary Club Tarpon Tournament

On the north side toward the mouth of the Neuse try:

- Pierce Creek at Whitehurst Point
- Orchard Creek
- another Broad Creek
- Brown Creek, which is really an arm of Broad Creek

Upriver on the south side, consider these areas:

- Brown Creek (short but sometimes worth a look)
- South River (hardly a river, it is more a wide creek)
- Adams Creek with the Adams Creek Canal at its lower end, which is part of the Atlantic Intracoastal Waterway that makes for a great shortcut between the Neuse and Newport Rivers, and Back Creek runs off of Adams Creek
- Clubfoot Creek and its offspring, Mitchell Creek
- Hancock Creek and Cahoogue Creek, which form a large fork beside Cherry Point Marine Corps Air Station
- Slocum Creek on the other side of the air station—Slocum has two prongs called Southwest and East, and a finger running off the north end called Tucker Creek
- the Trent River, which brings in a lot of fresh water, thus making largemouth bass just as likely, if not more so, as puppy drum and specks (lots of weed growth up here)

Speaking of Oriental, the Neuse is well known for its tarpon. Each summer, folks start looking for tarpon rolling around the US 17 bridge connecting New Bern to Bridgeton. When tarpon can be seen below the bridge, it's time to head for the river or sound to catch the silver kings.

I think the Neuse has a great deal of potential as a striper fishery. I first fished it for stripers many years ago with Captain Bill Harris of Atlantic Beach and my buddy, Rick Pelow. It was at the confluence of the Neuse and the Trent that Rick took his first striper. He still talks about it today—he was stunned at the ferocity of the attack and the power the striper had in reserve.

The Neuse has a lot of backcountry water with stumps, rocks, oysters, flats, holes, points, creeks, rips, sunken trees, and other structure that attracts and holds fish. Naturally, there are enough ramps to serve the river. A big, nice one is just off US 70 beside the bridge crossing the Trent. Flanner Beach has one (take Flanner Beach Road off US 70), as does Minnesott near the ferry terminal on SR 306, Hancock Creek off Cahoogue Creek Road, Temple Road at the mouth of Mitchell Creek in downtown Oriental, and also just off Janeiro Road inside Dawson Creek.

CAPE LOOKOUT TO NEW RIVER INLET

This region receives its fair share of boat traffic and angling pressure, but that shouldn't preclude visiting here. With easy access via US 17 and regional airports, such as Beaufort-Morehead City, Jacksonville, and Wilmington, and moderate prices, this stretch of coast can be rewarding in many ways.

Barden Inlet to Beaufort Inlet

Flounder, specks, and Spanish mackerel are the primary attractions heading northwest from Barden Inlet inside the hook of the cape toward the North River. Flies, lures, and bait fished around Great Marsh Island, Cedar Hammock, Morgan

The dean of North Carolina saltwater flyfishers, Tom Earnhardt, admires a fat Albert taken at Cape Lookout in November 1998, which was a super false albacore season. Many of the greats in the flyfishing world—Tom, Lefty Kreh, Bob Clouser, Ed Jaworowski, Bob Popovics, Jon Cave, and other notables—showed up for the annual gathering of flyfishing writers and tiers at Tom's home on Harkers Island. I was invited because I paid Tom five dollars.

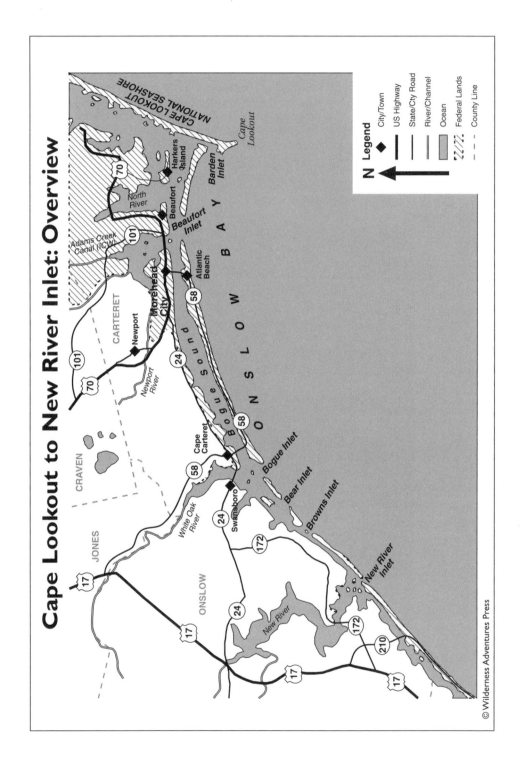

Cape Lookout to New River Inlet: Overview

Legend
N
City/Town
US Highway
State/City Road
River/Channel
Ocean
Federal Lands
County Line

© Wilderness Adventures Press

North River

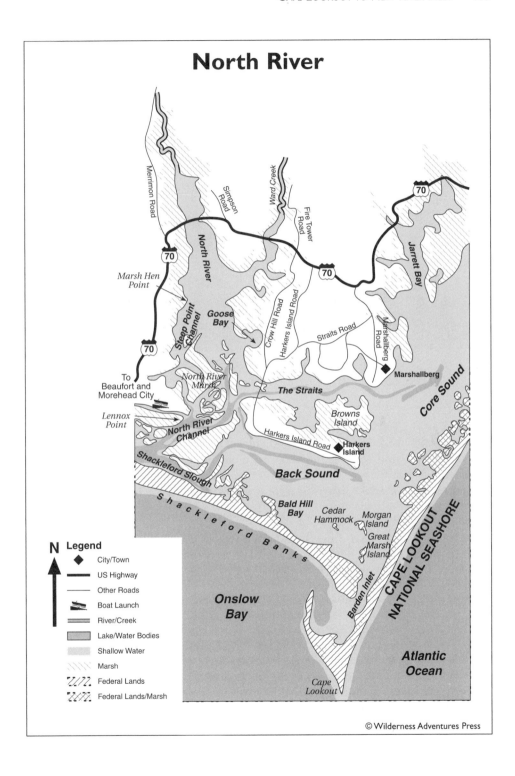

Legend

- ◆ City/Town
- ▬ US Highway
- — Other Roads
- 🛥 Boat Launch
- ═ River/Creek
- ▨ Lake/Water Bodies
- ▨ Shallow Water
- ▨ Marsh
- ▨ Federal Lands
- ▨ Federal Lands/Marsh

© Wilderness Adventures Press

A classic Cape Lookout false albacore.

Island, Bald Hill Bay, and Shackleford Slough can all be productive. It is especially useful to watch for feeding pelicans and gulls in this area.

At the cape itself, some of the best false albacore action on the Eastern Seaboard can be found. This fishery is astounding at times and has become extremely popular, as I mentioned earlier. Flyfishers and spin casters alike can catch a great many albies in the hook of the cape from October through December, with November being prime time.

While the boats can be thick, especially on the weekend, the fish are there, sometimes in mobs that stretch from the cape all the way to Beaufort Inlet, which was the case for a couple of days in early November 1998. Small chartreuse Clousers produce all the time and in great numbers.

The broad indentation of Shackleford Banks is Spanish mackerel country. Trolled spoons with feather dusters in front of them are excellent.

North River

Because it is so broad and short, the North River is really more like a bay with a creek at the upper end. Beginning at the North River Channel between Lennox Point and Harkers Island, motor up the North River to these five areas, the primary fish attractors in the North River and all good bets for successful fishing:

The subject of many paintings, photos, sketches, and other forms of art, the fabled lighthouse at Cape Lookout today marks the best false albacore area along the North Carolina coast. The Jones Brothers Cape Fisherman has become one of the most popular fishing boats among knowledgeable anglers, with flyfishers and light tackle buffs finding it especially practical inshore, near-shore, and offshore. Jones Brothers Marina is located in Morehead City, North Carolina. Photo by Tom Earnhardt.

- North River Marsh to the west
- Steep Point Channel
- Goose Bay (flounder and speck country)
- Marsh Hen Point
- Ward Creek (some very good puppy drum action)

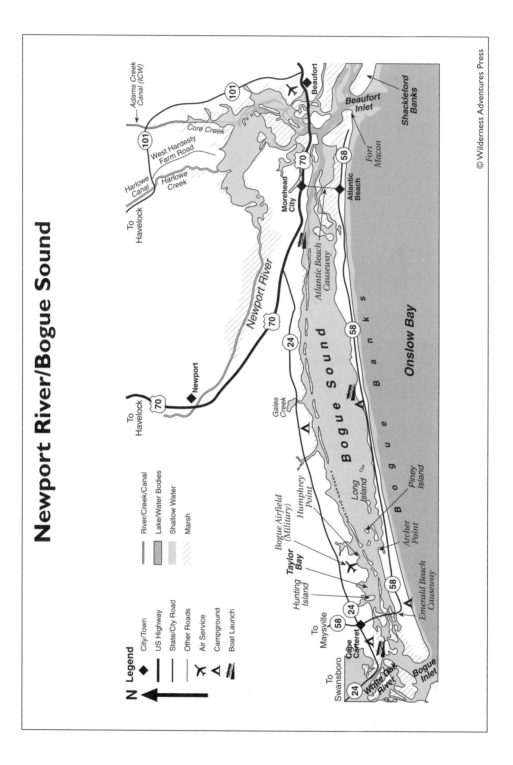

Newport River/Bogue Sound

© Wilderness Adventures Press

Morehead City–Newport River

Heading west toward Morehead City, it becomes almost impossible to find a quiet place to wet a line. This is due to the heavy boat traffic using Beaufort Inlet, which includes commercial shipping and vessels belonging to the US Navy and Coast Guard.

However, there are fish in this area for those who know where to look and what to offer. For example, in the Morehead City Channel, some very nice kings can be tempted by trolling live menhaden. Or back in the Newport River, try these spots:

- Core Creek (one of the best red drum and speck creeks in the region)
- Harlow Creek
- the bridges along US 70 between Morehead City and Beaufort (for sheepshead and black sea bass);
- the "Turning Basin" (for specks)
- the Atlantic Beach Causeway (especially for cobia and sheepshead)
- the Fort Macon rock jetty (gray trout, specks, albies, flounder, and bluefish)

Bogue Sound

West of the causeway things begin to quiet down somewhat. This is Bogue Sound, which separates Beaufort Inlet from Bogue Inlet. Bogue is North Carolina's southernmost major sound, with the White Oak River at its lower end. The southern end of Bogue Sound is bordered by the Emerald Isle Causeway, a high-rise bridge linking Emerald Isle on lower Bogue Banks with Cape Carteret.

Creek mouths, coves, docks, and spartina points are the key to successful fly-fishing and spin casting Bogue Sound. Check these:

- Gales Creek off SR 24
- Humphrey Point and Taylor Bay around Bogue Field (a Marine Corps auxiliary airfield)
- Hunting Island
- Long Island
- Piney Island
- Archer Point
- the Emerald Isle Causeway (SR 58 from Cape Carteret to Emerald Isle)—the channel below the bridge on the Emerald Isle side and the dock ruins on the Cape Carteret side are both good places to look for specks and reds

White Oak River

The White Oak River begins between Bogue Inlet and the SR 24 bridge connecting Swansboro to Cape Carteret. It winds its way well into the White Oak Pocosin, which is a treacherous swamp, but it only stays salty to about the Stella region and the White Oak River Impoundment, which is a waterfowling area that is also a very good seatrout spot.

This is a very diverse river, with many species of game fish and a lot of water to fish, and more nooks and crannies than many other rivers. Of all the rivers in North

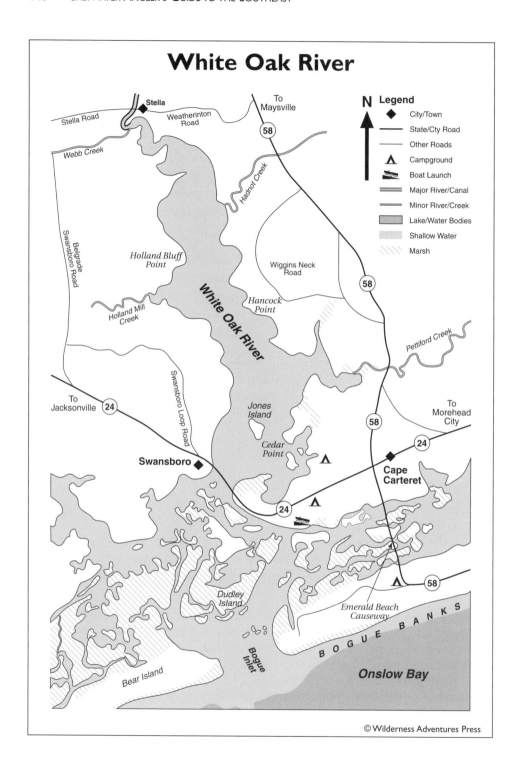

White Oak River

Legend

- ◆ City/Town
- State/Cty Road
- Other Roads
- Λ Campground
- Boat Launch
- Major River/Canal
- Minor River/Creek
- Lake/Water Bodies
- Shallow Water
- Marsh

Stella

Stella Road

Weatherinton Road

To Maysville

58

Webb Creek

Hadnot Creek

Belgrade Swansboro Road

Holland Bluff Point

Wiggins Neck Road

58

Holland Mill Creek

White Oak River

Hancock Point

Pettiford Creek

To Jacksonville

24

Swansboro Loop Road

Jones Island

58

To Morehead City

24

Cedar Point

Λ

58

Swansboro ◆

24

Λ

Cape Carteret ◆

Dudley Island

Λ

58

Emerald Beach Causeway

Bogue Inlet

B O G U E   B A N K S

Bear Island

Onslow Bay

© Wilderness Adventures Press

Tom Earnhardt beat this cobia on the fly. Cobia are great game fish on the fly rod. They are found around structure in inlets quite often. Photo courtesy of Tom Earnhardt.

Carolina that I have fished, I have spent more time on the White Oak than any other because it is so dependable—fish can usually be found on the White Oak.

To get onto the White Oak from the Atlantic Intracoastal Waterway, which runs through Bogue Sound, look for the marinas around this confluence and the SR 24 bridge, which isn't a high-rise bridge. Traveling south, be on the lookout for Dudley's Marina on the right, then bear to the north (right) when the channel swings to the southwest. Coming from the south, just look for the SR 24 bridge. After passing under it, you are on the White Oak River proper, although it really begins just below the bridge somewhere.

The first order of business when fishing the White Oak is to work the spartina lining the creeks above the park in Swansboro. There are some docks belonging to restaurants and other businesses that hold the occasional puppy drum and flounder, and baby grouper (tiny things no more than 6 inches long) can even be caught there. Spartina holds average specks, and the mud shelves around spartina are home to

King mackerel can be reached without big offshore boats.

quite a few average flounder. There's a good chance of fishing alone in this area, at least from a boat. However, this isn't the case out in the river, and elsewhere there will likely be anglers fishing from the docks and sea wall of the park.

Around the SR 24 bridge, a really fun method to take fish is to drift the channel between the aforementioned spartina and docks and the flat opposite them, which is to say between Jones Island and the bridge. The falling tide is best. Put a boat in at the ramp in Cape Carteret (right off SR 24) and motor around the bend and under the bridge up to Jones Island, about a mile above the bridge. Just before reaching the island, look for a small marker. Start there and drift back down to the bridge with a sinking line and short leader and a bottom-hugging fly such as a Clouser soaked in menhaden oil. Many game fish, especially snapper blues and flounder, hang in this part of the channel waiting to intercept the baitfish running off the flat and out from spartina marshes. Jigs and live alligator minnows (striped killifish) fished on the bottom are excellent with spinning gear.

On the eastern shore adjacent to Jones Island is Cedar Point and the Cedar Point Tideland Trail, a boardwalk that wanders through a spartina marsh (access to this trail is off SR 58 to Dudley Road). Small fiddler crabs infest the many tiny creeks in this area, and puppy drum get up into the creeks and spartina as the tide comes in. I

This pair of seatrout made for a fine dinner. Jigs did the trick.

have been back in here during low tide, too, and am always amazed at the fiddler population. At times it can seem as if the mud is alive with them.

Fiddlers are easy to catch—simply dig a hole in the mud the size of a #10 can (a restaurant-sized vegetable can) so that the top of the can is flush with the mud, kind of like a large pin hole on a golfing green. Take a couple of two-by-fours about 4 feet long each and place them on the mud on their narrow side so that they look like low walls. One end of each board goes over the can, and the boards are set so that they form a V, with the can at the point. Now leave the mud flat and wait for a few minutes. Soon the fiddlers will reemerge from their holes.

Once there are plenty of fiddlers out and about again, walk back onto the mud herding the crabs toward the open V and can. Walk slowly so that the crabs stay headed toward the can rather than running for their holes. They'll be herded into the V and drop into the can.

On light tackle, fiddlers make great drum and sheepshead bait, and specks eat many more fiddlers than most anglers realize. After all, specks are in the drum family.

Openings in the spartina at high tide or where thinner spartina is found amid thicker are good for casting crab imitations and Clousers. Approach these holes quietly and watch for tailing puppy drum. Be careful not to spook other drum in the

King mackerel action can be fast and furious just outside of Bogue Inlet.

area, because once one drum blows out of a hole, they all leave. One of the most common ways a flyfisher scares a drum in this situation is by casting across an unseen drum. Drum are also spooked if they see a flyfisher on the bow platform or see a rod moving during the casting cycle. By crouching or kneeling on the bow platform and using sidearm casts, these mistakes are reduced.

From the Cedar Point area on up the White Oak, it becomes a matter of hitting likely spots, some of the best of which are creek mouths. These include:

- Pettiford Creek and Pettiford Creek Bay (can be good for flounder and specks)
- Hadnot Creek
- Holland Mill Creek below Stella
- Webb Creek at the Stella impoundment (a few excellent trout holes; there are lots of duck hunters up here come autumn, so watch carefully)

A stringer attached to your belt is invaluable if you intend to keep some specks for dinner, such as these taken at the swing bridge.

Bogue Inlet to New River Inlet

Some of the best flounder fishing in the state exists from here down to the swing bridge at Onslow Beach. I highly recommend:

- Great Neck Landing
- Bear Inlet
- the warren of cuts and creeks behind Bear Island (Hammocks Beach State Park)
- Bear Creek

I was trained to catch giant flounder in this area by none other than Fred Kluge, one of the most successful flounder anglers in the region. Fred taught me how to use a fine-mesh cast net on the shallow, sandy flats just inside Bear Inlet to catch striped killifish, which are called alligator minnows in North Carolina. The killifish are then fished live on the bottom for flounder. One of the best places to do this is in the

Bogue Inlet to Brown's Inlet

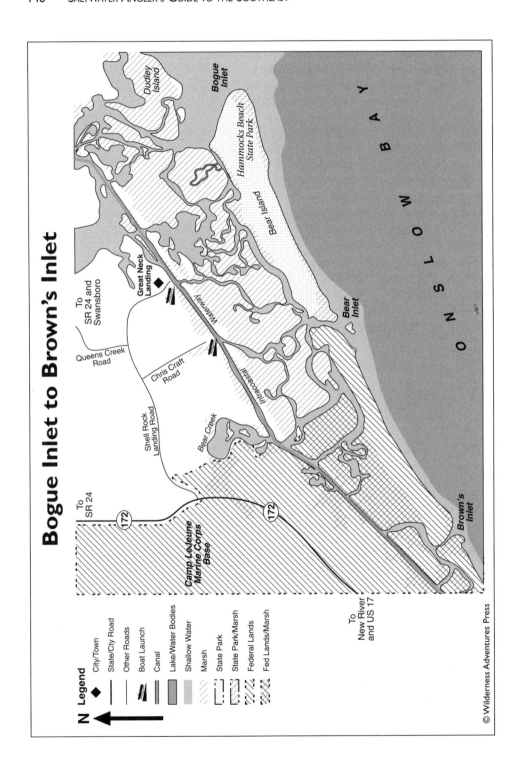

© Wilderness Adventures Press

Brown's Inlet to New River Inlet

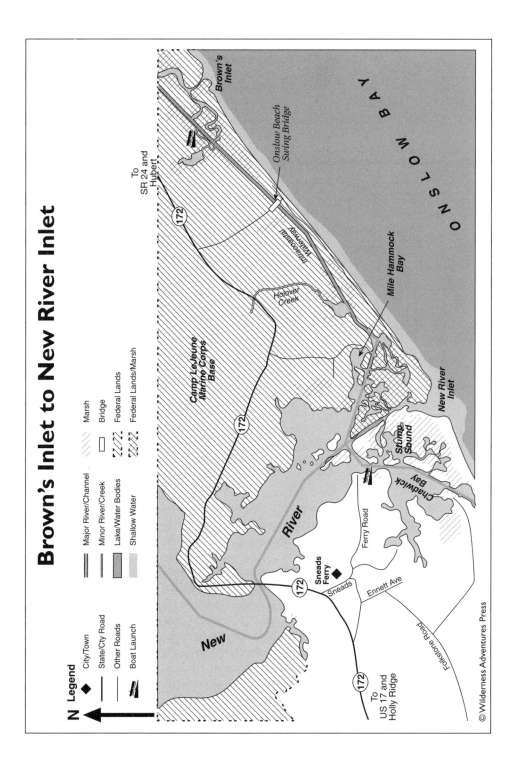

N

Legend

◆ City/Town

State/Cty Road

Other Roads

⚓ Boat Launch

Major River/Channel

Minor River/Creek

Lake/Water Bodies

Shallow Water

Marsh

Bridge

Federal Lands

Federal Lands/Marsh

Brown's Inlet

Onslow Beach Swing Bridge

To SR 24 and Hubert

172

Intracoastal Waterway

Holover Creek

Camp LeJeune Marine Corps Base

Mile Hammock Bay

ONSLOW BAY

New River Inlet

172

Stump Sound

Chadwick Bay

Ferry Road

River

Sneads Ferry

Sneads

Ennett Ave

172

New

172

To US 17 and Holly Ridge

Folkstone Road

© Wilderness Adventures Press

This classic Cape Lookout false albacore elected to eat a Clouser.

slough adjacent to the old Chris Craft factory on the Intracoastal Waterway just down from Swansboro. The flounder in here get very big.

Proceeding down the waterway toward Onslow Beach, one reaches Brown's Inlet. The creek that attaches the inlet to the waterway is shaped like a loop, and the southern part of the loop has some outstanding trout holes. Look for troughs lining the loop and oyster rocks, as well as other boats working the area, especially during the fall from about late October into mid-December.

The next hot spot is the very popular swing bridge at Onslow Beach. The flat shelf lining the eastern bank sees many waders in November who are after specks that pile up in there. This spot is nothing short of great much of the time. Curltail jigs in chartreuse with a bright orange lead head worked from the channel back up over the lip of the shelf are murder. Flies worked in the same manner (Clouser Deep Minnows, in particular) with fast sinking lines (like Teeny 400s) will do the trick, but a floating line to work Clousers and poppers along the banks lined with spartina also works. Use caution when entering the water just up from the little pier by the bridge because there is a lot of riprap in the water there. Otherwise the wading is easy.

This area is on Camp Lejeune, so if you aren't in or retired from the military, you have to get a visitor's pass (free) at the gate. Access to Lejeune is made from three major points:

- SR 172 in Hubert off of SR 24
- the base's main gate off SR 24 just north of Jacksonville
- the Snead's Ferry gate on SR 172 at the south end of the base

Farther down the waterway is Holover Creek, which holds mostly specks and flounder. Just past Holover Creek is Mile Hammock Bay and an anchorage. Both sides of the anchorage have earthen piers, but the one on the left while entering the anchorage is best for specks and flounder. I like wading around in Mile Hammock Bay because I don't usually run into any other wading anglers, and there are specks and flounder all through the spartina marshes lining the bay.

New River

The northern tip of the New River Inlet is a popular surf-casting spot, and there are lots of blues in there. The occasional black drum is also caught there, and specks, flounder, pompano, and northern whiting round out the action.

I think that the New River Inlet changes more than any other inlet in the area. After hurricanes Bertha and Fran in the summer of 1996, the inlet underwent major changes, and the sand that was moved around is still moving, so never fully trust markers thereabouts, although never assume that they are wrong, either. Play it safe and go slowly.

The New River is adequate by and large for fishing, but the real hot spot is the deep hole just east of the old 172 bridge, where many large specks are taken. Jigs fished deep on the bottom are best, but live shrimp and finger mullet can be equally effective from time to time. The pilings of both the old and new bridges are good for sheepshead, too—use live fiddler crabs or Jack Samson Fighting Crabs.

Morehead City
Population–6,000

ACCOMMODATIONS

Best Western Buccaneer Inn, 2806 Arendell Street / 252-726-3115

Hampton Inn, 4035 Arendell Street / 252-240-2300

Sundowner Motel, (Atlantic Beach) Atlantic Beach Causeway / 252-726-2191

Calico Jack's Inn & Marina (Harkers Island), 1698 Island Road / 252-728-3575 /
Owned and operated by Captains Donny and Rose Hatcher, this is a great place
to stay during the great false albacore run at Cape Lookout come autumn /
Right on the water with its own marina and store / Launch a boat at their
ramp, tie it up in one of the slips in a nicely protected marina, go to a clean
room, and get up the next morning ready to fish—the cape is only minutes
away / Still relatively inexpensive

CAMPGROUNDS

Salter Path Campgrounds, 1620 Salter Path Road (Salter Path) / 252-247-3525

Squatter's Campsite, 1475 Salter Path Road (Salter Path) / 252-247-3063

Guest Inn and Campground (Atlantic Beach), 303 Henderson Boulevard /
252-726-5818

Arrow Head Campsite (Atlantic Beach), 1550 Salter Path Road / 252-247-3838

Whispering Pines Campground (Newport), 2791 Hwy 24 East / 252-726-4902

Indian Beach Pier and Campground (Atlantic Beach), 1960 Salter Path Road /
252-247-3411

Long Creek Family Campground (Havelock), 3560 Adams Creek Road /
252-447-7076

Camp Ocean Forest (Emerald Isle), PO Box 4069 / 252-354-3454

RESTAURANTS

Mrs. Willis', 3002 Bridges Street / 252-726-3741 / Fresh seafood, barbecue,
steaks, and other goodies / A local hangout

Beach Tavern (Atlantic Beach), SR 58 (just south of the Atlantic Beach Causeway /
252-247-5554 / My friend, "Squash," owns this tavern restaurant, which offers
a large menu of traditional tavern fare only at very good prices / Squash specializes in some outstanding spicy entrees and is himself an accomplished
angler

Trattoria Da Franco's (Atlantic Beach), Intersection of Fort Macon Road and
Kinston Avenue / 919-240-3141 / Italian fare at reasonable prices is the thing
here / Good food

Yana's (Swansboro), 119 Front Street / 919-326-5501 / Perched on a knoll above
the Atlantic Intracoastal Waterway, Yana's is one of my favorite restaurants in
North Carolina / I highly recommend the club sandwich with an order of
Yana's very fresh onion rings, which are outstanding; for dessert have a huge
chocolate sundae, then waddle down the hill to the little pier across SR 24 and
catch a speck

TACKLE AND FLY SHOPS

Pete's Tackle, 1704 Arendell Street / 252-726-8644

Cape Lookout Fly Shop (Atlantic Beach), 601-H Atlantic Beach Causeway / 800-868-0941 / This fly shop is attached to Captain Joe Shute's Bait & Tackle / Stocked with everything you need for saltwater game fish available in this region

Captain Joe Shute's Bait & Tackle (Atlantic Beach), 601-H Atlantic Beach Causeway / 800-868-0941 / The long-time operation of Captain Joe Shute, one of the best known light-tackle guides on the North Carolina coast, this is a great shop / Has virtually everything you could possibly need, including a huge jig and MirrOlure selection, rods, reels, line, live and cut bait, and good information / The proverbial one-stop shop in Atlantic Beach, which services Cape Lookout, Harkers Island, and all of Bogue Sound

Calico Jack's (Harkers Island), PO Box 271 / 252-728-3575 / Just about to the end of the island, Calico Jack's has tackle for inshore and nearshore, and does a lot of business during the fall when the fat Alberts are running

Custom Marine Fabrication (New Bern), 2401 Hwy 70 East / 252-638-5422 / This shop has some fly tackle, including Fenwick and G. Loomis rods, and an assortment of light tackle

AIR SERVICE

Nearest Commercial Airport: 40 miles (New Bern)

MARINAS

Coral Bay Marina (Atlantic Beach), Hwy 70 East / 252-247-6900 / 300 Atlantic Beach Causeway / 252-726-6977

Calico Jack's (Harkers Island), PO Box 271 / 252-728-3575 / A nicely protected marina with well-maintained slips and a good ramp, plus fuel, tackle, food, and most everything else you might need

Dudley's Marina (Swansboro), Hwy 24 East / 252-393-2204

FOR MORE INFORMATION

Chamber of Commerce
801 Arendell Street
Morehead City, NC 28557
252-726-6350

New Bern

Population–21,770 • Located on the Neuse River

ACCOMMODATIONS

Sheraton, 100 Middle Street / 252-638-3585
Comfort Suites, 218 East Front Street / 252-636-0022
Hampton Inn, 200 Hotel Drive / 252-637-2111
Economy Inn, 3465 Clarendon Boulevard / 252-638-8166

RESTAURANTS

Chelsea's Restaurant, 335 Middle Street / 252-637-5469
Harvey Mansion Restaurant, 309 Middle Street / 252-638-3205
Kress Cafe, 309 Middle Street / 252-633-9300
Latitude 35 Waterfront Restaurant, 100 Middle Street / 252-638-3585

HOSPITAL

Craven Regional Medical Center, 2000 Neuse Boulevard / 252-633-8111

MARINAS

Bridgepointe Marina, 101 Howell Road / 252-637-7372
Northwest Creek Marina, 104 Marina Drive / 252-638-4133
River Bend Yacht Club and Marina, 1 Marina Road / 252-633-2006

AIRPORT

Craven County Regional Airport, 1501 Airport Road / 252-638-5891

FOR MORE INFORMATION

New Bern Area Chamber of Commerce
316 South Front Street
New Bern, NC 28560
252-637-3111

This black drum was taken in the surf just south of the New River Inlet shortly after Hurricane Bertha roared through the area laying waste to Topsail Island.

NEW RIVER INLET TO LITTLE RIVER INLET

Past the New River Inlet is Chadwick Bay, with Stump Sound to seaward. The shallows of this sound hold pretty good flounder. Next is Alligator Bay and then the bridge linking the mainland to Topsail Island, which was devastated during Hurricanes Bertha and Fran. If ever there was plain evidence that people shouldn't build houses on a barrier island, this is it. The little island, which is barely above sea level, was wiped out.

Sloughs lined with spartina grass around the SR 210 bridge are good for specks as well as some puppy drum and flounder. Some good spots can be seen by driving slowly over the bridge and looking down into the marshes—wade back in there and have fun. There's a boat ramp at the bridge, too, and another one at Turkey Creek a little farther south.

Speaking of Turkey Creek, this whole area (Ashe Island, Spicer Bay, Everett Bay, and the Permuda Islands) all carry specks and flounder, but there aren't all that many anglers in there, and certainly very few, if any, flyfishers.

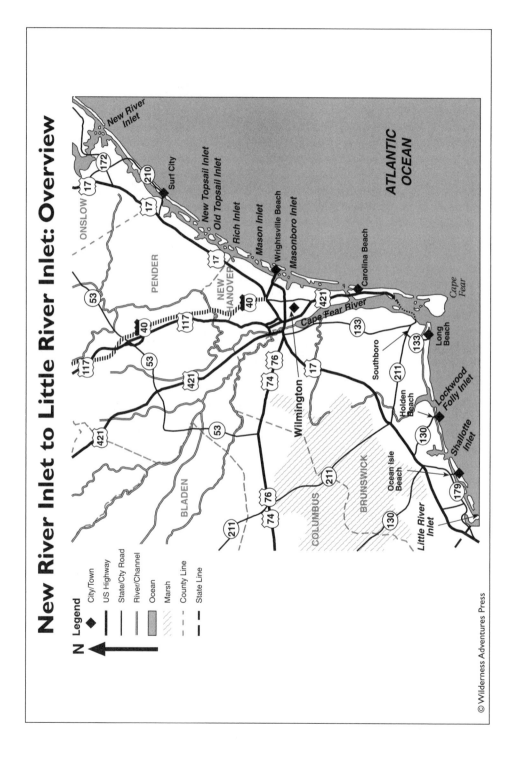

New River Inlet to Little River Inlet: Overview

Legend

- ◆ City/Town
- US Highway
- State/Cty Road
- River/Channel
- Ocean
- Marsh
- County Line
- State Line

N

ATLANTIC OCEAN

New River Inlet

Surf City

New Topsail Inlet

Old Topsail Inlet

Rich Inlet

Mason Inlet

Wrightsville Beach

Masonboro Inlet

Carolina Beach

Cape Fear

ONSLOW

PENDER

NEW HANOVER

Cape Fear River

Wilmington

Southboro

Long Beach

Lockwood Folly Inlet

Holden Beach

Shallotte Inlet

Ocean Isle Beach

BRUNSWICK

COLUMBUS

BLADEN

Little River Inlet

17

172

210

17

17

53

40

117

40

117

53

421

421

53

74

76

74

76

211

211

211

130

130

179

133

133

211

421

© Wilderness Adventures Press

New River Inlet to Surf City

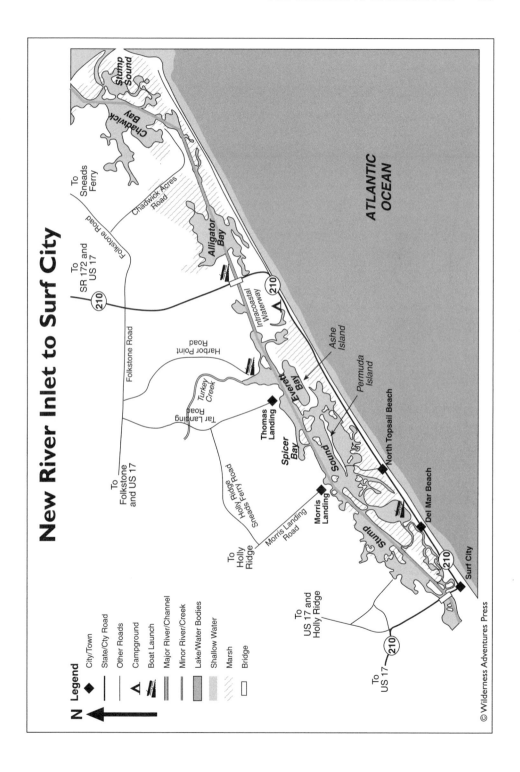

Legend

- ◆ City/Town
- State/Cty Road
- Other Roads
- ⛺ Campground
- Boat Launch
- Major River/Channel
- Minor River/Creek
- Lake/Water Bodies
- Shallow Water
- Marsh
- Bridge

N

© Wilderness Adventures Press

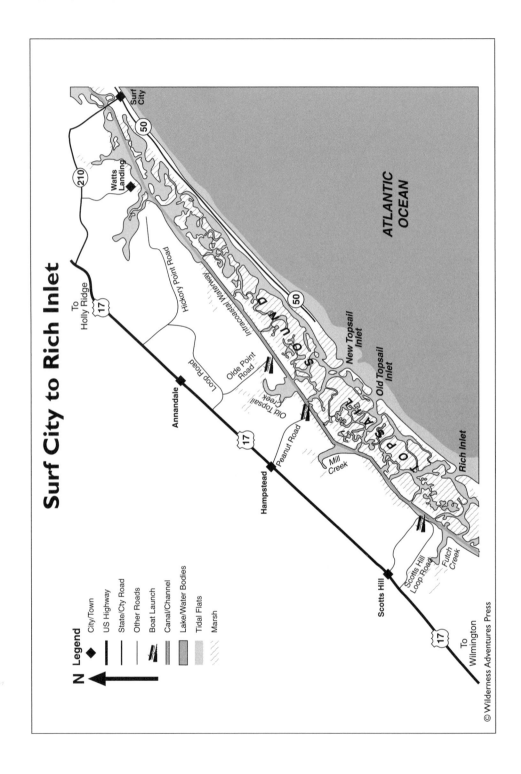

Surf City to Rich Inlet

© Wilderness Adventures Press

Rich Inlet to Masoboro Inlet

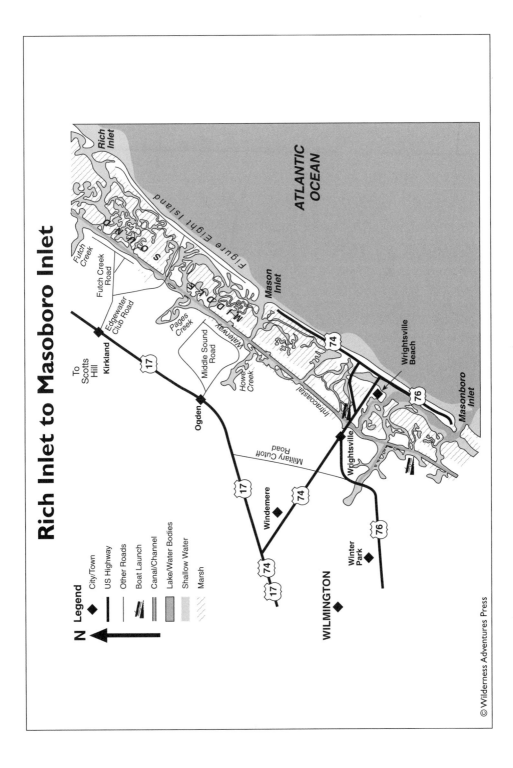

N Legend

- ◆ City/Town
- US Highway
- Other Roads
- Boat Launch
- Canal/Channel
- Lake/Water Bodies
- Shallow Water
- Marsh

Rich Inlet

ATLANTIC OCEAN

Futch Creek

Futch Creek Road

Edgewater Club Road

To Scotts Hill

Kirkland

17

Pages Creek

Middle Sound Road

Howe Creek

Figure Eight Island

Waterway

Mason Inlet

74

Wrightsville Beach

Intracoastal

Masonboro Inlet

Ogden

Military Cutoff Road

Wrightsville

76

17

Windemere

74

WILMINGTON

74

17

Winter Park

76

© Wilderness Adventures Press

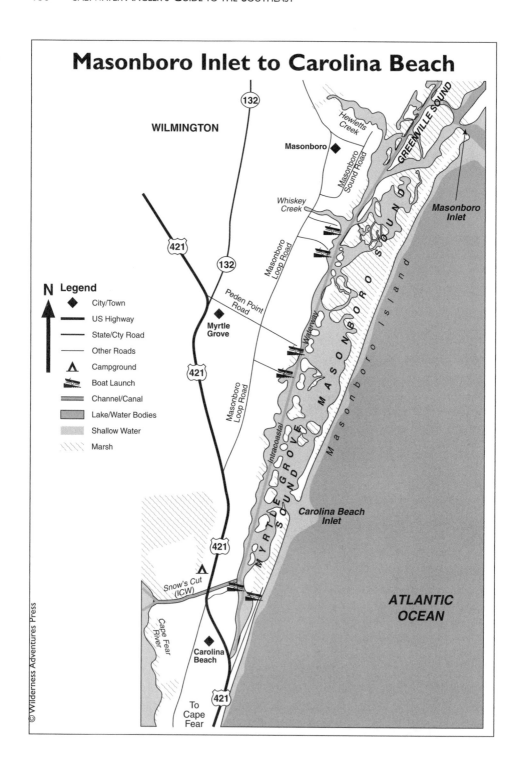

After passing Surf City, there's an area that sees even fewer anglers. It stays this way all the way down to Wrightsville. This stretch is home to plenty of good fishing locations, including:

- Watts Landing
- New Topsail Inlet
- Old Topsail Inlet
- Topsail Sound in general (although this really isn't a sound at all—it's more like a big spartina marsh)
- Rich Inlet
- Middle Sound
- Figure Eight Island (Captain Tyler Stone tells me that one of his favorite speck holes is Mason Inlet, which sits at the southern end of the island)

Land access to this entire area is best accomplished via US 17 (SR 210).

Wilmington to Cape Fear

Now you arrive in the Wilmington region. The city of Wilmington is fairly large, and when you add summer traffic and people to the equation, it grows enormously. Plan accordingly.

The spartina banks lining the Intracoastal Waterway along Masonboro Sound hold mostly flounder and specks. After passing Wilmington you come down the waterway until you get to Snow's Cut, which links the dug waterway to the Cape Fear River at Carolina Beach.

Cape Fear to the Little River Inlet

This is the southernmost coast of North Carolina, a region very popular as a summertime beach attraction (Long Beach is packed tight with beach homes), but it isn't known for stupendous fishing. That isn't to say that the fish aren't here, because they certainly are. It is just that the area isn't known for the fishing. Of course, locals know where the fish are and like it just fine.

The Cape Fear River is perhaps best known locally for sheepshead and flounder fishing, but farther south, as you approach Cape Fear itself, is Snow's Marsh and Walden Creek, and then Smith Island. The latter isn't an island, of course, but a maze of marshes made up of spartina grass, creeks (Bald Head and Cape), and Buzzard Bay. Cape Fear is located at the very end of Bald Head Island, which is a barrier island. The creeks and bays of Smith Island are good for specks and flatties.

Now comes the final stretch before South Carolina, including:

- Long Bay
- Oak Island (hit the Elizabeth River in the marshes of Oak Island)
- Long Beach
- Lockwood Folly Inlet (Lockwood Folly River is the best bet here—work the oyster bars as far up as possible)
- Holden Beach

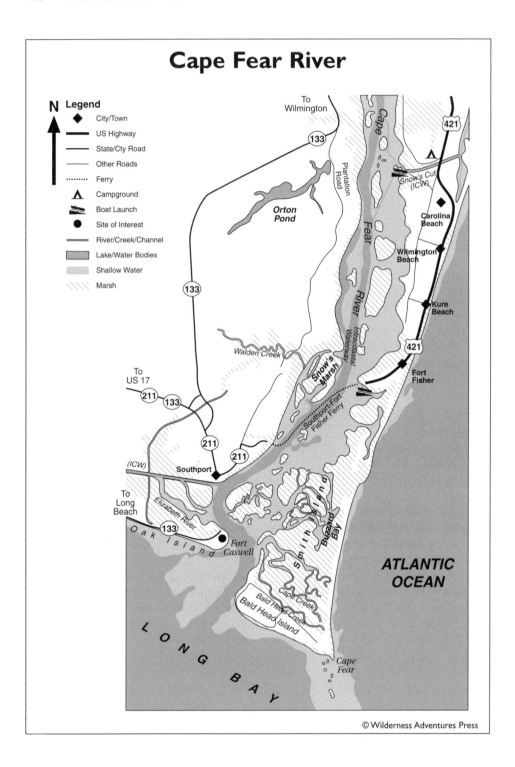

Cape Fear River

Legend

N

◆ City/Town
━━ US Highway
── State/Cty Road
── Other Roads
········· Ferry
⛺ Campground
🛥 Boat Launch
● Site of Interest
━━ River/Creek/Channel
▨ Lake/Water Bodies
░ Shallow Water
▨ Marsh

To Wilmington

133

421

Plantation Road

Snow's Cut (ICW)

Orton Pond

Carolina Beach

Wilmington Beach

Kure Beach

133

Walden Creek

Snow's Marsh

421

Fort Fisher

To US 17

211 133

Southport-Fort Fisher Ferry

211

211

(ICW)

Southport

To Long Beach

Elizabeth River

133

Oak Island

Fort Caswell

Smith Island

Buzzard Bay

ATLANTIC OCEAN

Cape Creek

Bald Head Creek

Bald Head Island

L O N G   B A Y

Cape Fear

© Wilderness Adventures Press

Southport to Holden Beach

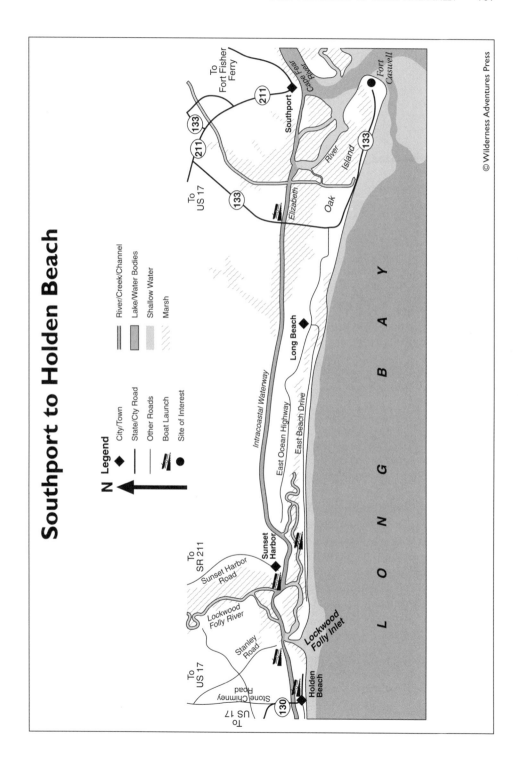

N Legend

City/Town
State/Cty Road
Other Roads
Boat Launch
Site of Interest

River/Creek/Channel
Lake/Water Bodies
Shallow Water
Marsh

To Fort Fisher Ferry

Cape Fear River

211

Fort Casuvell

Southport

133

211

133

To US 17

Elizabeth

Oak Island

133

River

LONG BAY

Long Beach

Intracoastal Waterway

East Ocean Highway

East Beach Drive

To SR 211

Sunset Harbor Road

Sunset Harbor

Lockwood Folly River

Stanley Road

To US 17

Lockwood Folly Inlet

Holden Beach

Stone Chimney Road

130

To US 17

Holden Beach to Little River Inlet

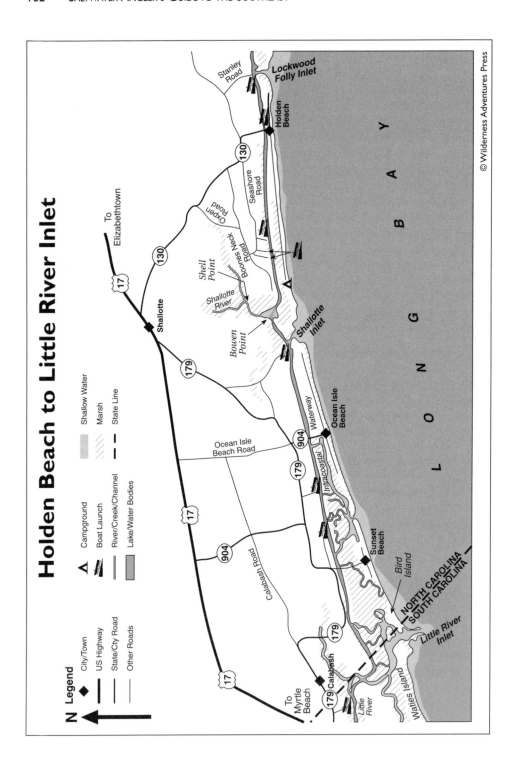

© Wilderness Adventures Press

Legend

N

- City/Town
- US Highway
- State/Cty Road
- Other Roads

- ▲ Campground
- Boat Launch
- River/Creek/Channel
- Lake/Water Bodies

- Shallow Water
- Marsh
- State Line

Anglers on the Fin Quest *are used to big drum. Photo by Joel Arrington.*

- Shallotte Inlet (the Shallotte River and the marsh islands between Bowen Point and Shell Point are best)
- Ocean Isle Beach (the creeks of the waterway are good)
- Sunset Beach
- Bird Island

Into the Frying Pan

Frying Pan Shoals off Cape Fear holds countless game fish, including some giant king mackerel and tarpon. Using the tarpon tactics mentioned in the game fish chapter, I highly recommend trying the silver kings of Frying Pan Shoals. Most anglers will be after kings, but don't be dissuaded—the tarpon show up there in late June and often stay right into October if the water and weather stay warm enough for their subtropical tastes.

There are those who feel that tighter restrictions on king tournaments are in order.

A WORD ABOUT TROPHY GAME FISH IN NORTH CAROLINA

No matter what area is being fished or what type of tackle is being used, it is very important for the future of fisheries to release as many game fish as possible, especially trophy game fish, such as the giant black drum caught aboard the *Fin Quest* out of Cape Hatteras (see picture previous page). Taken on a 20-pound test tippet, the 74½-pound beast was safely released.

One of the problems in North Carolina insofar as trophy fish numbers is tournaments. North Carolina has many big-money king mackerel tournaments, and I have to say that I used to participate in these events from time to time. But the fact of the matter is that these events put a lot of pressure on the king fishery, and kings are migratory for the most part, which means that pressure gets put on them from state to state.

We must all take a closer look at the reasons—all the reasons—why trophy saltwater game fish are becoming less and less common. We have to be honest with ourselves when we do so, too.

Wilmington
Population–70,000

ACCOMMODATIONS

Catherine's Inn, 410 South Front Street / 800-476-0723

The Curran House, 312 South 3rd Street / 910-763-6603 / A three-star bed and breakfast

The Inn at St. Thomas Court, 101 South 2nd Street / 800-525-0909

Taylor House Inn, 14 North 7th Street / 910-763-7581 / A small but nice bed and breakfast

The Verandas, 202 Nun Street / 910-251-2212

Wilmington Hilton, 301 North Water Street / 910-763-5900

The Worth House, 412 South 3rd Street / 910-762-8562 / A three-star bed and breakfast

The Docksider Inn (Carolina Beach), 202 Ft. Fisher Boulevard / 910-458-4200 / With a complimentary breakfast, the Docksider is really meant for couples, but if you tell them you intend to be romantic with your redfish, they will let you stay

Blockade Runner (Wrightsville Beach), 275 Waynick Boulevard / 800-541-1161 / Not for the summer season due to many sandy kiddies running up and down the hallways, but at other times it is fine

CAMPGROUNDS

Camelot Campground, 7415 Market Street / 910-686-7705

Carolina Beach Campground, 9641 River Road / 910-392-3322

RESTAURANTS

The Tides, 1125 Military Cutoff Road / 910-256-1118 / Gourmet seafood with some imaginative offerings / Owned by fishermen who know the importance of fresh fish and seafood / Don't show up in your fishing clothes, but this is a great place for a nice dinner

The Fish House, 1410 Airlie Road / 910-256-3693 / Located on the Intracoastal Waterway across from Wrightsville Beach on scenic Airlie Road / Sit outside and enjoy sandwiches and seafood, as well as the famous Fish House fish stew / Both The Fish House and its neighbor, The Dockside, are home to several charter boats and offer transient space for diners

The Dockside, 1308 Airlie Road / 910-256-2752 / A favorite spot for fishermen, boaters, and tourists / Can be crowded during the summer and also on nice weekends during the fall / Typical sandwich and fired seafood offerings, famous for its view of Wrightsville Beach and the fried softshell crab sandwich

Clarence Foster's, 22 North Lumina Avenue / 910-256-0224 / Located on Wrightsville Beach, Foster's is known more for its night life than for its dining, although the food is good / It is a good spot for younger anglers / Those wanting a quiet dinner should probably pass

TACKLE AND FLY SHOPS

Intracoastal Angler Fly Shop, 1900 East Wood Road, Suite 7 / 888-325-4285 / Owned and operated by Captain Tyler Stone, this shop is fully stocked for all flyfishing needs

Digh's Country Sports Gallery, 1988 Eastwood Road (Plaza East Mall in Wrightsville Beach) / 910-256-2060 / Full Orvis shop with other lines available

Great Outdoor Provision Company, 3501 Oleander Drive #A9 / 910-343-1648

MARINAS

Boat House Marina, 6334 Oleander Drive / 910-350-0023

Canaday's Yacht Basin, 7624 Mason Landing Road / 910-686-9116

Coastal Carolina Yacht Yard, 2107 Middle Sound Loop Road / 910-686-0004

Johnson Marine Services, 2029 Turner Nursery Road / 910-686-7565

Mason's Marina, 7421 Mt. Pleasant Drive / 910-686-7661

Pages Creek Marine Services, 700 Market Street / 910-799-7179

Wilmington Marine Center, 3410 River Road / 910-395-5055

FOR MORE INFORMATION

Chamber of Commerce
1 Estelle Lee Place
Wilmington, NC 28401
910-762-2611

Chamber of Commerce
100 Eastwood Road
Wilmington, NC 28403
910-395-2965

FLYFISHING AND LIGHT-TACKLE GUIDES IN NORTH CAROLINA

If you decide to use the services of a guide, the two most important things to check are how well the guide communicates with you and good references from other clients.

Don't necessarily only consider guides in the area to which you are traveling; many guides travel considerable distances and fish waters nowhere near their home port. Also, guides listed herein focus on flyfishing and light tackle. The vast majority of other saltwater guides are offshore, heavy tackle trollers.

The sudden proliferation of light-tackle and flyfishing guides along the coast of North Carolina is astounding. Not long ago, one could count the number of such guides on one hand. Today, they are everywhere, which is a potential problem. It is absolutely necessary to check a guide out very well before chartering a trip. The guides listed below have good reputations, however, take the time to talk with a guide and be sure that you agree on what type of fishing is to be done. There are far more working guides in North Carolina than the other states in this guidebook, so guides for the entire state are listed separately. In the following chapters on South Carolina and Georgia, guides are listed in the nearest hub city.

ATLANTIC BEACH

Captain Joe Shute, 601-H Atlantic Beach Causeway / 800-868-0941 / I have known Joe Shute for a very long time and can attest to his skills as a light-tackle guide with a great reputation as a speckled trout pro. He also loves cobia. Joe's knowledge of flyfishing is coming on strong, too, as he adapts to the growing demand—try him for false albacore.

AURORA

Captain Scott Austin, PO Box 312 / 252-322-5542 / E-mail: castaway@pamlico.net / Scott Austin is a marine biologist who fishes for red drum, specks, blues, tarpon, stripers, and other inshore species.

HARKERS ISLAND

Captain Robert "Stick" Sandlin, PO Box 402 / 800-544-6039 / Stick knows Portsmouth Island better than anyone, I suspect. His drum records are impressive. False albacore have become a big part of his business, too, especially in fall. He also fishes offshore.

Captain Rob Pasfield, PO Box 400 / 252-504-3823 / Website: www.charternet.com/charters/harkers / Pasfield works the waters of North Carolina's central coast for cobia, false albacore, Spanish mackerel, spotted seatrout, king mackerel, red drum, bluefish, and dolphin.

Captain Bobby Moore / 252-728-4688 / E-mail: c/change@aol.com / Moore fishes both offshore and inshore—flyfishers are welcome.

Captain Sam Sellars, 125 Ann Street (Beaufort) / 252-728-3735 / Sellars specializes in flyfishing and light tackle and is one of the top names in the false albacore fishery / He also pioneered a summertime flats fishery for blacktip sharks that has become very popular.

LONG BEACH

David Mammay, 115 Northeast 15th Street / 910-278-7717 / David fishes the Southport region for specks, focusing on trophy specks.

MANTEO

Captain Bryan DeHart, 141 Blackwood Drive / 252-473-1575 / Website: www.chaela.com/coastaladventures / DeHart has been featured on ESPN's *Fly Fishing America*. He goes after stripers in the famous Roanoke River fishery, some of the hottest striper fishing anywhere. He also angles for puppy drum, specks, flounder, and blues.

MOREHEAD CITY

Captain Dave Dietzler, 252-240-2850 / Based out of Atlantic Beach, Dietzler knows barracuda, blues, Spanish, red drum, kings, dolphin, and most everything else, inshore and offshore.

NAGS HEAD

Captain Brian Horsley, 227 South Woodlawn Drive / 252-449-0562 / Horsley is a very well known and respected guide. His knowledge of spotted seatrout, red drum, and stripers is unsurpassed for this region. He also ties and sells excellent flies.

Captain Sarah Gardner, PO Box 387 / 252-449-2251 / Sarah is the only woman guide I know of along the North Carolina coast. She is known for her striper expertise.

OCEAN ISLE BEACH

Captain Brant McMullan, 72 Craven Street / 910-575-4885 / Website: www.captainbrant.com / McMullan uses light tackle and live bait for kings and other game fish. A mere 22 years old and a captain for only four years, I am surprised that he uses terms like "Big catches of wahoo are GUARANTEED!!!" when advertising about the wahoo fishing he offers. I spoke with him about this and he danced around the issue by talking about the water temperature info he gets from a satellite, but after I pressed him on what he meant by his claim of wahoo being guaranteed, he said that he didn't really guarantee wahoo because he would not refund a client's money if the client didn't catch any wahoo. To his credit, however, Captain McMullan is an aggressive young captain with a reputation for finding kings and other game fish.

Captain Brandon Sauls, 72 Craven Street / 910-575-4885 / Sauls runs one of Captain McMullan's boats for kings and other offshore game fish.

OCRACOKE

Captain Norman Miller, PO Box 742 / 252-928-6111 / Miller is a very experienced and effective light-tackle and flyfishing guide. Big red drum are one of his specialties, and I have watched him work a school of "happy" reds (gigantic reds that are running around outside the surf zone apparently going crazy chasing bait), all monsters, with Tom Earnhardt on Tom's popular television show *Fishing the Tidewaters.*

Captain David Nagel, PO Box 434 / 800-825-5351 / Wrecks, Pamlico Sound, Ocracoke Inlet, and the Gulf Stream are all worked by Nagel.

ORIENTAL

Captain George H. Beckwith, Jr., PO Box 403 / 252-249-3101 / Cellular: 252-671-3474 / Website: www.pamlico-nc.com/guide / E-mail: guide@pamlico-nc.com / I have caught a lot of fish with George and can attest to his prowess. He is personable and informed and goes after big reds, stripers, specks, tarpon, and flounder in and around Pamlico Sound. He knows those fat Alberts at Cape Lookout, too. A top choice for a guide, Beckwith has his pulse on the coast of North Carolina and is very active in conservation issues.

Captain Gary Dubiel, PO Box 1029 / 252-249-1520 / Gary is a very good guide and a top choice. You simply can't go wrong with him / An IGFA fly rod world-record holder.

ROANOKE RAPIDS

Captain Jack Eudy, PO Box 2024 / 252-537-1386 / Roanoke River stripers are a primary target species for Jack.

SOUTHPORT

Captain Jimmy Price, 10425 Fish Factory Road / 910-457-9903 / A popular speaker, Price is very well known for his ability to catch giant flounder.

SWANSBORO

Captain Lee Manning, PO Box 64 / 252-354-3035 / Manning can set up a light-tackle trip including king mackerel and other offshore game fish out of Bogue Inlet. One of the most experienced charter captains on the North Carolina coast.

WILMINGTON

Captain Rick Bennett, 910-799-6120 / Website: www.outdoorsworld.com/rodman.htm / E-mail: rbfishrods@aol.com / Bonito, kings, Spanish, cobia, flounder, specks, and drum are all sought by Bennett.

Captain Bill Douglass, PO Box 3456 / 888-813-0445 or 910-392-5520 / E-mail: bccharters@aol.com / Douglass seeks red drum and most any other game fish in the Cape Fear region.

Captain Lee Parsons, 6404 Head Road / 910-350-0890 / Parsons, an Orvis-endorsed guide, specializes in stripers on the Roanoke River.

Captain Tyler Stone, 1900 Eastwood Road, Suite 7 / 888-325-4285 or 910-256-4545 / Stone is a very knowledgeable and proven flyfishing and light-tackle guide. A solid choice for false albacore, red drum, specks, and just about anything else you might want. One of the top flyfishing guides in the state.

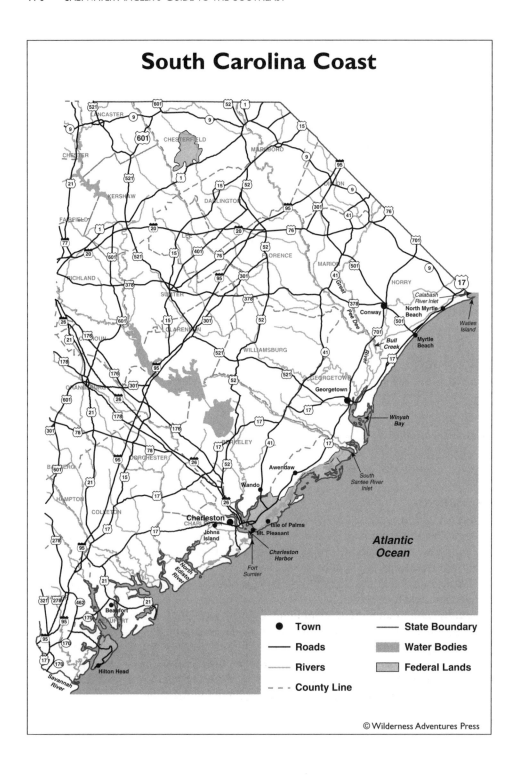

South Carolina Coast

Atlantic
Ocean

● Town	— State Boundary
— Roads	Water Bodies
— Rivers	Federal Lands
- - County Line	

© Wilderness Adventures Press

South Carolina

I love South Carolina—it's gentle, beautiful, and has saltwaters with loads of great game fish. It is a state that treasures its marine resources, managing it as the property of everyone rather than strictly the commercial fishing industry. The people of South Carolina are warm and friendly, and they have a fine tradition of extending their famous Southern hospitality to any and all who would come to visit their historic state. South Carolina is indeed an enchanting Southern belle.

When it comes to angling along the coast, South Carolina is helping to ensure a bright future by requiring an inexpensive saltwater license (a few dollars), which is put directly into maintaining the fishery. You can pick one up at any tackle shop or contact the South Carolina Wildlife and Marine Resources Department at 843-762-5000 for a copy of the current regulations and more information.

Getting There

The littorals of South Carolina are easier to reach than those of North Carolina because US 17 runs parallel to most of the coast and is less circuitous than in North Carolina. There are also two major airports that lend instant access to the South Carolina shore.

By Road

The main coastal highway is US 17, which can be unpleasant during the summer because of heavy beach traffic. Many travelers use Interstate 95 to get into the region and then lesser highways and routes to reach US 17.

For the Myrtle Beach area, take US 501 toward Dillon, Marion, and Conway. Georgetown is best approached by taking US 521 through Manning. Charleston is simply reached via Interstate 26. The beautiful Beaufort region can be reached by US 17 and 21 through Pocotaligo, Sheldon, and Gardens Corner. Take US 278 to Hilton Head Island.

By Air

For the northern coast of South Carolina, flying into Myrtle Beach may be the best option. Of course, because this is a small airport, it probably means making at least one plane change to a commuter or small jet.

South Carolina's fabled "Low Country" is immediately at hand by flying right into Charleston, which is serviced by jets from major national carriers and turboprop aircraft belonging to regional commuter airlines. When flying into Charleston, catch the view of the area's beautiful spartina marshes, which are very well known for their redfish and speckled trout. You can be catching those game fish as little as 15 minutes after picking up your baggage since Charleston International Airport is situated in North Charleston next to the Ashley River.

For the southernmost coast of South Carolina, consider going straight into Savannah, Georgia, directly across the Savannah River from South Carolina.

By Water

Charleston is a fairly busy seaport, and the Atlantic Intracoastal Waterway runs the length of the state's coast. Access is therefore quite easy.

Game Fish Species

South Carolina has the very same saltwater game fish inshore, near-shore, and offshore that are available to the light-tackle angler and flyfisher in North Carolina, with one addition: the lovely ladyfish (ladyfish are uncommon in North Carolina).

- Amberjack
- Black drum
- Bluefish
- Bonito
- Cobia
- Crevalle jack
- Croaker
- Dolphin
- False albacore
- Gray Trout
- King mackerel
- Ladyfish
- Pompano
- Red drum
- Sheepshead
- Spanish mackerel
- Spotted seatrout
- Striped bass
- Tarpon
- Tripletail
- Yellowfin tuna

WATIES ISLAND TO THE MYRTLE BEACH AREA

The northern coast of South Carolina is known for its Calabash seafood, which is a style named after the North Carolina town of Calabash just over the border on the Calabash River. And it is that river where we begin our journey down the coast of South Carolina.

Calabash River Inlet to North Myrtle Beach

From what most people consider its inlet just south of Sunset Beach, behind Waties Island and across almost to the town of Little River, the Calabash River is the primary area where inshore game fish can be found. Specific places to investigate include:

- the Calabash River Inlet (Spanish mackerel, cobia, king mackerel, bluefish, and sometimes crevalle jacks, among others)
- the spartina banks lining much of the channel running from the inlet back to the main river, which is part of the Atlantic Intracoastal Waterway (Spanish mackerel, blues, specks, and the occasional drum)
- the backwaters between the channel and the Myrtle Beach RV resort on Little River Neck (specks and flounder mostly)
- the banks of islands in the middle of the channel northeast of Little River (again, specks and flounder)
- the dropoffs between those islands and Little River in the waterway (specks)

Most red drum in this region are small to midsized. The speck fishing is usually better than drum fishing, generally speaking.

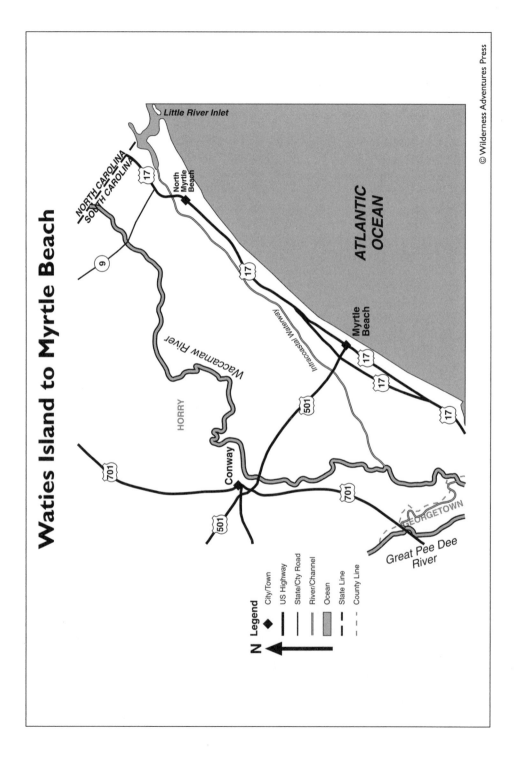

Waties Island to Myrtle Beach

Calabash River Inlet to North Myrtle Beach

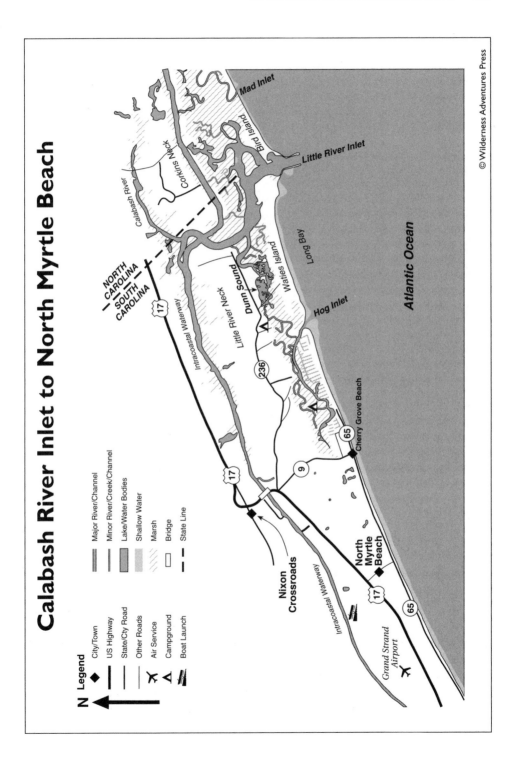

N

Legend

◆ City/Town
— US Highway
— State/City Road
— Other Roads
✈ Air Service
△ Campground
⚓ Boat Launch

— Major River/Channel
— Minor River/Creek/Channel
▨ Lake/Water Bodies
▨ Shallow Water
▨ Marsh
□ Bridge
— State Line

Mad Inlet

Bird Island

Little River Inlet

Corkins Neck

Calabash River

NORTH CAROLINA

SOUTH CAROLINA

17

Dunn Sound

Waties Island

Long Bay

Hog Inlet

Little River Neck

Intracoastal Waterway

236

Cherry Grove Beach

65

9

17

Nixon Crossroads

North Myrtle Beach

Intracoastal Waterway

17

65

Grand Strand Airport

Atlantic Ocean

© Wilderness Adventures Press

Structure—rock piles, bridge abutments, wrecks, dock pilings—draw all sorts of game fish species, including the popular and tasty black sea bass. A piece of cut bait (squid is good) fished only inches off the bottom will usually entice them to strike.

Some large specks hang out in the slough behind Cherry Grove Beach. Work jigs and MirrOlures along the banks, in holes, over lips, across rips, and near structure, such as boat docks and mooring buoys.

North Myrtle Beach to the U.S. Route 501 Bridge

This stretch of the Atlantic Intracoastal Waterway, like so many other stretches of this water highway, seems uneventful to the casual observer, but like those other stretches, it is all a matter of finding microstructure. To be successful with the many specks that inhabit this seemingly mundane portion of the waterway, look for the following:

- flats along the banks that have steep lips leading to the channel bottom
- spartina banks on a rising tide, with plenty of fiddler crabs and baitfish
- bottom variances that attract and hold specks (use a depth finder)

North Myrtle Beach to the U.S. Route 501 Bridge

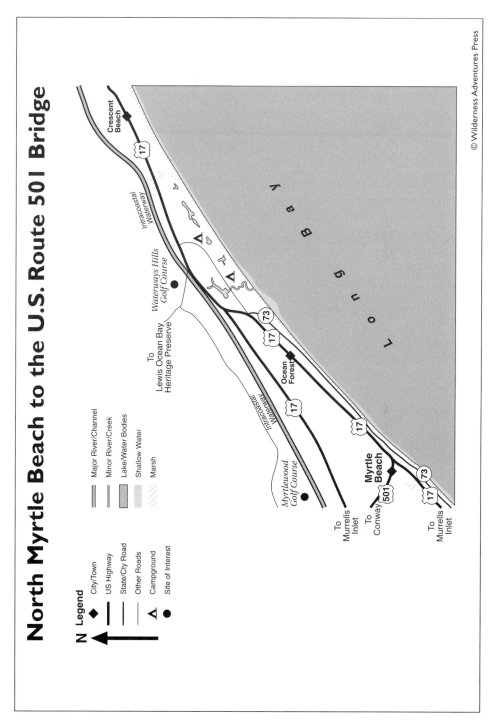

Legend
N

◆ City/Town
⬢ US Highway
━━ State/Cty Road
─── Other Roads
▲ Campground
● Site of Interest

━━ Major River/Channel
─── Minor River/Creek
▨ Lake/Water Bodies
░ Shallow Water
▨ Marsh

Crescent Beach

17

Intracoastal Waterway

Waterway Hills Golf Course

To Lewis Ocean Bay Heritage Preserve

73
17

Ocean Forest

17

Intracoastal Waterway

Long Bay

Myrtlewood Golf Course

To Murrells Inlet

To Conway

Myrtle Beach

501

73

17

To Murrells Inlet

17

© Wilderness Adventures Press

Speckled trout.

- tufts or tiny islands of spartina that have broken off from the main bank and are now separated from the bank by a few feet or several yards
- depressions in the bottom that were formed long ago by fallen trees
- deep holes in the channel in winter, where specks congregate (oftentimes some very big specks)
- the mouths of the many tiny creeks that enter the waterway, mostly on the north side, from about the Waterway Hills Golf Course down to the Myrtle-wood Golf Course

Two main lures that have always produced in this area are curltail jigs (char-treuse and dark green with orange or red heads) and MirrOlures (floaters and sinkers in silver or white with red heads). On the rising tide (as spartina becomes flooded),

Hundreds of small fiddler crabs swarm over a creekbed at low tide. Thousands more are still hiding in the spartina. Red and black drum, spotted seatrout, and even sheepshead get back into these creeks and onto the flats at high tide to feast on this nutritious and apparently tasty meal. The fly-fisher with a few good crab patterns can have a ball.

floating MirrOlures twitched against the banks as if they were wounded baitfish and jigs hopped along the bottom parallel to the bank both do well.

Another tactic to be tried here is to fish a live shrimp below a popping cork. The best results usually seem to come by drifting the shrimp over a channel dropoff on a fast-moving tide, particularly the falling tide. Trout move along these dropoffs in search of forage that is being swept along by the tide, and they have a hard time turning down a plump, scared shrimp that appears to be unable to escape.

Other than shrimp, try a live finger mullet or menhaden. And because spotted seatrout are members of the drum family, they love to eat crabs, with fiddlers being special favorites. A fiddler crab impaled on a hook without any weight and drifted with the current works well.

Flyfishers need to have sinking lines in this area—dropoffs can be 20 feet deep, and a sinking line is needed to get a fly down to trout. When the tide is running hard, which is when trout seem to want to feed most heavily, a fast-sinking line will result in more fish seeing the fly—it's that simple.

One of the largest South Carolina specks I have taken came from just north of the US 501 bridge at Myrtle Beach. I was using an Orvis Depth Charge line, which has a 30-foot, fast-sinking head and 70 feet of intermediate running line, to present a Cave's Rattlin' Minnow (the work of Florida guide and flyfishing writer Jon Cave) down deep below a rip. This fly consists of some materials that reflect light and add color to the equation, including red Flashabou for the cheeks, a gold Mylar body, and wings consisting of Krystal Flash, peacock herl, and yellow and olive bucktail. The underbody is flat lead foil and a glass rattle. The final touch is the large yellow eye with a big black pupil. All this added up to an 8-pound speck that attacked the fly more like a big bluefish than a speck.

Myrtle Beach and The Grand Strand
Population–25,000 (not including surrounding communities of The Grand Strand)

The most important piece of advice for a flyfishing or light-tackle angler looking for digs along the South Carolina coast is to avoid the hotels and motels of Myrtle Beach during the spring, summer, and early fall. Maybe even the winter, come to think of it. These places are geared to tourist families seeking beach fun, not anglers. Instead, get into a hotel, motel, or bed and breakfast that doesn't try to attract beach tourists.

ACCOMMODATIONS
Harbor Inn (Little River), 1564 US 17 North / 843-249-3535
The Cypress Inn (Conway), 16 Elm Street / 843-248-8199
Ashfield Manor, 3030 South Island Road / 843-546-0464
Du Pre House (Georgetown), 921 Prince Street (Georgetown) / 843-546-0298
King's Inn at Georgetown (Georgetown), 230 Broad Street / 843-527-6937
1790 House (Georgetown), 630 Highmarket Street / 843-546-4821
The Shaw House (Georgetown), 613 Cypress Street / 843-546-9663

CAMPGROUNDS
These campgrounds are either in the hub city or nearby:
Myrtle Beach Travel Park, 10108 King Road / 843-449-3714
Apache Family Campground, 9800 Kings Road / 843-449-7323
Myrtle Beach KOA, 613 5th Avenue South / 843-626-6748
Myrtle Beach Travel Park, 10108 Kings Road / 843-449-3714
Ocean Lakes Family Campground (Surfside Beach), 6001 South Kings Hwy / 843-238-5636
Apache Pier and Family Campground, 9700 Kings Road / 843-449-7323
Briarcliffe RV Resort, 10495 North Kings Hwy / 843-272-2730
Pirateland Family Camping Resort, 5401 South Kings Hwy / 843-238-5155
Lakewood Camping Resort, 5901 South Kings Hwy / 843-238-5161

RESTAURANTS
These establishments are in Myrtle Beach unless otherwise specified:
Aunt Maude's Seafood Beef, 7001 Kings Hwy North / 843-449-1434 / Very good meals made with Low Country fare / Seafood, beef, casseroles, etc.
Key West Grille, 1214 Celebrity Circle / 843-444-3663 / Eclectic menu of ethnic dishes including Cuban offerings—try the blackened frog legs
The Trestle Bakery and Cafe (Conway), 308 Main Street / 843-248-9896 / Inexpensive but pleasant, this little cafe offers tasty fare
Vintage House Café, 1210 North Kings Hwy / 843-626-3918 / Imaginative dishes well prepared and delicious
Yamato, 1213 Celebrity Circle / 843-448-1959 / Perhaps the most extensive authentic sushi menu in the state

Captain Dave's Dockside Restaurant (Murrells Inlet), 4037A US 17 Business
   Route / 843-651-5850

TACKLE AND FLY SHOPS
Chapin Company, 951 10th Avenue North / 843-448-7025
City Bait and Tackle, 713 8th Avenue North / 843-448-2543
Low Country Gun and Tackle, 6371 Hwy 544 / 843-236-3039
Myrtle Beach Outfitters (North Myrtle Beach), 2701 Kings Hwy / 843-488-0943 /
   A full-line Orvis dealer

MARINAS
Myrtle Beach Yacht Basin, 1 Hague Drive / 843-293-2141
Osprey Marina, 8400 Osprey Road / 843-215-5353

FOR MORE INFORMATION
Chamber of Commerce
1200 Oak Street
Myrtle Beach, SC 29577
843-626-7444

MYRTLE BEACH AREA TO WINYAH BAY

When compared to the water between the Calabash River and Myrtle Beach, this region is much more complex and fishy looking. It is home to many nuances (twists and turns, holes and flats, channels and sloughs), and for a region that is so close to so many people, it is often surprising how good the fishing can be.

Intracoastal Waterway: U.S. Route 501 Bridge to Bull Creek

The waterway here continues straight only until the Arrowhead Country Club, at which time it bends to the northwest and then back to the southwest at Socastee Swamp Creek. This is a small creek, but any time a confluence presents itself along the waterway, work the area hard to cover the entire water column. Confluences attract crabs and small baitfish because streams add nutrients to the waterway at these junctures. The additional activity of prey species attracts predators, such as spotted seatrout and flounder—never underestimate the value of even a small confluence.

I like to concentrate on natural routes of departure on falling tides, and this area is as good as any to practice tactics. As the tide drops, specks, flounder, and red drum that have been feeding up in Waccamaw River between Lake Busbee and the waterway where it splits Big Swamp (part of the Bucksport Wildlife Management Area) begin to move downriver with the falling tide. Poppers worked in the mouth of the river can be very productive, with red, yellow, white, and green being the most productive. But also consider popper style—chuggers (with an indented face), sliders (bullet shaped), and pushers (flat faced) are three styles that should always be at hand. Sometimes, for whatever reason, specks get very picky and demand a certain color and style of popper, just as brown trout get finicky when a certain hatch is on.

Red, yellow, white, and green are four colors that flyfishers need to have ready, whether for use in poppers, streamers, or other types of patterns.

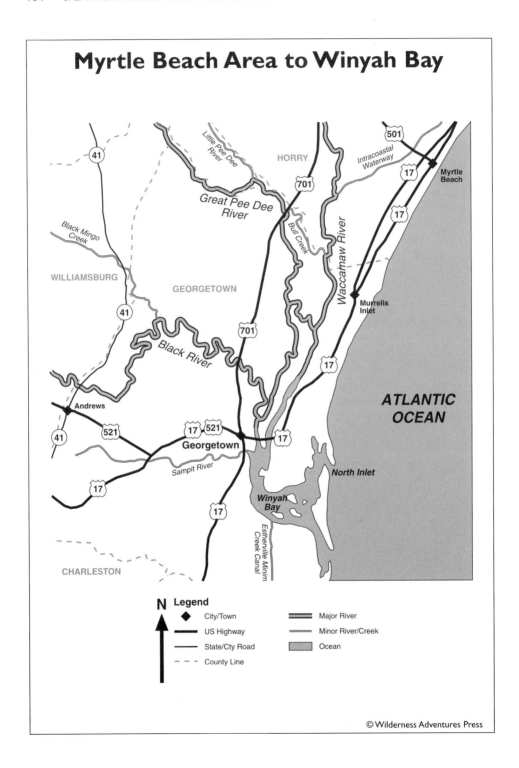

Myrtle Beach Area to Winyah Bay

Intracoastal Waterway: U.S. Route 501 Bridge to Bull Creek

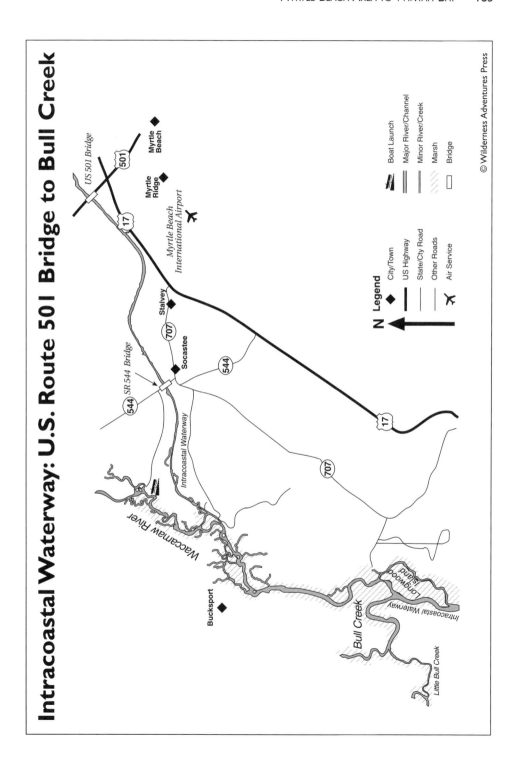

Legend

N

City/Town ◆

US Highway

State/Cty Road

Other Roads

Air Service ✈

Boat Launch

Major River/Channel

Minor River/Creek

Marsh

Bridge

© Wilderness Adventures Press

Myrtle Beach

Myrtle Ridge

US 501 Bridge

501

17

Myrtle Beach International Airport

Stalvey

707

Socastee

544

SR 544 Bridge

544

544

Intracoastal Waterway

17

707

Waccamaw River

Bucksport

Bull Creek

Longwood Island

Intracoastal Waterway

Little Bull Creek

Spartina, a type of cord grass, is acutely important to the health of coastal ecosystems in the Southeast. As the tide floods these rich flats, redfish, seatrout, and black drum search the grass for crabs, shrimp, and small baitfish. By stalking very quietly and carefully, flyfishers and light-tackle anglers can see feeding activity in the grass. Redfish tails often poke above the surface as they rummage for food.

I suggest trying even a small Clouser dropper fished below a larger popper. You might be very pleasantly surprised to see how many strikes this system gets.

The Waccamaw River is very snaky, winding its way through Big Swamp in a torturous series of turns, loops, twists, dead ends, sloughs, backwaters, and split channels. You could fish this little river all day long and not even scratch the proverbial surface.

There are two easy ways to get into the Waccamaw River: turn into it from the waterway (it's a short run down the waterway from the SR 544 bridge at Socastee) or put in at the boat ramp at the end of SR 611, off SR 544 on the north side of the bridge.

I have had fun with soft jerkbaits in the lower Waccamaw, such as those used for largemouth bass. (The Intracoastal becomes the Waccamaw—or is it the other way around?—just east of Bucksport. This area is brackish and a pickerel could be caught just as easily as a speck.) Twitching along the bank can really get specks excited, especially when baitfish are being chased and specks aren't thinking all that much about positive identification of their prey before striking.

Bonefish flies (upper left corner) should be added to your usual arsenal of drum and speck flies, such as Clousers, Deceivers, and Bend Backs.

Farther down the waterway toward Bull Creek is a large island formed by a split in the channel. Fish all around this island—don't be in a hurry to get somewhere else. After this nameless island, the channel widens a bit and gets deeper in some areas. Keep in mind that deep holes sometimes get shallower and that new deep holes can appear. Casting jigs or Clousers on sinking lines all through this area will sometimes yield a speck or two—once in a while a good-sized one.

A side channel just above Bull Creek is narrow but don't skip over it. This channel is the one before the side channel that helps form Longwood Island.

Intracoastal Waterway: Bull Creek to the Great Pee Dee River

The confluence of Bull Creek and the Intracoastal Waterway marks the beginning of an area that has many side channels, sloughs, holes, and other features that hold fish. Wherever the waterway has these features, it is a place to be explored slowly and thoroughly, being sure to work the little nooks and crannies that are oftentimes overlooked. It is also important to work the entire water column, which calls for assorted flies and lines that allow a flyfisher to cover all the water.

Although one seldom sees such flies in action along the Southeast coast, traditional bonefish flies, such as Crazy Charlies and Gotchas in sizes 4 to 8, can be highly effective on trout and reds. To work deep holes or otherwise stick close to the bottom,

Intracoastal Waterway: Bull Creek to the Great Pee Dee River

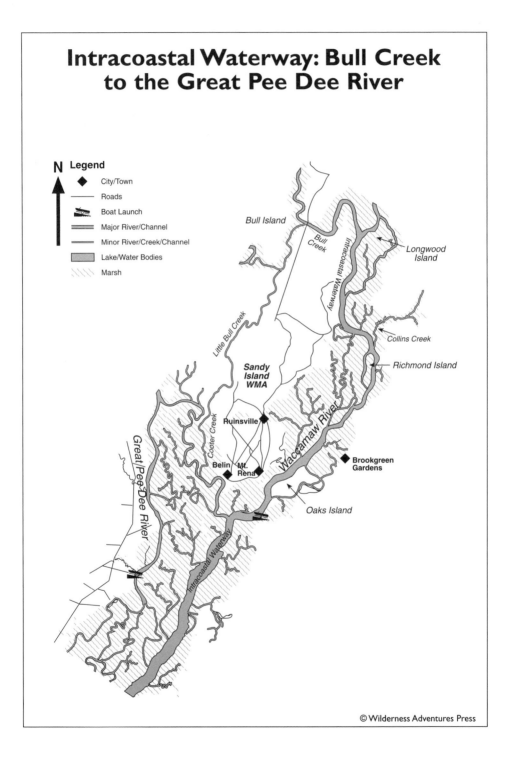

N

Legend

◆ City/Town

— Roads

Boat Launch

Major River/Channel

Minor River/Creek/Channel

Lake/Water Bodies

Marsh

Bull Island

Bull Creek

Intracoastal Waterway

Longwood Island

Little Bull Creek

Collins Creek

Richmond Island

Sandy Island WMA

Cooter Creek

Waccamaw River

Ruinsville

Great Pee Dee River

Belin Mt. Rena

Brookgreen Gardens

Oaks Island

Intracoastal Waterway

© Wilderness Adventures Press

Just inside an inlet at current rips, bluefish gather to attack their favorite victims, which are finger mullet and menhaden. Soft jigs can bring lots of fast action. Photo by Fred Kluge.

use large lead eyes on the Crazy Charlies and Gotchas. Other patterns to try are Borski's Fur Shrimp, Ruoff's Absolute Flea and Deep Flea (first tied by Florida Keys guide Rick Ruoff), and crab patterns like Jack's Fighting Crab (fly tier and respected permit specialist Jack Samson's creation), Dell's Merkin, and Peterson's Spawning Crab in sizes 2 to 8.

Soft jerkbaits worked deep right along the bottom in either a hopping or skittering motion can bring vicious strikes. I have found that lifelike, versatile baits, such as Lunker City's Fin-S series, are extremely good. Two of the best are the Fin-S Fish, which has a thinner, slightly tapered body, and Fin-S Shad (the 3¼-inch model), which has a fat body that radically tapers to a thin, forked, wobbly tail. Try such colors as silver phantom, albino shad, gold pepper shiner, alewife, and smoke pepper shad.

When using the Fin-S series, be sure to use the lead belly weights that are designed explicitly for these baits. They come in weights up to one-half ounce and are designed to keep the bait acting properly—standard lead heads can't do this with these baits.

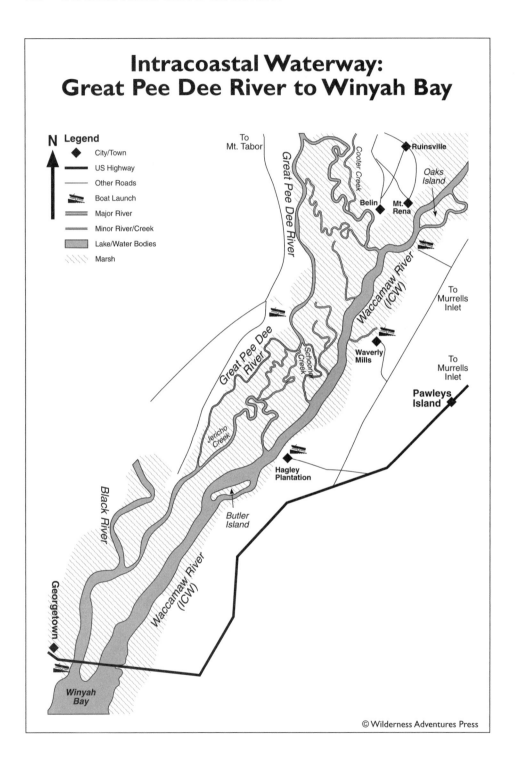

Intracoastal Waterway:
Great Pee Dee River to Winyah Bay

N

Legend
◆ City/Town
━━ US Highway
─── Other Roads
Boat Launch
Major River
Minor River/Creek
Lake/Water Bodies
Marsh

To Mt. Tabor

Great Pee Dee River

Cooter Creek

◆ Ruinsville

Oaks Island

Belin ◆   Mt. Rena ◆

Waccamaw River (ICW)

To Murrells Inlet

Great Pee Dee River

Schoola Creek

Waverly Mills

To Murrells Inlet

Pawleys Island ◆

Jericho Creek

Hagley Plantation ◆

Black River

Butler Island

Waccamaw River (ICW)

Georgetown ◆

Winyah Bay

© Wilderness Adventures Press

Murrells Inlet

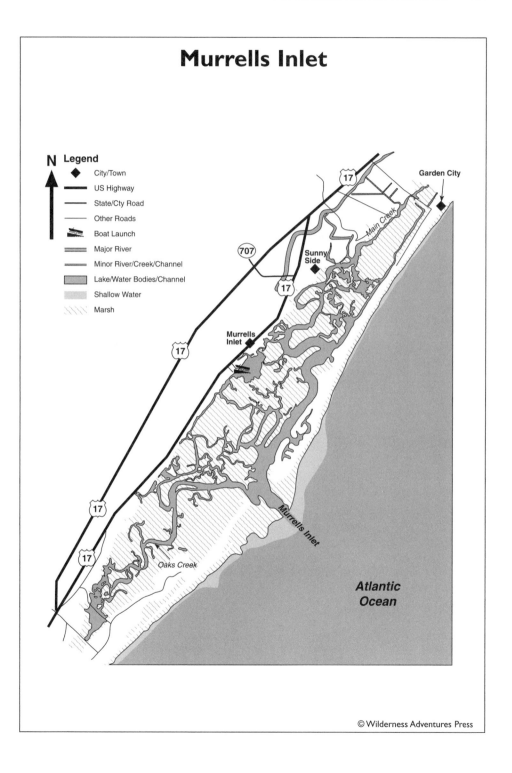

© Wilderness Adventures Press

This puppy drum demonstrates how effective a Beetle Spin can be.

Kalin's Super Floozy soft jerkbait is also good. The best colors are Texas shad, diamond shiner, fishy, and Arkansas shad.

Crankbaits can also be worked in these holes. The Excalibur Fat Free Shad series in threadfin shad and citrus shad, Rapala Shad Raps (silver, shad, and silver/gold), and Risto Raps in the same colors can do well.

Hot spots for this area include the mouth of Collins Creek, the islands behind Brookgreen Gardens, and the sloughs abutting Ruinsville.

On the other side of US 17 is Murrells Inlet. The jetty on the south side of the inlet attracts puppy drum, bluefish, and flounder, but there will probably be plenty of angling competition, and a fly rod can get downright dangerous during the back cast. Instead, I recommend spartina lining the marshes between the inlet and the highway. Lots of specks, flounder, and puppy drum move in here. Be sure to work all the dropoffs and docks and watch for puppy drum tails at high tide way back in spartina.

Back in the waterway, things really begin to get interesting at this point. Here, the Waccamaw River widens and many, many creeks, sloughs, loops, and flats are available, but most of the game fish in here—specks, reds, and flounder mostly—are overlooked because of the number of good-looking spots.

From the Sandy Island Wildlife Management Area at about Cooter Creek all the way down to where the Great Pee Dee and Waccamaw join at Winyah Bay, puppy drum can be taken using small spinnerbaits, such as Beetle Spins. The better colors include chartreuse and yellow, but white can work, too. A steady, slow retrieve about two feet off the bottom with these supposed crappie and bass lures can be deadly. Spinnerbaits are particularly effective worked through a stump field. I have even taken puppy drum in here with small marabou jigs soaked with menhaden oil.

Georgetown
Population–10,000

ACCOMMODATIONS
Ashfield Manor, 3030 South Island Road / 843-546-0464
Du Pre House, 921 Prince Street / 843-546-0298
King's Inn at Georgetown, 230 Broad Street / 843-527-6937
1790 House, 630 Highmarket Street / 843-546-4821
The Shaw House, 613 Cypress Street / 843-546-9663

CAMPGROUNDS
See Myrtle Beach and The Grand Strand

RESTAURANTS
Caribbean Connection, 1501 Front Street / 843-546-7282
Hook Line & Sinker, 706 Church Street / 843-546-5191
Huddle House, 1730 South Fraser Street / 843-527-3628
King Street Jazz Co., 129 King Street / 843-527-2209
Land's End Restaurant, 444 Marina Drive / 843-527-1376
Low country Bar-B-Que, Highway 701 North / 843-527-2697
Quincy's Family Steakhouse, 219 Church Street / 843-546-9510

FLY AND TACKLE SHOPS
Ali's Bait & Tackle Shop, 4496 Frasier Street / 843-545-9082
Blade & Barrel, 2022 Highmarket Street / 843-527-4298
Hewitt's, 7113 South Island Road / 843-527-1991
Tailwalker Tackle & Outfitters, 2903 Highmarket Street / 843-527-2495

GUIDES
Captain George Gallager (Awendaw area), 1290 Eden Road / Paradise Island / 843-884-6410 / Website: www.charternet.com/flyfish/gallager / E-mail: grgallager@aol.com / The beautiful 64,000-acre Cape Romain National Wildlife Refuge is Gallager's primary haunt / Reds on the fly and light tackle are his specialties

MARINAS
Belle Marina, Belle Isle Road / 843-546-8491
Blade & Barrel, 2022 Highmarket Street / 843-527-4298
Hewitt's, 7113 South Island Road / 843-527-1991
Mansfield Plantation, Highway 701 North / 843-546-6961
Tailwalker Tackle & Outfitters, 2903 Highmarket Street / 843-527-2495

FOR MORE INFORMATION
Chamber of Commerce
1001 Front Street
Georgetown, SC 29440
843-526-8436; 800-777-7705

Winyah Bay to Charleston Harbor

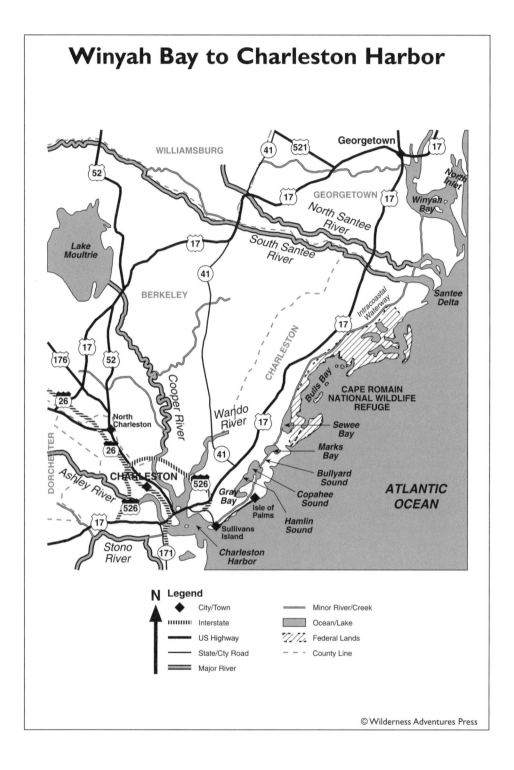

WINYAH BAY TO CHARLESTON HARBOR

This region is some of the best known water in the Low Country. Guides work the southern end (around Charleston and Cape Romain) quite thoroughly, but don't ignore the northern end. The region is one marked by big water and numerous creeks and sloughs. It is a place of active inlets, broad bays, vast flats covered with thick spartina, tiny islands and spits of land, and a great many game fish. If there is one word that aptly describes this area, it is potential.

Winyah Bay

A trio of rivers (the Great Pee Dee, Waccamaw, and Sampit) come together here to form a broad piece of water above Winyah Bay. The bay itself begins at Waccamaw Neck and contains several islands, including the Marsh Islands and Malady Bush Island, around which specks and flounder can be found. Spanish mackerel also come

Inlets, bays, river and creek mouths, and even harbors are all likely game fish locations. Here the author works a Deceiver. Photo by Michael Janich.

Winyah Bay

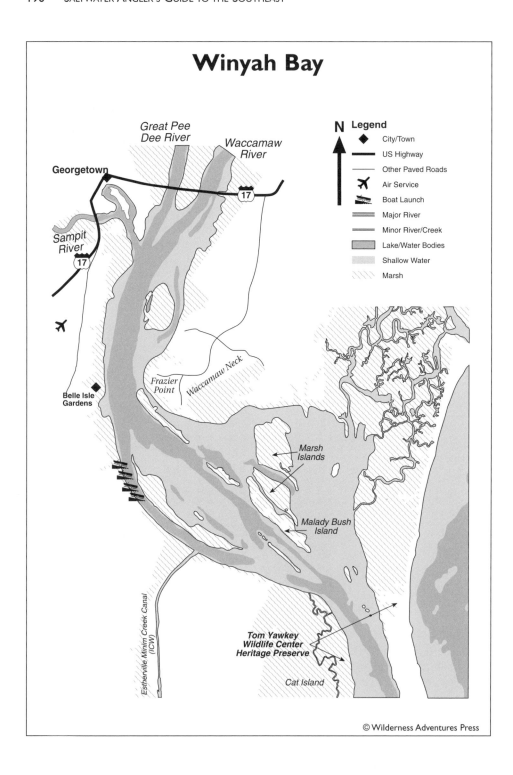

Great Pee
Dee River

Waccamaw
River

Georgetown

Sampit
River

17

17

Legend

N

◆ City/Town
━━ US Highway
── Other Paved Roads
✈ Air Service
🚤 Boat Launch
▬▬ Major River
── Minor River/Creek
▨ Lake/Water Bodies
▨ Shallow Water
▨ Marsh

Belle Isle
Gardens

Frazier
Point

Waccamaw Neck

Marsh
Islands

Malady Bush
Island

Estherville Minim Creek Canal
(ICW)

Tom Yawkey
Wildlife Center
Heritage Preserve

Cat Island

© Wilderness Adventures Press

If you are unfamiliar with the bottom, use caution when wading in rivers, near inlets, and on flats; there can be unseen bottom obstructions and holes.

into this bay through the inlet, and Got-Cha plugs with gold hooks can produce nice catches of these pretty mackerel. Bluefish can get thick in here, so consider curltail jigs with trailer hooks that help prevent blues from biting off the tails and getting away clean.

Across Waccamaw Neck is the North Inlet and its associated sloughs, creeks, and spartina marshes. The name of the game in here is trout, flounder, and some puppy drum. Finger mullet and shrimp drifted below popping corks can really get things going when the tide begins to fall and the marshes begin to drain. Look for rips or strong currents running off points. In the winter, check for deep holes and slow your retrieves down to a crawl, whether using jigs, jerkbaits, crankbaits, or flies.

The Estherville Minim Creek Canal links lower Winyah Bay to North Santee Bay and forms Cat Island, which is home to the Tom Yawkey Wildlife Center Heritage Preserve. Everyone just calls it Cat Island, though. The inlet has submerged jetties and rocks that hold flounder, specks, and drum. There are no roads leading down to the beaches here, but there will be boat anglers in the area.

Minim Island above North Santee Bay and Crow Island on the west side of North Santee Bay both hold specks along the banks. The area comprised of Cat Island, Crow Island, North Santee Bay, and Cedar Island is called the Santee Delta and contains

North Inlet

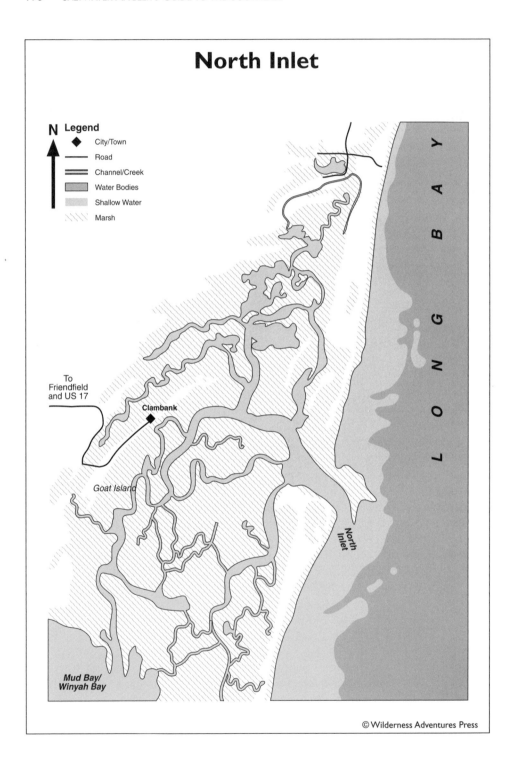

N

Legend

◆ City/Town

── Road

══ Channel/Creek

Water Bodies

Shallow Water

Marsh

To
Friendfield
and US 17

◆ Clambank

Goat Island

North
Inlet

Mud Bay/
Winyah Bay

L O N G   B A Y

© Wilderness Adventures Press

Cat Island

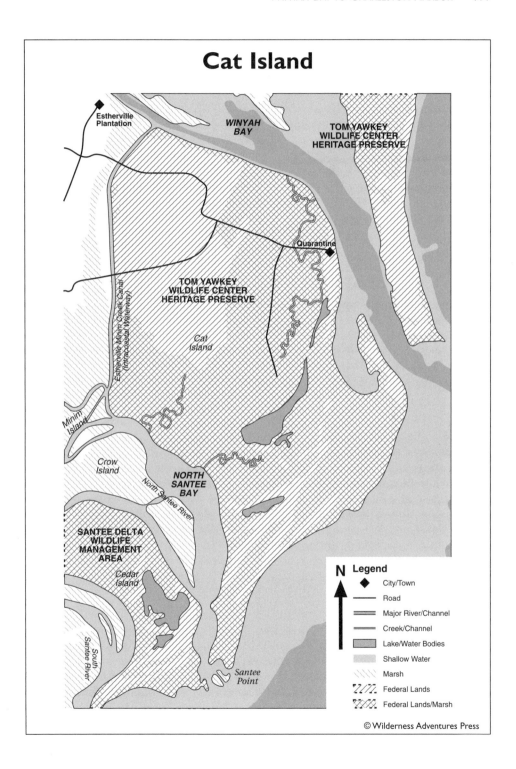

Estherville
Plantation

*WINYAH
BAY*

TOM YAWKEY
WILDLIFE CENTER
HERITAGE PRESERVE

Quarantine

TOM YAWKEY
WILDLIFE CENTER
HERITAGE PRESERVE

*Cat
Island*

*Estherville Minim Creek Canal
(Intracoastal Waterway)*

*Minim
Island*

*Crow
Island*

**NORTH
SANTEE
BAY**

North Santee River

SANTEE DELTA
WILDLIFE
MANAGEMENT
AREA

*Cedar
Island*

*South
Santee River*

*Santee
Point*

N

Legend

◆ City/Town

—— Road

═══ Major River/Channel

—— Creek/Channel

▨ Lake/Water Bodies

░ Shallow Water

▨ Marsh

▨ Federal Lands

▨ Federal Lands/Marsh

© Wilderness Adventures Press

the Santee Delta Wildlife Management Area located between the North and South Santee Rivers.

Due to the amount of fresh water just a short way up the South Santee River, the best fishing on the South Santee River is on the lower end around the Santee Coastal Wildlife Management Area on Murphy Island and Grace Island, situated on the first big bend inside the South Santee Inlet.

Next is the fabulous Cape Romain National Wildlife Refuge, where guides working the Charleston area spend a lot of time chasing red drum in spartina. The refuge is well managed, and every guide in the territory knows how important it is to protect this awesome game fish. They remember that not so long ago the redfish was in peril because of commercial overfishing. Now the reds are back, and everyone is enjoying catch-and-release with only the occasional red being kept for supper, and then always a puppy drum, which taste better than adult fish and aren't prime breeders.

Above Bulls Bay, the Cape Romain NWR is a complicated warren of creeks, bays, beaches, islands, and much spartina. This diversity helps attract drum (red and black), seatrout, and flounder. The area's primary features include:

- the banks lining Cape Romain Harbor
- Horsehead Creek
- the back side of Cape Island
- Lighthouse Island
- Raccoon Key
- the banks of Muddy Bay
- Five Fathom Creek
- holes and dropoffs along the waterway
- the Romain River

MirrOlures, assorted other crankbaits, as well as poppers, Clousers, Bend Backs, and Deceivers for flies are the ticket—but the spoon fly is the best of all. This gold fly makes red drum crazy and is being used more and more by flyfishers and guides who have discovered its great value. It has the ability to sink fairly quickly amid the spartina and reflects light very well. When drum see it, they think it is a baitfish or shrimp and go after it. I wouldn't be caught dead anywhere on a spartina flat without several spoon flies; you can get them from Orvis.

Take time and work slowly when in the upper end of Cape Romain. There are many game fish in here, so watch for tails, swooshes, and "muds" (mud suspended in the water like a cloud that indicates a drum is in the area).

Holes in spartina, where grass spreads out into quiet little backwaters, must be approached with absolute stealth. Drum that feed in these openings are nervous because they are exposed to danger from above and elsewhere. If poling, stay as low as possible. When casting, use as few false casts as possible. If a drum sees a rod waving around or anything else to scare it, it will "blow out" in a sudden burst of speed and fright. This can also blow out other drum in the same opening. Once a drum blows out, forget about catching it, even if you can see it.

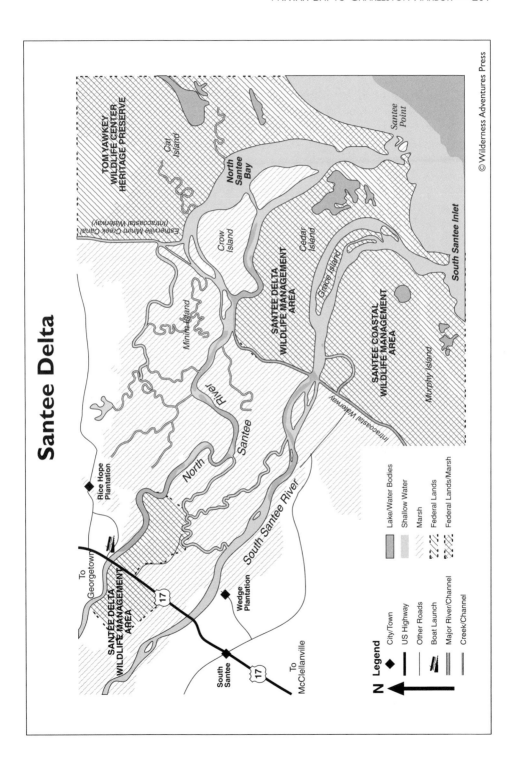

Santee Delta

© Wilderness Adventures Press

Legend

- ◆ City/Town
- US Highway
- Other Roads
- Boat Launch
- Major River/Channel
- Creek/Channel
- Lake/Water Bodies
- Shallow Water
- Marsh
- Federal Lands
- Federal Lands/Marsh

N

Cape Romain National Wildlife Refuge

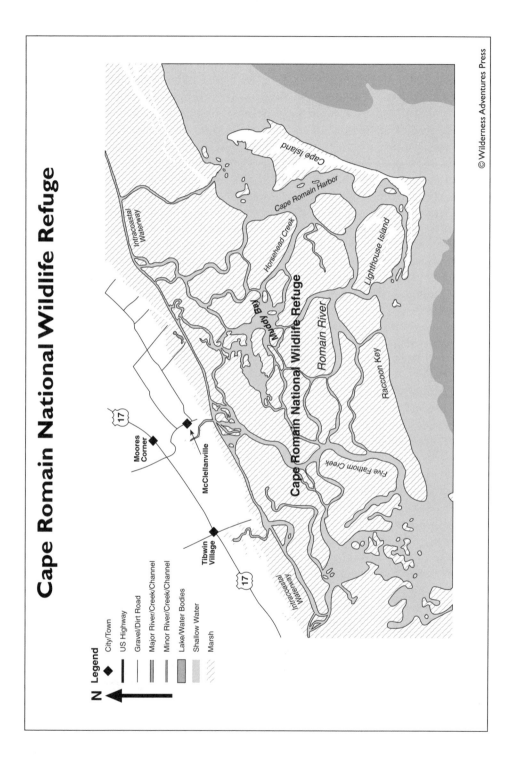

Legend

N

City/Town
US Highway
Gravel/Dirt Road
Major River/Creek/Channel
Minor River/Creek/Channel
Lake/Water Bodies
Shallow Water
Marsh

Intracoastal Waterway

Moores Corner

McClellanville

Tibwin Village

Cape Romain National Wildlife Refuge

Cape Island

Cape Romain Harbor

Horsehead Creek

Muddy Bay

Romain River

Lighthouse Island

Raccoon Key

Five Fathom Creek

Intracoastal Waterway

© Wilderness Adventures Press

Cape Romain NWR and Bulls Bay

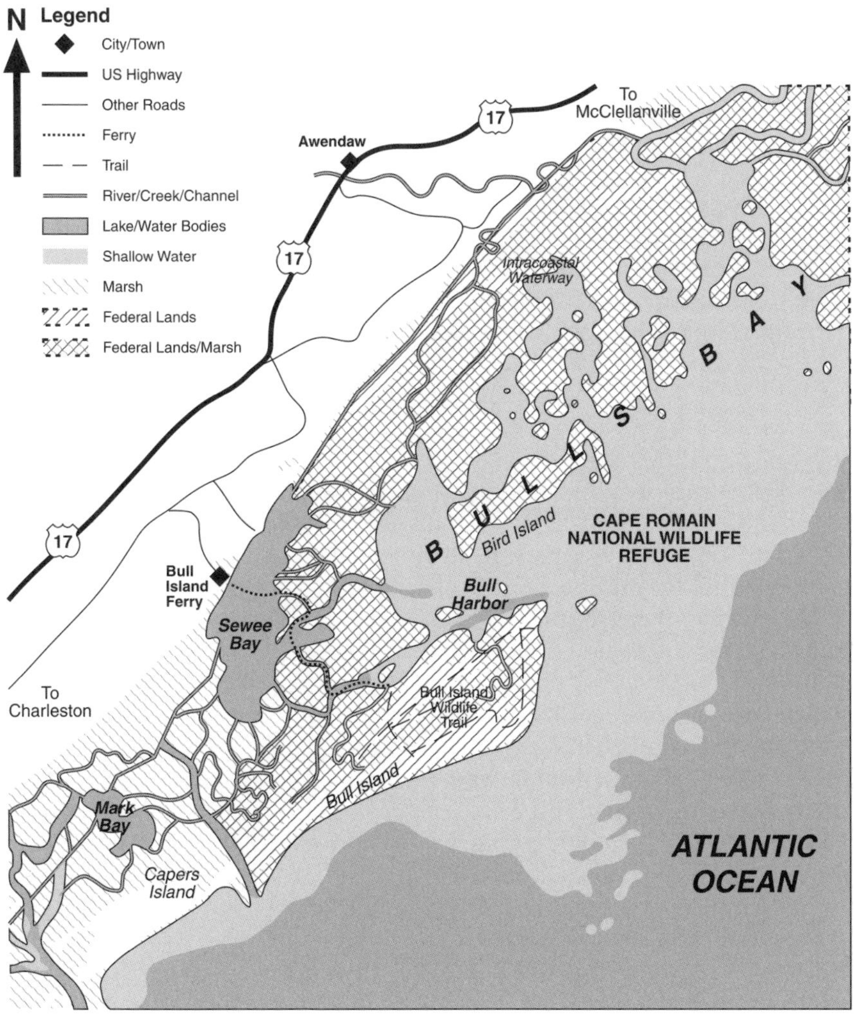
N
Legend
City/Town
US Highway
Other Roads
Ferry
Trail
River/Creek/Channel
Lake/Water Bodies
Shallow Water
Marsh
Federal Lands
Federal Lands/Marsh
17
To McClellanville
Awendaw
17
Intracoastal Waterway
B U L L S B A Y
Bird Island
CAPE ROMAIN NATIONAL WILDLIFE REFUGE
17
Bull Island Ferry
Bull Harbor
Sewee Bay
Bull Island Wildlife Trail
To Charleston
Bull Island
Mark Bay
Capers Island
ATLANTIC OCEAN

© Wilderness Adventures Press

Captain Richard Stuhr, a guide who knows the Cape Romain
National Wildlife Refuge well, releases a nice red drum after tagging it.

It is highly entertaining and very educational to watch drum feed in a spartina opening. Sometimes they can become so engrossed in foraging that they seem to forget about everything else. They stand on their heads to root out a crab or marine worm, with their tails flipping back and forth in the air entirely out of the water. They get so excited that they turn quickly back and forth trying to suck in crabs, shrimp, and other goodies that are around them. Such an actively feeding red can be a thrilling target for a flyfisher.

Bulls Bay is broad and quite crammed with birds and other wildlife, especially porpoises. Knowing that baitfish can be easy to trap in the bay, pods of porpoises enter the bay to feed in what can sometimes be stunning charges against shoals of bait. These marine mammals also chase puppy drum and specks, and it isn't often you catch one of these game fish while a pod of porpoises are feeding nearby (drum can hear and perhaps see the feeding activity and get out of there). If you see porpoises feeding, please approach carefully, if at all, to watch them. Have a camera ready—an autofocus comes in handy, as does a long lens that allows taking photographs without disturbing the porpoises. And never think for a second about hopping in to swim with porpoises as in *Flipper*. These are wild creatures that are very large and strong. You could easily be hurt and would certainly be breaking the law. Watch from a safe distance.

The southernmost end of Cape Romain consists of several creeks linking to Sewee Bay, Bull Harbor, and Bull Island. Redfish can be thick down here at times.

A little known fact about spartina is that it can even attract such game fish as false albacore. When baitfish are in flooded spartina and false albacore know it, these

These oyster beds are lying exposed on the falling tide just north of Charleston. As water levels drop and the spartina drains, red drum use the sloughs that form between the beds as avenues of escape.

powerful fish invade the grass looking like fat torpedoes speeding through the stuff eating crazily. I have seen this happen in Bull Harbor and at Cape Lookout, too.

Oyster beds are also an extremely important feature in Southeast coastal ecosystems. Oysters attract myriad forms of life in the lowermost end of the food chain, which in turn attract crabs and baitfish. Naturally, reds, specks, and flounder come looking for crabs and baitfish, and then flyfishers come looking for the reds, specks, and flounder. But it's important to know how to work oysters.

On a rising tide, drum are anxious to get into spartina flats where they can hunt crabs and other delectables. They stay as long as possible until skinny water forces them back out. When they leave spartina flats, they use the sloughs (gaps) between oyster beds as routes leading to deeper water, but on their way they continue to forage.

These gaps are good places to watch for "pushes," which are slight humps on the surface of the water created by drum as they swim. Drum know that baitfish are in these gaps and that baitfish will flee ahead of them. Flies stripped in front of and away from these drum can get fast and furious results. One good fly for this technique is Lefty's Deceiver, which is an outstanding imitation of a baitfish.

The Cape Romain National Wildlife Refuge ends at Capers Island. Mark Bay, where reds are found, is just west and a bit north of the island. There is a lot more water between here and Charleston Harbor, including:

- Copahee Sound
- Bullyard Sound
- Hamlin Sound
- Gray Bay

The little island fragments found between Mark Bay and Gray Bay deserve a close look due to the many specks and reds to be found there. The larger islands—Dewees between Capers Island and Isle of Palms, and Eagle between Hamlin Sound and Gray Bay—are also productive.

Check the creeks for specks behind Isle of Palms, as well. Isle of Palms was hit very hard by Hurricane Hugo but is now fully recovered. The inlet is good for Spanish mackerel, and if there is any debris floating in the water there, look for tripletail. A shrimp pattern tossed in front of a tripletail can result in a tremendous battle that won't soon be forgotten. Tripletail love surface structure near inlets and are powerful fighters, although they aren't much to look at.

Mark Bay to Gray Bay

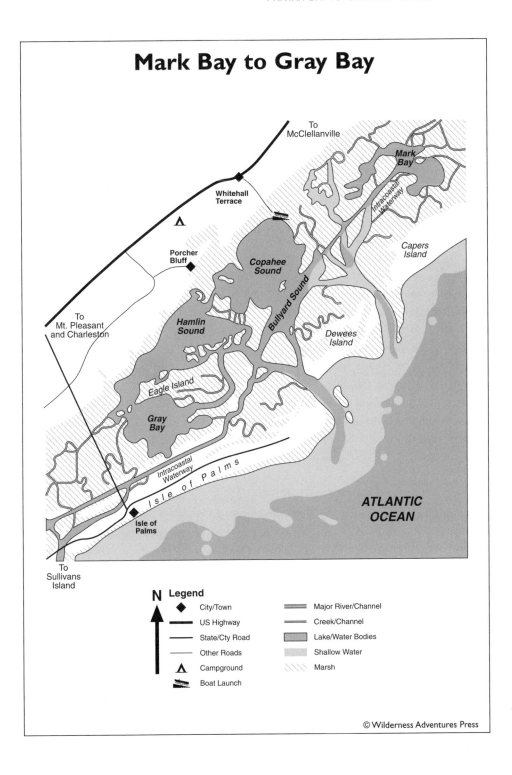

To
McClellanville

Mark
Bay

Intracoastal
Waterway

Whitehall
Terrace

Capers
Island

Porcher
Bluff

Copahee
Sound

Bullyard Sound

To
Mt. Pleasant
and Charleston

Hamlin
Sound

Dewees
Island

Eagle Island

Gray
Bay

Intracoastal
Waterway

Isle of Palms

ATLANTIC
OCEAN

Isle of
Palms

To
Sullivans
Island

N

Legend

◆ City/Town
— US Highway
— State/Cty Road
— Other Roads
⋀ Campground
Boat Launch

Major River/Channel
Creek/Channel
Lake/Water Bodies
Shallow Water
Marsh

© Wilderness Adventures Press

Charleston
Population–81,000

Charleston is rich in history, style, and grace. The area around The Battery is quite beautiful, with many old, gracious homes, inns, and pleasing sights for the eye. With an impressive plethora of historic inns and a setting that reminds us of the War Between the States and a time when our country's future was imperiled, Charleston is a Southern city not to be missed.

ACCOMMODATIONS

Two Meeting Street Inn, address / 843-723-7322 / One of the most beautiful inns in Charleston and a top choice of accommodations / Afternoon tea, fresh, homemade pastries, such as carrot cake, haystacks, and pecan squares, and proper Southern hospitality make the Two Meeting Street Inn something special

Fulton Lane Inn, 202 King Street / 800-720-2688 / Canopy beds, whirlpool baths, and antebellum architecture round out this inn

Indigo Inn, 1 Maiden Lane / 800-845-7639 / An historic antebellum inn with a private courtyard

Kings Courtyard Inn, 198 King Street / 800-845-6119

The Lodge at Lofton's Landing, PO Box 245 / 803-720-7332 / E-mail: makairal@aol.com / This lovely lodge is situated on the edge of a spartina marsh in the Cape Romain National Wildlife Refuge on Doe Hall Creek / Available for private rentals and comes fully equipped / Very tastefully furnished and decorated / Captain Richard Stuhr will drive his Action Craft flats boat right up to the lodge's private dock and pick you up / For something out of the bustle of Charleston's Battery area, this is the place / Proprietors are Pam and Bright McConnell

The Mills House Hotel, 115 Meeting Street / 800-874-9600 / Exceptional hotel, classy / Built in 1853

Planters Inn, 112 North Market Street / 800-845-7082 / Website: www.plantersinn.com / Built in 1844 at the corner of Market and Meeting, this very nice inn is located in one of the most historic areas of the city

Victoria House Inn, 208 King Street / 800-933-5464 / From the Victorian era, this inn features Romanesque styling

CAMPGROUNDS

These campgrounds are either in or near Charleston.

Lake Aire RV Park and Campground (Hollywood), 4375 Hwy 162 / 843-571-1271

The Campground at James Island, 871 Riverland Drive / 843-795-9884

Kampgrounds of America, 9494 Hwy 78 / 843-797-1045

Peperhill Campsites (North Charleston), 2801 Ashley Phosphate Road / 843-873-7060

Oak Plantation Camp Ground (Johns Island), 3540 Savannah Hwy / 843-766-5936
Fain's RV Park (North Charleston), 6309 Fain Boulevard / 843-744-1005

RESTAURANTS

There is a large selection of all types of restaurants available in this beautiful city, here are a few of the more interesting ones.

Anson, 12 Anson Street / 803-577-0551 / Casually elegant restaurant featuring good seafood

Blossom Café, 171 East Bay Street / 803-722-9200 / Pasta, seafood, Mediterranean dishes

Charleston Grill, 224 King Street / 803-577-4522 / Live jazz / Fare consists of traditional Low Country offerings

Fulton Five, 5 Fulton Street / 803-853-5555 / Northern Italian cuisine that is better than most

Peninsula Grill, 112 North Market Street / 803-723-0700 / One of the best restaurants in the city. Impressive wine list / Outstanding fare

Saracen Restaurant, 141 East Bay Street / 803-723-6242 / Fresh seafood and top choice meat dishes

TACKLE AND FLY SHOPS

Captain Ed's Fly Fishing Shop, 47 John Street / 843-723-0860 / Well stocked with flyfishing tackle

Carolina Rod and Gun, 1319 Savannah Hwy / 843-571-7972

Charleston Angler, 946 Orleans Road / 843-571-3899 / An outfitter with several good guides and well stocked for light tackle and flyfishing / All your guide and/or tackle needs for reds, specks, ladyfish, cobia, flounder, tarpon, and more

Folly Road Tackle Shop, 805 Folly Road / 29412 / 843-762-7397

Gone Fishin, 2289 Furman Drive /

John's Rod and Reel, 47 Windemere Boulevard / 29407 / 843-766-7300

J.J.W. Luden, 360 Concord Street / 29401 / 843-723-7829 / Luden's is a full-line Orvis dealer and is one of the best equipped shops for flyfishers in the Low Country / Also has many good guides with plenty of experience both flyfishing and casting with light spinning tackle / All inshore game fish species

West Ashley Tackle, 1117 Magnolia Road / 29407 / 843-556-1828

FLY FISHING & LIGHT-TACKLE GUIDES

Captain Richard Stuhr, 547 Sanders Farm Lane / 803-881-3179 / One of the very best and most experienced flyfishing and light-tackle charter guides I have ever met, Stuhr goes after redfish and spotted seatrout in the spartina flats surrounding Charleston, giant crevalle jack in Charleston harbor, and ladyfish near Fort Sumter, among other species / Richard encourages beginners to give flyfishing a try with him, too / Stuhr is an Orvis-endorsed guide who receives my very highest recommendation

Captain Chris Chavis, 1287 Hampshire Road / 843-795-4707 / Reds, specks, jacks, blues, and tarpon are Chavis's primary targets / He has been guiding for four years in the Charleston area

Captain Chad Ferris, c/o Charleston Angler, 946 Orleans Road / 843-732-3277

Captain Champ Smith, c/o Charleston Angler, 946 Orleans Road / 843-928-3990 / Smith is a respected guide with a lot of experience

Captain Wally Burbage, c/o Charleston Angler, 946 Orleans Road / 843-556-8004

Captain Randy Hamilton, c/o Charleston Angler, 946 Orleans Road / 843-763-6499 / Hamilton is a well-known guide who works the McClellanville area a great deal

Captain Lee Taylor, c/o Charleston Angler, 946 Orleans Road / 843-971-1200

Captain Peter Brown, c/o J.J.W. Luden, 360 Concord Street / 843-830-0448

Captain John Cox, c/o J.J.W. Luden, 360 Concord Street / 843-884-1371

Captain Rich Moore, (Isle of Palms) No. 4 Dolphin Row / 843-886-6927 / E-mail: shpk18@aol.com / Moore targets Tarpon, Spanish mackerel, specks, reds, jacks, and ladyfish

Captain Bill Glenn (Mt. Pleasant), 1558 Fiddlers Marsh Drive / 843-884-8627 / Specks, reds, ladyfish, jacks, and tarpon are the big five for Glenn, who is endorsed by Orvis / He fishes the Charleston region

MARINAS

Ashley Marina, 33 Lockwood Drive / 843-722-1996

Charleston Maritime Center, 10 Wharfside Street / 843-853-3625

City Marina, 17 Lockwood Drive / 843-853-4386

Cooper River Marina, 861 Riverland Drive / 843-554-0790

Dolphin Cove Marina, 2079 Austin Avenue / 843-744-2562

Duncan's Boat Harbour, 4354 Bridge View Drive / 843-744-2628

Ripley Light Marina, 56 Ashley Point Drive / 843-766-2100

Bohicket Marina (Johns Island), 1880 Andell Bluff Boulevard / 803-768-1280\

Daniel Island Marina (Wando), 669 Marina Drive / 843-884-1000

FOR MORE INFORMATION

Chamber of Commerce
81 Mary Street
Charleston, SC 29403
843-853-8000

CHARLESTON HARBOR TO THE SAVANNAH RIVER

Many large game fish are hunted in these waters, many of which are found right around and even in Charleston Harbor. From the mighty silver king and brutish crevalle jack to the dainty but acrobatic ladyfish to the spotted seatrout and many more species, this region is fabulous.

Charleston Harbor

My most memorable event surrounding Charleston Harbor is of a fish I failed to catch because I underestimated the size and strength of the beast. This was back in the summer of 1994. My wife, Susan, and I had gone to Charleston to flyfish with Captain Richard Stuhr and Captain Bramblett Bradham (the latter now retired from guiding).

On a hot, still weekday morning, with Susan in Richard's boat and me in Bramblett's, we looked out over the glassy surface of the harbor hoping to see golden tails glistening in the sun. It was only a few minutes before we spotted them—crevalle jacks—a big school of them. I had seen many schools of jacks in my life, but this school was clearly large and the fish huge, their big tails shining in the bright morning sun as they slowly cruised along the surface. I knew I was about to experience some incredible jack action.

This midsized jack was brought in, but others...

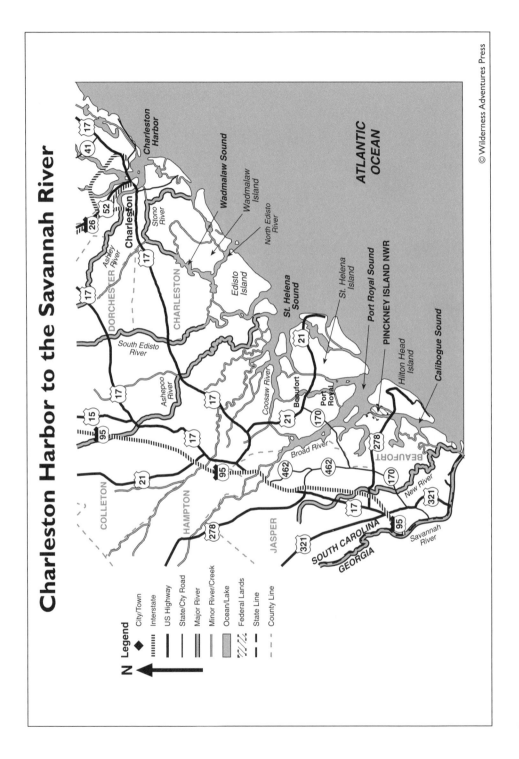

Charleston Harbor to the Savannah River

© Wilderness Adventures Press

Legend

- ◆ City/Town
- Interstate
- US Highway
- State/Cty Road
- Major River
- Minor River/Creek
- Ocean/Lake
- Federal Lands
- State Line
- County Line

N

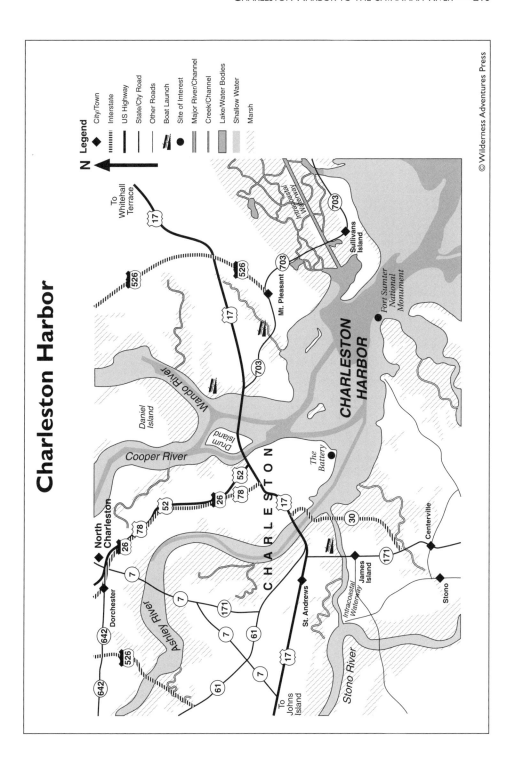

Charleston Harbor

*Captain Richard Stuhr casts toward a school of large jacks
in Charleston Harbor as Susan watches the action unfold.*

I stripped line off the reel and allowed it to pile in large coils at my feet. Bramblett warned me that the fish were coming and to get ready. Quickly, I double-hauled and sent the big popper toward the front of the mob, which landed four feet in front of the lead fish, a big bruiser that dashed forward to attack the fly.

Bramblett told me to get ready again, which only served to make me even more tense, and let me tell you, I was tense. The jack opened its mouth and ate the fly.

With Bramblett shouting from the platform, I strip struck the fish. My rod bent to the cork and line began leaving the reel at a most alarming rate, the drag putting great pressure on the jack to stop. The rod bent under the bow, and I quickly flipped the rod under it in an attempt to keep the jack on. Then the tippet went south. The jack had popped it because it was just too light, apparently. It was one of the shortest and most exciting fights I have ever gotten into with a game fish.

But jacks are not the only game fish in and around Charleston Harbor. Ladyfish, tarpon, and even cobia are available, with redfish, specks, flounder, black drum, Spanish mackerel, and every once in a while, some kings.

Shark fishing has become very popular around the mouth of the harbor, with many anglers fishing from and around Sullivan's Island. Some surprisingly large sharks are caught from and near bridges and even off the beach. I am hoping that this shark fishery will fall out of style because of the severe pressure being placed on

*Captain Bramblett
Bradham poles a
Charleston area spartina
flat in search of redfish.*

many shark populations by commercial fishermen who kill sharks for their fins and then toss the carcass back in. Shark fin soup is a delicacy in the Orient, and commercial fishermen will do anything for the dollars shark fins produce regardless of what effect their callous actions have on the ecosystem.

Three rivers help to form Charleston Harbor: Wando and Cooper from the north, and Ashley from the northwest. A creek links the Stono River to the harbor from the west. Add features like the neck on which the city of Charleston sits, numerous points, spartina marshes, creeks, and islands, and what you get is an elaborate ecosystem that fosters life at all levels. The result is a superb fishery that every fly-fisher and light-tackle kook should try—frequently.

The rivers themselves are home to many drum, flounder, and specks. Spartina flats abutting rivers and similar flats that lie on creeks feeding the rivers are prime drum habitat. By exploring these flats and creeks, one can come upon surprising numbers of game fish, with redfish being the main target of many anglers. Seemingly countless potential hot spots present themselves on these waters, and I have found up to 10 large reds feeding in one opening on a spartina flat that was no larger than 30 feet by 20 feet.

Charleston Harbor is also home to a large sheepshead population. Most dock and bridge pilings hold these strong game fish, but very few anglers, especially flyfishers, ever go after them. This is a real shame because the spunky sheepshead, a member in good standing of the porgy family, is a smashing (I cleared the use of this adjective with my friends in Great Britain) game fish that will take live fiddler crabs impaled on small hooks and small flies (mostly crab patterns, but also shrimp) if presented very close to their structure. Sheepshead also get back into spartina flats and congregate around oyster rocks, both in the spartina and away from it. But be careful: sheepshead are quite nervous and scoot quickly if they think someone is looking for them.

One bright summer day many years ago, I was fishing with Captain Bramblett Bradham back on a flat covered with tall spartina. Bramblett was on the poling platform and I was on the bow platform with a fly rod in my hand. I was looking around for some redfish when Bramblett suddenly but softly told me to look in the grass about six feet off the bow at one o'clock. I did so but saw nothing. Bramblett insisted that I look harder.

Then it materialized: a 10-pound or so black drum quietly feeding on fiddler crabs. It was obviously too close to cast to, so I dropped the gold size 2 spoon fly beside it. Maddeningly, the fish apparently saw my rod tip and bolted in a huge blowout of water, mud, and no doubt confused fiddlers. I told Bramblett—as the fish fled—that I was surprised to find a black drum so far back in the grass, but he said they were quite common there if fiddlers were around. I had always thought that black drum only hung out around jetties and such, but that long-ago day I learned that I needed to pay more attention and never assume that the so-called rules I learned long ago were based in absolute fact. Of particular importance to me regarding this lesson was just how big black drum can get.

This lesson reminds me of another lesson about cobia. No, cobia won't get up into spartina grass—at least I don't think they will—but they do occasionally show up in places where they aren't exactly expected. For example, back in the early to mid-1990s I was the outdoor columnist for the *Daily News* of Jacksonville, North Carolina. One day I received a letter in the mail from a fellow who had been surf fishing for puppy drum and other smallish game fish on Emerald Beach just north of Bogue Inlet. He was using cut bait or something when suddenly his rod began to depart for Europe. He grabbed it, set the hook, and the fight was on.

After quite a while, and with many onlookers having gathered to watch the fracas, the angler hauled a cobia up onto the beach that weighed about 60 pounds, if my memory serves. A photo of the fish was included with the letter he sent. It—the fish, not the picture—was as big as the angler! Everyone was surprised with the catch because cobia are supposed to be game fish that hang around wrecks offshore and buoys in inlets, not surf zones.

Captain Richard Stuhr works a Clouser for redfish on a flat bordering Charleston Harbor.

My point—and yes, I do have one—is that you should always be on the lookout for cobia and other game fish that aren't necessarily supposed to be in the area. And cobia go up rivers—Rick Pelow lost a huge one right in front of me that he was fighting on 8-pound test mono, the fish having appeared beside a small pier below the SR 210 bridge over the New River at Snead's Ferry in North Carolina. The estimated weight of the cobia was easily 40 pounds.

Charleston Harbor itself, within view of The Battery, is home to redfish. This fact was proved to me by Captain Richard Stuhr years ago, and it was a lesson I have remembered. Never assume that because of boat traffic or the proximity of a city that game fish aren't nearby. Check the harbor flats—reds will be there.

Ladyfish are an exquisite and very athletic game fish found around Charleston Harbor, principally around Fort Sumter, where the Civil War finally began (I am a military historian and use the term "finally" to indicate how long in coming this terrible war was).

I caught my first ladyfish on a live shrimp in 1971. When it picked up the shrimp, it immediately shot into the air and spun wildly, then crashed back into the water. It

On a flat beside Charleston Harbor, this redfish fell
for Captain Richard Stuhr's chartreuse and white Clouser.

did this several times until finally netted, after which I released it. I recall exclaiming to my father how I thought it was a "baby tarpon," because it went nuts on the surface, but it did seem a bit skinny to me. As I examined it in the net, I realized that it wasn't a baby tarpon, although it appeared to be something like one.

That night I looked the ladyfish up in one of my reference books and learned that, indeed, the ladyfish is a very close cousin of the tarpon. Since then I have always pursued ladyfish whenever the opportunity presented itself, and Fort Sumter presents itself very nicely.

Being subtropical in nature, ladyfish are warmwater fish, so they are around Charleston only during late spring, summer, and very early fall. Once they feel a bit of a chill in the water, they are off to points south and more tepid climes. I suggest curltail jigs in green, gray, silver, and chartreuse, with lead heads of white, red, yellow, or orange. When using live bait, a live shrimp is pretty much irresistible. Flies for ladyfish include any shrimp imitation, but baitfish imitations also work very well. A 9-foot, 7-weight rod is just right, and the reel need not be anything special when it comes to drags—ladyfish can be handled by palming the rim. Just be sure to bow to the fish when it jumps, and it will jump frequently.

A word of caution when it comes to catching and safely releasing ladyfish. These are delicate fish that require quick fights and minimal handling for a good release. If

Bull reds can be found anywhere within their range, but certain locations are favored by the huge game fish, such as the mouth of Charleston Harbor, the Outer Banks of North Carolina, Pamlico Sound in North Carolina, and Florida's Banana River Lagoon. Here, Rick Pelow hugs his favorite bull red prior to release.

you can avoid handling it at all, i.e., using a Ketchum Release or other method of releasing without actually touching it with your hands, do so.

Before we move on, consider the mouth of Charleston Harbor for bull reds. Drifting freshly cut menhaden on the bottom can entice some monstrous reds. Be ready for a battle—and be ready for a tarpon to pick up the menhaden, too. The silver kings in these parts can go well over 100 pounds. Bull reds can push 40 pounds and then some.

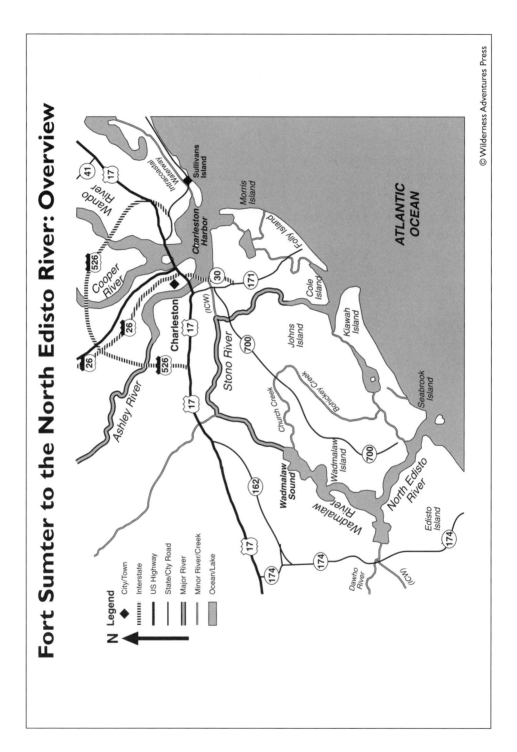

Fort Sumter to the North Edisto River

Fort Sumter sits on a very small island at the mouth of Charleston Harbor. The inshore waters south and southwest of the fort are a typical warren of creeks, marshes, holes, flats, bays, bridges, pilings, and islands, all of which are important to game fish.

Keeping Fort Sumter to starboard and Cummings Point to port (James Island is to starboard and ahead, whereas Morris Island is to port and ahead), enter a small bay fed by three primary and two secondary creeks. The mouths of these creeks are havens for specks, drum, flounder, and sometimes tarpon. The main creek at the bay's southwest corner leads to many more creeks on another bay at the southwest corner of which is the Fort Lamar Heritage Preserve. Five major islands are located here:

- Goat Island
- Long Island
- Oak Island
- Folly Island (includes Folly Beach and many beach homes)
- Cole Island

The creeks and flats in this area can be good for specks and puppy drum, with the occasional good-sized redfish being found. The usual lineup of baits and flies work fine, but also try live shrimp, menhaden, and finger mullet for trout, and live crabs for drum. Sheepshead around the SR 171 bridge are also an option.

Now comes the Stono River and its inlet, in the mouth of which is a small island called Bird Key. Jigs tossed around this island are effective on trout, and spoons and Got-Cha plugs take Spanish mackerel. Heading upriver the first creek is on Kiawah Island (to port, er, your left) and then the Kiawah River. On the right is Cole Island. The Kiawah River separates Kiawah Island from Johns Island, and some people don't realize it is an island because it is formed only by the Stono River, which is very narrow between the enclave of Johns Island and Wadmalaw Sound. After the Kiawah River comes the Stono River proper, which makes a large semicircle up past the Charleston Executive Airport and winds around to Wadmalaw Sound, emptying into the sound northwest of Church Creek. The marshes lining the river, particularly between Johns Island and Wadmalaw Sound, are worthy of attention using MirrOlures and soft jerkbaits.

Between Wadmalaw Sound and Deveaux Bank at the mouth of the North Edisto River are some productive fishing grounds, including:

- the islands, points, and cuts of the Wadmalaw River, which really isn't much of a river but more like a small sound
- Toogoodoo Creek (both arms)
- Tom Point Creek across from Bears Bluff
- the Dawho River (around the SR 174 bridge, in particular, and Whooping Island)
- Little Edisto Island
- all the creeks that are part of Wadmalaw Island, including Bohicket Creek
- Seabrook Island
- the banks and creeks of Edisto Island (outermost Fishing Creek is often a good choice)

Although I would select a chartreuse curltail jig with a bright orange lead head if I had but one jig to use, a variety of body styles, tail designs, and lead head colors can result in many more trout, particularly when there is only one type of bait in the water at the moment. But style and color aren't the only things to consider; action and precisely where the jig is presented are equally important. The right style and color scheme are of no use if the jig lands where there are no trout or if the action is all wrong for the situation.

These spots amount to a lot of water to be covered—don't rush it. Puppy drum and trout can be found in any of these spots at almost any time, but concentrate on deep holes in the river and creeks during winter.

Many fish occupy the spartina flats from spring through fall, and with so many flats available, it is important to have an experienced guide if you are not familiar with the region. The guide should have a flats boat with a poling platform and be a very adept poler, as well.

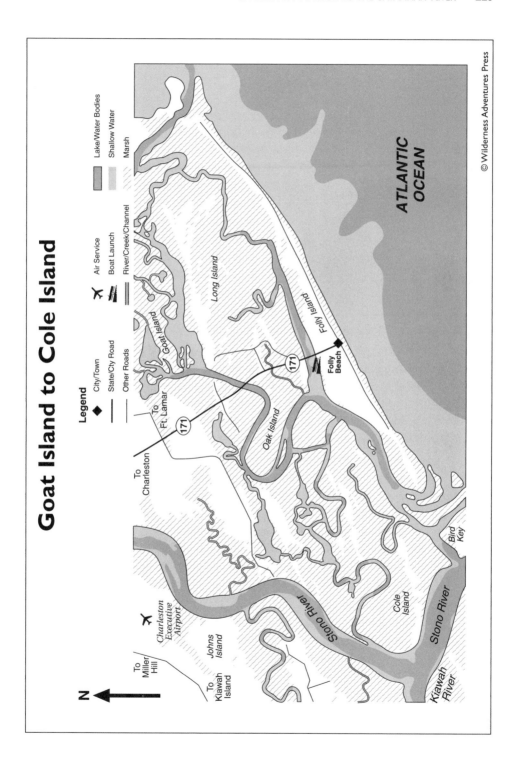

Goat Island to Cole Island

Legend
City/Town
State/Cty Road
Other Roads
Air Service
Boat Launch
River/Creek/Channel
Lake/Water Bodies
Shallow Water
Marsh

N

To Miller Hill
To Kiawah Island
Charleston Executive Airport
Johns Island
To Charleston
To Ft. Lamar
171
171
Goat Island
Long Island
Oak Island
Folly Island
Folly Beach
Stono River
Cole Island
Bird Key
Kiawah River
Stono River
ATLANTIC OCEAN

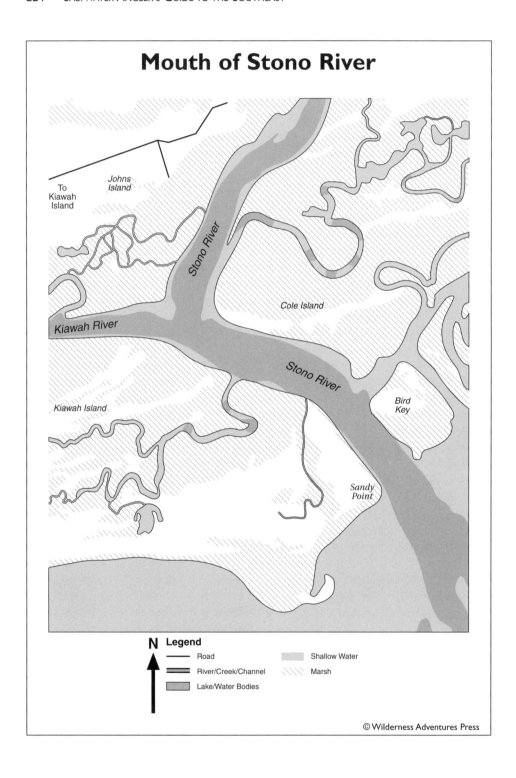

Mouth of Stono River

To Kiawah Island

Johns Island

Stono River

Kiawah River

Cole Island

Stono River

Kiawah Island

Bird Key

Sandy Point

N

Legend

——— Road

═══ River/Creek/Channel

▓ Lake/Water Bodies

░ Shallow Water

╱╱╱ Marsh

© Wilderness Adventures Press

Stono River: Johns Island to Wadmalaw Sound

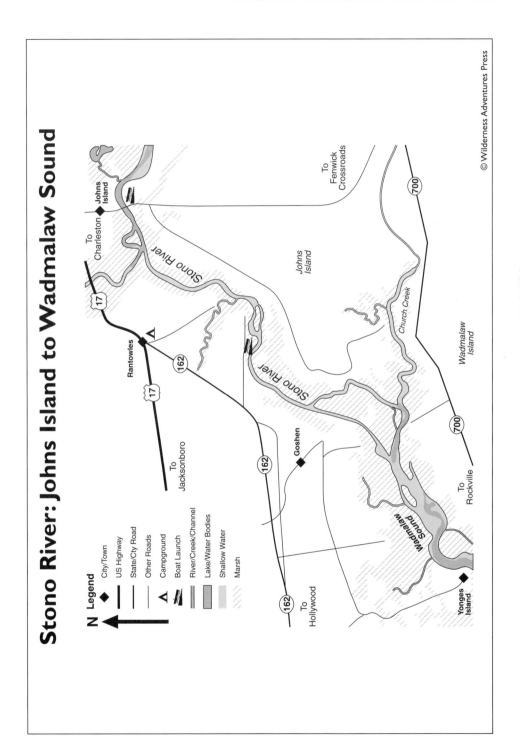

Legend

N

- ◆ City/Town
- ━━ US Highway
- ── State/Cty Road
- ── Other Roads
- ⚠ Campground
- 🚤 Boat Launch
- ▬ River/Creek/Channel
- ▬ Lake/Water Bodies
- ▬ Shallow Water
- ▨ Marsh

To Charleston

Johns Island

To Fenwick Crossroads

700

Stono River

17

Rantowles

17

162

To Jacksonboro

Stono River

Johns Island

Church Creek

Stono River

Goshen

162

To Hollywood

162

Wadmalaw Island

700

To Rockville

Wadmalaw Sound

Yonges Island

© Wilderness Adventures Press

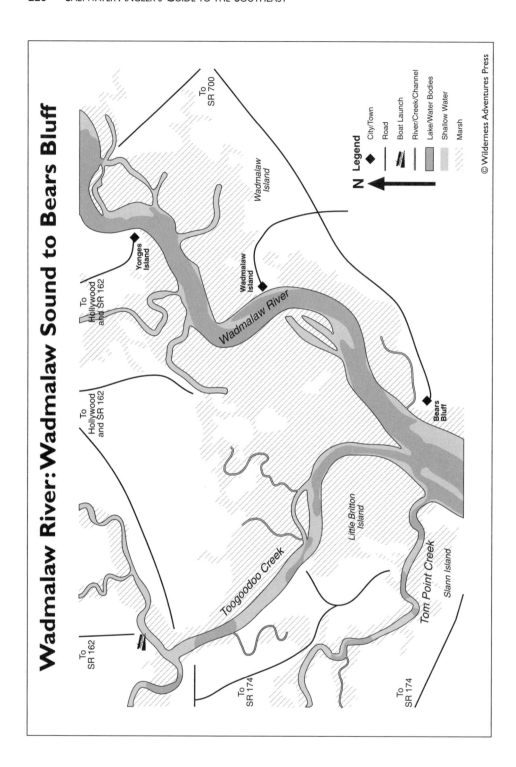

Wadmalaw River: Wadmalaw Sound to Bears Bluff

Legend

◆ City/Town

〿 Road

🚤 Boat Launch

River/Creek/Channel

Lake/Water Bodies

Shallow Water

Marsh

N

© Wilderness Adventures Press

To SR 700

Wadmalaw Island

Yonges Island

To Hollywood and SR 162

Wadmalaw Island

Wadmalaw River

To Hollywood and SR 162

Bears Bluff

Little Britton Island

Toogoodoo Creek

Tom Point Creek

Slann Island

To SR 162

To SR 174

To SR 174

Dawho River and Little Edisto Island

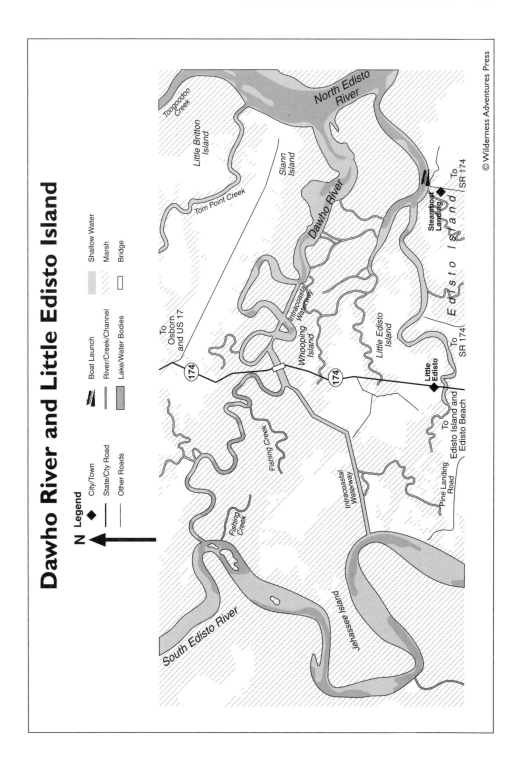

N
Legend
- ◆ City/Town
- — State/City Road
- — Other Roads
- 〰 Boat Launch
- | River/Creek/Channel
- ▨ Lake/Water Bodies
- ▨ Shallow Water
- ▨ Marsh
- ☐ Bridge

© Wilderness Adventures Press

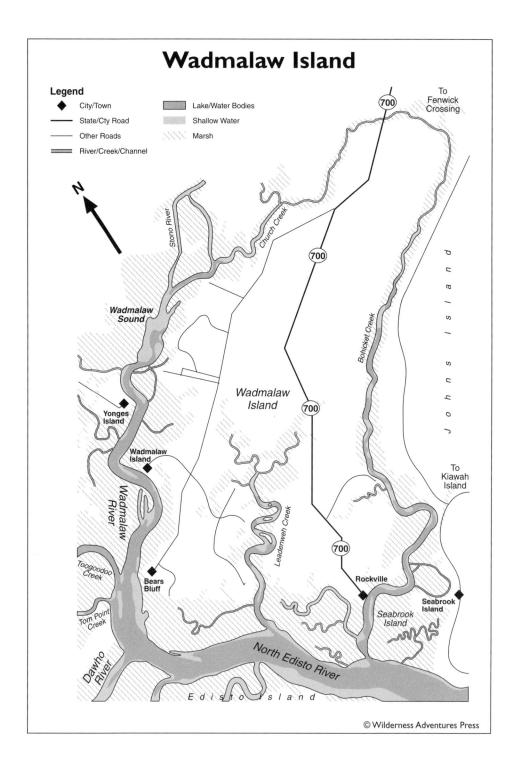

Wadmalaw Island

Legend

◆ City/Town

▬ State/Cty Road

— Other Roads

▬ River/Creek/Channel

▬ Lake/Water Bodies

▒ Shallow Water

░ Marsh

To Fenwick Crossing

700

N

Stono River

Church Creek

700

Wadmalaw Sound

Bohicket Creek

J o h n s   I s l a n d

◆ Yonges Island

Wadmalaw Island

700

Wadmalaw Island ◆

To Kiawah Island

Wadmalaw River

Leadenweh Creek

Toogoodoo Creek

700

◆ Bears Bluff

Rockville ◆

◆ Seabrook Island

Tom Point Creek

Seabrook Island

Dawho River

North Edisto River

E d i s t o   I s l a n d

© Wilderness Adventures Press

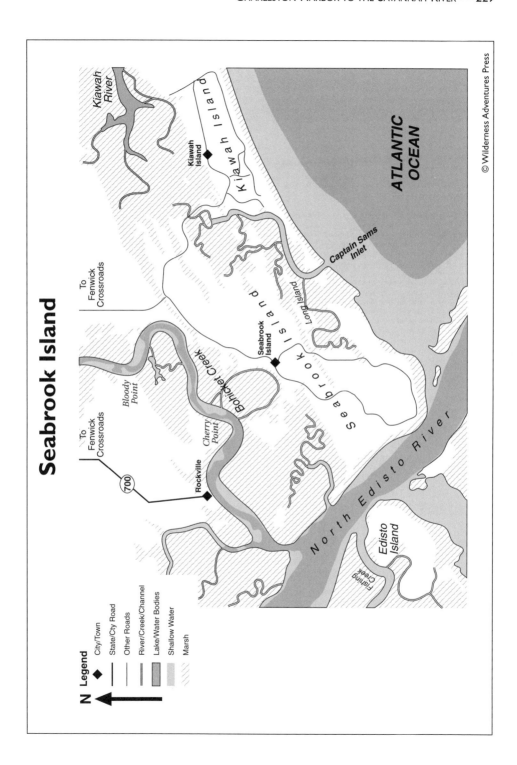

Seabrook Island

Kiawah River

Kiawah Island

Kiawah Island

Kiawah Island

ATLANTIC OCEAN

Captain Sams Inlet

Long Island

To Fenwick Crossroads

Seabrook Island

Seabrook Island

Bohicket Creek

Bloody Point

To Fenwick Crossroads

Cherry Point

Rockville

700

North Edisto River

Edisto Island

Fishing Creek

Legend

◆ City/Town

— State/Cty Road

— Other Roads

River/Creek/Channel

Lake/Water Bodies

Shallow Water

Marsh

N

© Wilderness Adventures Press

Edisto Island

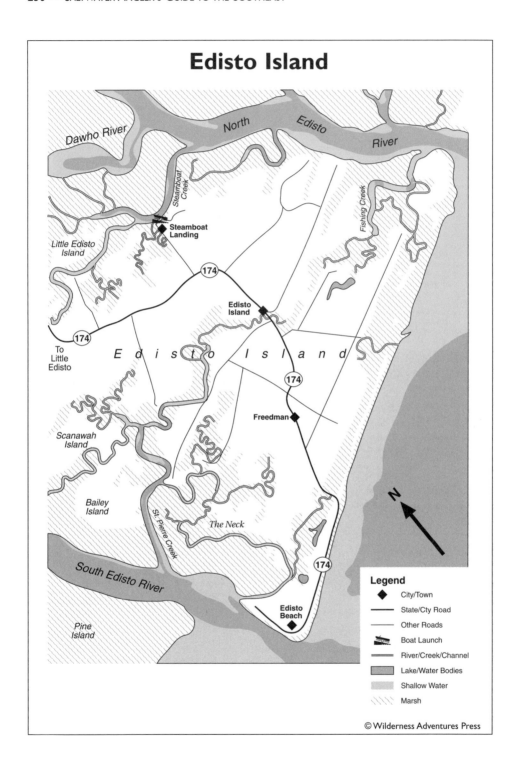

Dawho River

North Edisto River

Steamboat Creek

Fishing Creek

Steamboat Landing

Little Edisto Island

174

Edisto Island

174

To Little Edisto

E d i s t o   I s l a n d

174

Freedman

Scanawah Island

Bailey Island

St. Pierre Creek

The Neck

N

South Edisto River

174

Edisto Beach

Pine Island

Legend

◆ City/Town
— State/Cty Road
— Other Roads
🚤 Boat Launch
▬ River/Creek/Channel
▬ Lake/Water Bodies
▨ Shallow Water
▧ Marsh

© Wilderness Adventures Press

North Edisto River to the Savannah River

Edisto Island's southeast-facing shore is a long, mostly straight stretch of coast that runs from the mouth of the North Edisto River down to Edisto Beach, a small beach community. Trolling for Spanish mackerel is a popular pastime along this beach—watch for sea birds working bait on the surface and jumping Spanish mackerel. Sometimes false albacore show up along this beach, too, so be ready with 2/0 Clousers in chartreuse and white.

The South Edisto River cuts up into the hinterland between Edisto Beach and Pine Island. Drum, trout, and flatties can all be found fairly far upriver, at least as far as the upper branch of the Dawho River (the two branches of the Dawho River, along with the South Edisto River, form Jehossee Island). This was one of the first rivers on which I tried walleye jigs for specks—yes, walleye jigs. I had brought some "stand-up" style jigs (they have a flat head that allows the tail of the jig to stand up off the bottom when the jig is at rest) back from Minnesota's Leech Lake and decided to give them a try. They did work, although not as well as a curltail.

Four types of inlet structure are apparent here: the barrier sandbar, buoy, submerged rocks (indicated by the flat water amid the riffles near the shore), and the thin stumps of former trees, which are submerged at high tide. Seatrout, bluefish, flounder, cobia, and drum (red and black) can all be found in such areas.

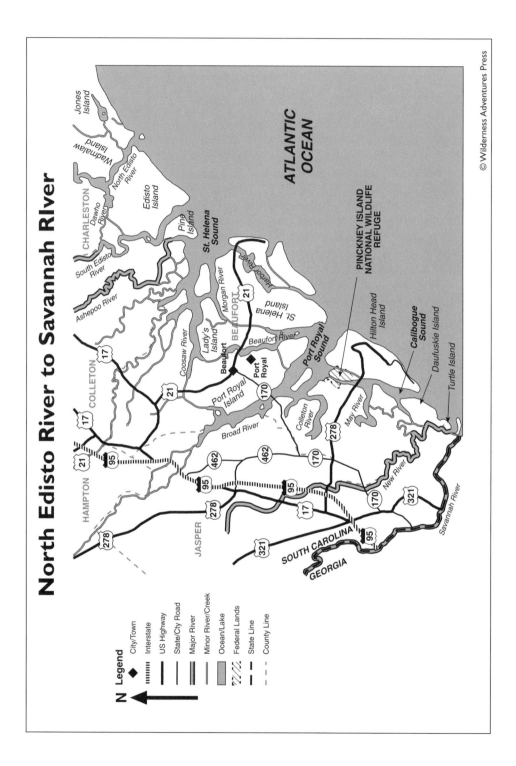

North Edisto River to Savannah River

ATLANTIC OCEAN

Jones Island

Wadmalaw Island

North Edisto River

CHARLESTON

Edisto Island

Dawho River

South Edisto River

Pine Island

Ashepoo River

St. Helena Sound

Harbor River

Morgan River

COLLETON

Coosaw River

Lady's Island

BEAUFORT

St. Helena Island

PINCKNEY ISLAND NATIONAL WILDLIFE REFUGE

Hilton Head Island

Calibogue Sound

Daufuskie Island

Beaufort River

Port Royal Sound

Beaufort

Port Royal

Port Royal Island

Broad River

Colleton River

May River

Turtle Island

HAMPTON

JASPER

Savannah River

New River

SOUTH CAROLINA

GEORGIA

© Wilderness Adventures Press

Legend
N

♦ City/Town

▪▪▪▪ Interstate

— US Highway

— State/Cty Road

— Major River

— Minor River/Creek

Ocean/Lake

Federal Lands

— State Line

– – County Line

A volunteer: This pinfish is just the right size for a "gator" trout.

Some spots worth checking out in this area are:

- the cut linking the South Edisto River to the smaller Ashepoo River
- the mouth of Sampson Creek on the South Edisto
- the inlets of both arms of the Dawho River
- the creeks of Edisto Island, Bailey Island, and Pine Island (between the South Edisto and Ashepoo)
- Mosquito Creek on the Ashepoo
- Two Sisters Creek
- Rock Creek

You will often find that at the mouths of creeks entering rivers that the water becomes deep quite quickly. A chubby crankbait retrieved along the bottom of these dropoffs so that the lip of the crankbait bounces off the bottom can be very productive for specks and flounder.

St. Helena Sound marks the beginning of what may be the most convoluted and challenging water along the Southeast coast. Challenging not in finding game fish but in simply learning the water. These are torturous waters with endless facets requiring a lot of time on the water to truly learn well. If this is your first time around Beaufort, I recommend a guide.

From St. Helena Sound back up the Coosaw River to the US 21 bridge, there are excellent trout, flounder, drum, and even shark waters. Indeed, shark fishing around Beaufort and Parris Island has been very popular for decades. It is said that there were never many sharks in this area until the Marine Corps established the Parris Island Marine Corps Recruit Depot nearly 80 years ago, at which time the Marines

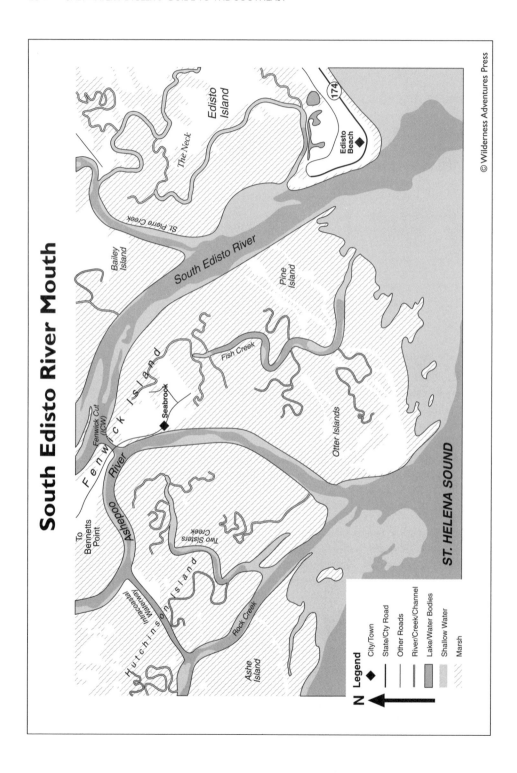

South Edisto River Mouth

Edisto Island

Edisto Island

The Neck

Edisto Beach

174

St. Pierre Creek

Bailey Island

South Edisto River

Pine Island

Fish Creek

Seabrook

F e n w i c k   I s l a n d

Fenwick Cut (ICW)

River

To Bennetts Point

Ashepoo

Two Sisters Creek

Otter Islands

H u t c h i n s o n   I s l a n d

Intracoastal Waterway

Rock Creek

Ashe Island

ST. HELENA SOUND

© Wilderness Adventures Press

Legend

N

- ◆ City/Town
- State/Cty Road
- Other Roads
- River/Creek/Channel
- Lake/Water Bodies
- Shallow Water
- Marsh

South Edisto River: Sampson Island Area

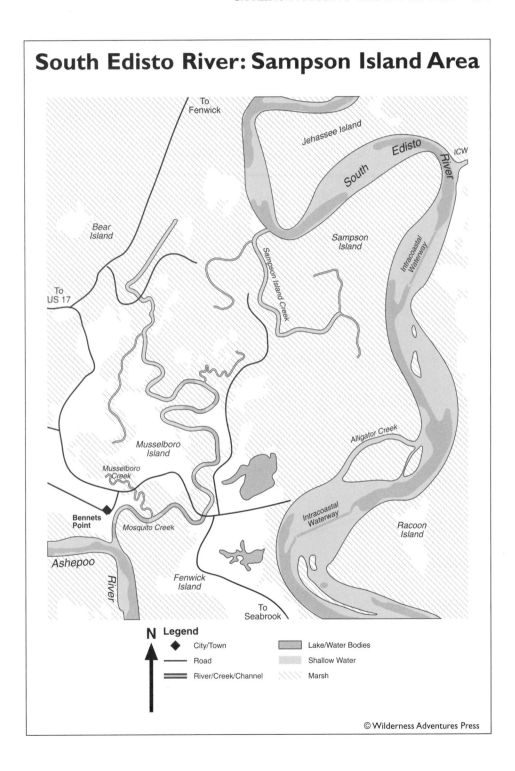

To
Fenwick

Jehassee Island

South Edisto River

ICW

Bear
Island

Sampson Island Creek

Sampson
Island

Intracoastal Waterway

To
US 17

Musselboro
Island

Alligator Creek

Musselboro
Creek

Bennets
Point

Mosquito Creek

Intracoastal
Waterway

Racoon
Island

Ashepoo

River

Fenwick
Island

To
Seabrook

N

Legend

◆ City/Town

Lake/Water Bodies

— Road

Shallow Water

River/Creek/Channel

Marsh

© Wilderness Adventures Press

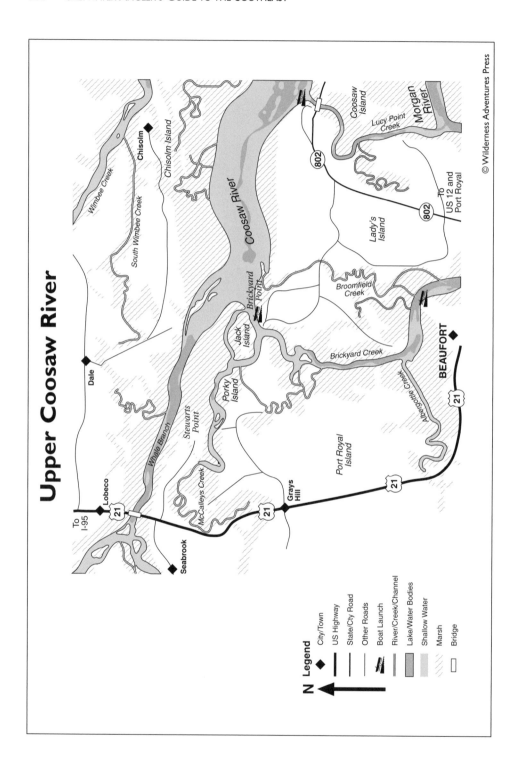

Upper Coosaw River

© Wilderness Adventures Press

Legend

N

City/Town
US Highway
State/Cty Road
Other Roads
Boat Launch
River/Creek/Channel
Lake/Water Bodies
Shallow Water
Marsh
Bridge

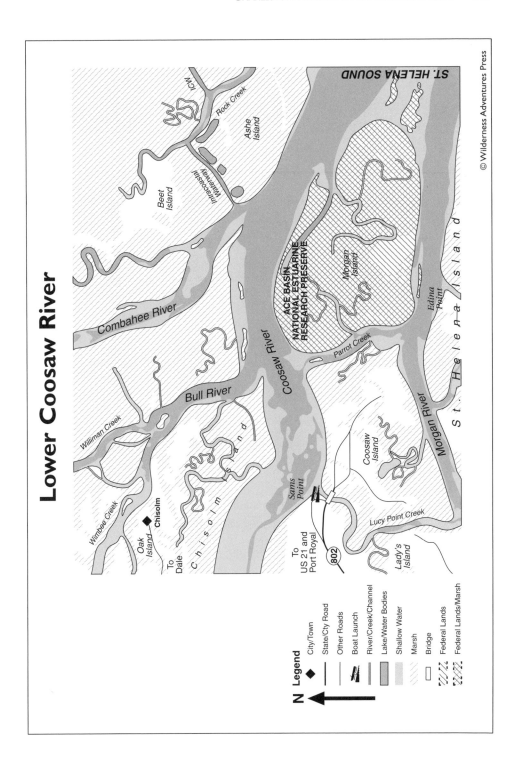

Lower Coosaw River

ST. HELENA SOUND

ICW

Rock Creek

Ashe Island

Intracoastal Waterway

Beet Island

ACE BASIN NATIONAL ESTUARINE RESEARCH PRESERVE

Morgan Island

Combahee River

Edina Point

Coosaw River

Parrot Creek

Bull River

St. Helena Island

Willliman Creek

Chisolm Island

Coosaw Island

Morgan River

Wimbee Creek

Oak Island

Chisolm

Sams Point

To Dale

Lucy Point Creek

To US 21 and Port Royal

802

Lady's Island

© Wilderness Adventures Press

Legend

N

- ◆ City/Town
- State/City Road
- Other Roads
- Boat Launch
- River/Creek/Channel
- Lake/Water Bodies
- Shallow Water
- Marsh
- Bridge
- Federal Lands
- Federal Lands/Marsh

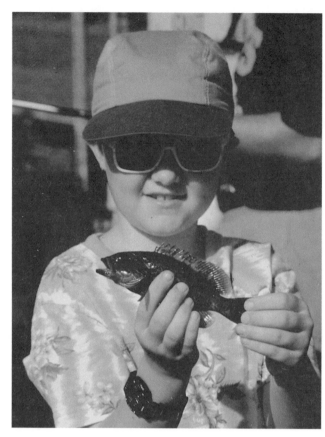

When after pinfish, be careful not to accidentally keep a juvenile grouper, which inhabit inshore waters. If you can't identify it, release it. Here, Britta admires a juvenile grouper destined for bigger and better things.

brought in many of the man-eating variety to dissuade unhappy victims (er, recruits) from swimming across the Broad River or Beaufort River to freedom. I am sure this is just a fanciful tale, however.

Features along the Coosaw River to examine are:

- Morgan Island (this island is part of the Ace Basin National Estuarine Research Reserve)
- the Bull River and its two arms, Wimbee Creek and Williman Creek
- Parrot Creek between Coosaw Island and Morgan Island
- Lucy Point Creek between Coosaw Island and Lady's Island
- the upper Beaufort River
- the creeks and sloughs of Porky Island

There are many species of baitfish in these waters, one of the most common being pinfish found among pilings. A live pinfish is of definite interest to "gator" trout, which are extra large seatrout. Fished beneath a popping cork along a rip, a pinfish

Some tarpon are migratory, whereas others remain in the same region all their lives. Photo by Captain Les Hill.

can be just what trophy trout are looking for. Pinfish can be caught very easily using a small, thin hook and a little piece of cut squid dropped down beside pilings.

Tarpon inhabit these waters, too, and many make great migrations to and from the Carolinas every summer from their starting point in Florida. By July they have reached Pamlico Sound, meaning that early summer is the beginning of tarpon action in South Carolina. They can sometimes be seen in schools coming up the beach, and once in a while a pier angler hooks into one and is in for the fight of his life.

St. Helena Island has trout and reds to offer, plus ladyfish in the warmer months. Try these:

- the Morgan River (just a broad cut between Morgan Island and St. Helena Island)
- Jenkins Creek and the other creeks of the island
- the US 21 bridge between St. Helena Island and Harbor Island (sheepshead)
- the creeks of Datha Island
- the Harbor River (I just can't fathom how this can be thought of as a river—it is really a sound)

St. Helena Island

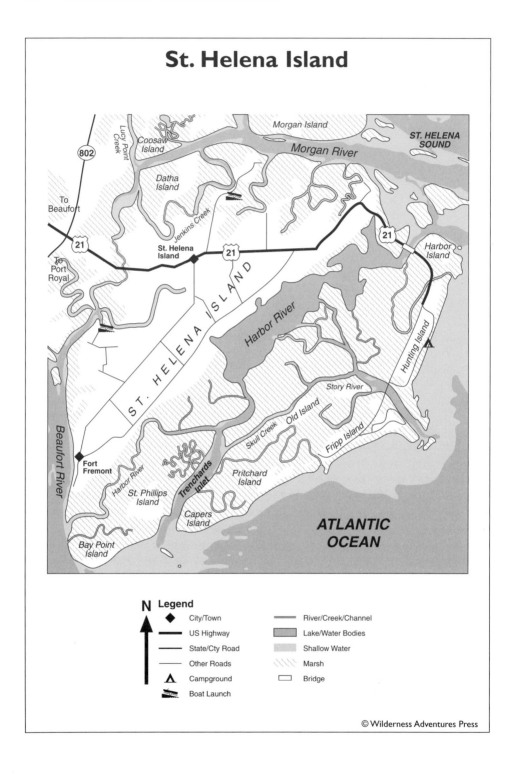

N Legend

- ◆ City/Town
- ▬ US Highway
- — State/Cty Road
- — Other Roads
- ▲ Campground
- 🚤 Boat Launch

- ▬ River/Creek/Channel
- ▨ Lake/Water Bodies
- ▨ Shallow Water
- ▨ Marsh
- ▭ Bridge

© Wilderness Adventures Press

These bass worms can be used for drum and are fished just as they would be for bass.

Between the lower Harbor River and Bay Point Island, check out the following:
- the Story River (just a little creek between Hunting Island and Trenchards Inlet)
- Old Island
- Fripp Island
- Skull Creek (no doubt a story there)
- Pritchards Island
- Capers Island

These are all potential trout and drum locations. Here's an idea: try plastic worms designed for largemouth bass. Such worms can be used to imitate marine worms and even eels, and drum pick them up if worked along the bottom where they spend most of their time looking for grub. They can be fished Texas style or with a short Carolina rig.

Trout also pick up these worms, but I have found that trout are more likely to bite the worm's tail off with their sharp teeth. On the other hand, trout do come to the surface to hit a plug faster than a drum, because drum have what are called "inferior"

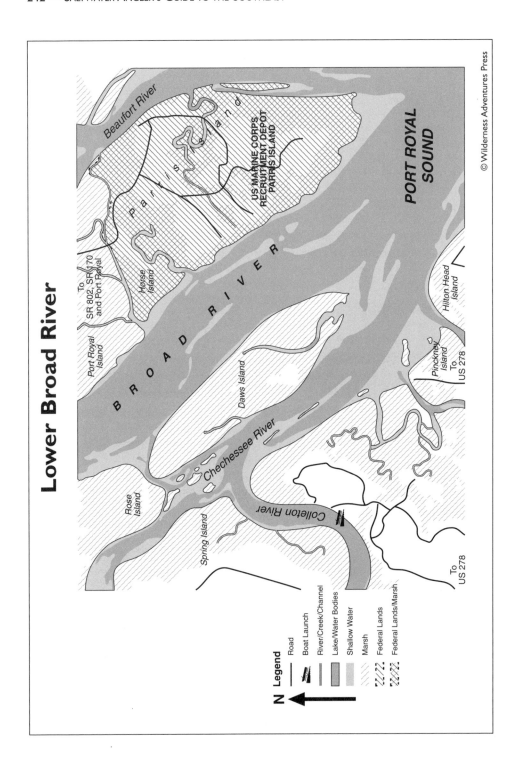

Lower Broad River

© Wilderness Adventures Press

Legend

N

- Road
- Boat Launch
- River/Creek/Channel
- Lake/Water Bodies
- Shallow Water
- Marsh
- Federal Lands
- Federal Lands/Marsh

Hilton Head Island

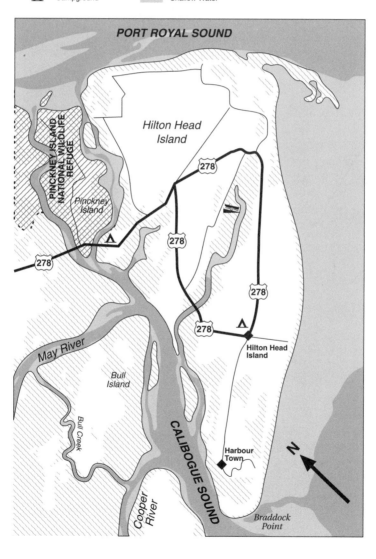

Legend

◆	City/Town	🚆	Boat Launch	╲╲╲╲	Marsh	
▬▬▬	US Highway	═══	River/Creek/Channel	╱╱╱╱	Federal Lands	
───	Other Roads		Lake/Water Bodies	╱╱╱╱	Federal Lands/Marsh	
▲	Campground		Shallow Water			

PORT ROYAL SOUND

Hilton Head Island

278

278

278

278

278

PINCKNEY ISLAND NATIONAL WILDLIFE REFUGE

Pinckney Island

Hilton Head Island

May River

Bull Island

Bull Creek

Cooper River

CALIBOGUE SOUND

Harbour Town

Braddock Point

N

© Wilderness Adventures Press

Turtle Island Area

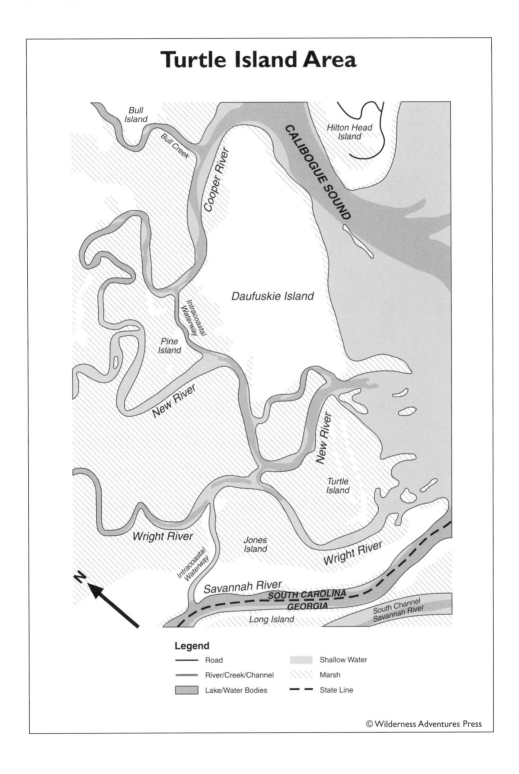

Bull Island

Bull Creek

Cooper River

Hilton Head Island

CALIBOGUE SOUND

Daufuskie Island

Intracoastal Waterway

Pine Island

New River

New River

Turtle Island

Wright River

Jones Island

Intracoastal Waterway

Wright River

N

Savannah River

SOUTH CAROLINA
GEORGIA

South Channel Savannah River

Long Island

Legend

——	Road	▨	Shallow Water
═══	River/Creek/Channel	▨	Marsh
▨	Lake/Water Bodies	– –	State Line

© Wilderness Adventures Press

Three crankbaits that can take tarpon.

mouths—that is, mouths that are shaped to feed primarily on the bottom. Spotted seatrout, although members of the drum family, do not have inferior mouths.

These plugs are best used along spartina banks and flats, worked the same way as for bass. I have even had flounder come off the bottom in up to four feet of water to attack these plugs. I am still surprised every time this happens.

The Broad River is a classic South Carolina coastal river. In its lower reaches between Port Royal Sound and about the SR 170 bridge are many stingrays (Atlantic, roughtail, smooth butterfly) and skates (clearnose, cownose, bullnose, little) that sharks feed on. Chunks of baitfish, ray, and skate often entice a passing shark.

Kingfish can be found just outside Port Royal Sound from spring through fall and out in the Gulf Stream and its tendrils in the dead of winter.

Ribbonfish are one of the king mackerel's all-time favorite meals. There are many ways to rig them, one being to attach it to a large, brightly colored bucktail jig. Used with or without a downrigger, this combination can be remarkably productive.

Cigar minnows, flyingfish, pinfish, and live menhaden trolled slowly are other good baits for kings, whether working just outside an inlet or sound or far offshore over a wreck or rock pile.

Above Port Royal Sound, the Broad River flows between Daws Island (a heritage preserve) and Parris Island, where Marines are made—I highly recommend a tour of the island.

Fish the creeks, bridge and dock pilings, and islands of both the Broad River and the smaller Chechessee River and Colleton River on the west side of Daws Island. Do not attempt to wade in the spartina creeks near Parris Island—the mud of these creeks can be very soft and can suck you down. Some Marine recruits and their drill instructor found this out a long time ago—some recruits perished.

A radically different island, at least insofar as fun is concerned, is Hilton Head Island, where the only pain you might feel is if you throw your back out setting the hook on a large tarpon, the only sweat you experience might be from fighting a big redfish, and the only toil you experience might be from carrying a cooler filled with cold drinks from your truck to your boat.

Hilton Head is a playground for many, some of whom are anglers after tarpon, redfish, trout, Spanish and king mackerel, black drum, cobia, and ladyfish. Tarpon are normally thought of as fish that are cast to with flies on scenic flats in the Keys, but they are also often caught in sounds and rivers in this region, and one need not be a flyfisher to catch them. In fact, most tarpon taken in this area are not taken by flyfishers but by bait soakers and lure draggers, and many are taken incidentally, meaning that the angler was really expecting something else. Crankbaits with strong, sharp, stainless steel hooks are the best performers.

Other potential fish hideouts include:

- Pinckney Island (home of Pinckney Island National Wildlife Refuge)
- the May River
- Bull Island
- Bull Creek
- the Cooper River
- Calibogue Sound

The last bit of water before hitting the Georgia border contains:

- Daufuskie Island
- the New River
- Turtle Island (home to the Turtle Island Wildlife Management Area)
- Jones Island

Redfish, specks, and ladyfish are the main draw in these waters.

Savannah, GA

Savannah, just over the Georgia border, provides the best services for fishing the southern waters of South Carolina. A full listing of services may be found on page 271 of the Georgia section of this guide.

Beaufort, SC

ACCOMMODATIONS

Atlantic Inn, 2249 US 21 / 843-524-6024
Battery Creek Inn, 19 Marina Village Lane #102B / 843-521-1441
Beaufort Inn & Restaurant, 809 Port Republic Street / 843-521-9000
Best Western Inn, 1015 Bay Street / 843-522-2090
Comfort Inn, 2227 Boundary Street / 843-525-9366
Hampton Inn, 2342 Boundary Street / 843-986-0600
Holiday Inn, US 21 / 843-524-2144
Lord Carteret Motel, 301 Carteret Street / 843-521-1121
Twosuns Inn Bed & Breakfast, 1705 Bay Street / 843-522-1122

CAMPGROUNDS

Kobuch's Campground, 246 Savannah Hwy / 843-525-0653

RESTAURANTS

Applebee's Neighborhood Grill, 2338 Boundary Street / 843-524-4322
Bank Grill & Bar, 926 Bay Street / 843-522-8831
Broad River Seafood Co., 2601 Boundary Street / 843-524-2001
Captain D's Seafood, 2427 Boundary Street / 843-522-3474
Duke's Barbeque of Beaufort, 3533 Trask Parkway / 843-524-1128
Factory Creek Landing, 67 Sea Island / 843-525-1165
Fuji Restaurant, 81 Sea Island / 843-524-2662
Huddle House, US 21 / 843-522-3447
                    1015 Ribaut Road / 843-524-1991
La Sirena, 822 Bay Street / 843-524-2500
Ollie's Seafood Grille & Bar, 71 Sea Island / 843-525-6333
Peking Gourmet Chinese Restaurant, 10 Sams Point Road #3 / 843-986-0166
Riverwalk, 19 Marina Village Lane / 843-525-6466
Salt Marsh Grill, 100 Marina Boulevard / 843-838-8444
Waffle House, 2344 Boundary Street / 843-770-0080
Whitehall Plantation Restaurant, 27 White Hall Drive / 843-521-1700

FLY & TACKLE SHOPS

Bay Street Outfitters Ltd., 815 Bay Street / 843-524-5250
Island Outfitters, 189 Sea Island Parkway / 843-522-9900
Sportsman Shop, 330 Robert Smalls Parkway #16 / 843-522-1547

GUIDES

Bay Street Outfitters, 815 Bay Street / 843-524-5250 / Fax: 843-524-9002 / Bay Street Outfitters are a well-known source for good guides and plenty of specks, reds, tarpon, jacks, cobia, and ladyfish around historic Beaufort, Charleston, and Savannah / They are Orvis endorsed, so you know you are getting with the right folks, and they also run The Redfish School

Low Country Outfitters, (Hilton Head), 1533 Fording Island Road / 843-847-6100 / Guides, tackle, information, advice, and more / Carries a full line of flyfishing tackle and light tackle

Captain Bill Parker (Hilton Head), 28 Eagle Claw / 843-689-2628 / Cellular: 843-384-6511 / Inshore and offshore game fish, including tarpon, grouper, cobia, dolphin, red drum, amberjack, kings, barracuda, wahoo, and even sharks

Captain Marty Pinkston (Hilton Head), No. 4 Dolphin Row / 843-886-6927 / E-mail: shpk18@aol.com / Tarpon, Spanish mackerel, Specks, reds, jacks, and ladyfish

MARINAS

Downtown Marina, 1010 Bay Street / 843-524-4422

Lady's Island Marina, 73 Sea Island Parkway / 843-522-0430

Marsh Harbor Boat Yard, 45 Colony Gardens Road / 843-521-1500

FOR MORE INFORMATION

Greater Beaufort Area Chamber of Commerce
1106 Bay Street
Beaufort, SC 29902
843-524-3163

A selection of proven freshwater bass plugs that work well for spotted seatrout.

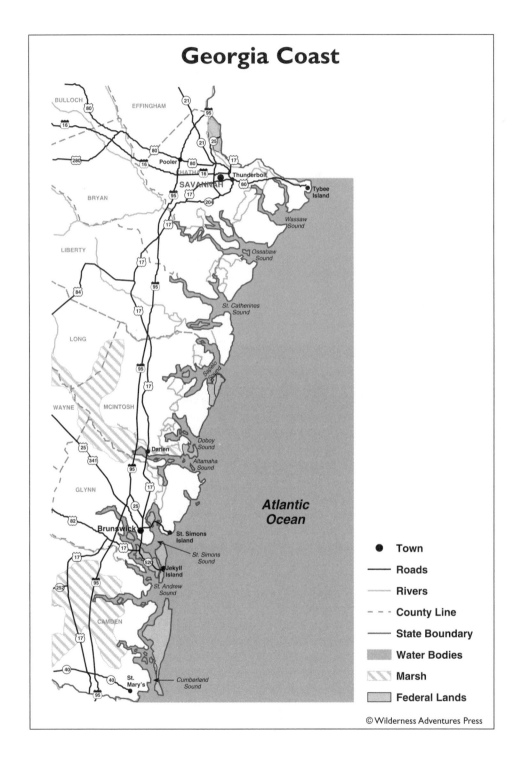

Georgia Coast

BULLOCH

EFFINGHAM

BRYAN

LIBERTY

LONG

WAYNE   MCINTOSH

GLYNN

CAMDEN

SAVANNAH

Pooler

CHATHAM

Thunderbolt

Tybee Island

Wassaw Sound

Ossabaw Sound

St. Catherines Sound

Sapelo Sound

Doboy Sound

Darien

Altamaha Sound

Brunswick

St. Simons Island

St. Simons Sound

Jekyll Island

St. Andrew Sound

St. Mary's

Cumberland Sound

Atlantic Ocean

● Town

— Roads

— Rivers

- - - County Line

— State Boundary

Water Bodies

Marsh

Federal Lands

© Wilderness Adventures Press

Georgia

I had already written this chapter's introductory words when I again returned to the Peach Tree State in February 1999. Landing in Atlanta, I was gripping the seat's armrests somewhat more tightly than usual. My memories of flying into Atlanta in the early 1990s were still too vivid. As we were about to touch down, a rather large gust of wind knocked the jet sideways, causing the pilot to abandon or "wave off" the landing just as the aircraft's wheels were about to touch down. I had recently returned from the Gulf War and didn't need any more rude surprises, but the pilot did the right thing, and we circled to land safely 15 minutes later.

Atlanta has grown into a sprawling metropolis, but when you head southeast on Interstate 75 and then on Interstate 16, things change rapidly. It quickly becomes apparent that Georgia has remained largely unchanged, defiant in the face of the unrepentant progress to the north and west. This is the land of boiled peanuts, Vidalia onions, and sweet tea, and if you head far enough southeast on I-16, red drum, tarpon, striped bass, spotted seatrout, crevalle jack, cobia, and a host of other worthy saltwater game fish.

Coastal Georgia: Where Time Stands Defied

The coast of Georgia is very different by and large from the coasts of the Carolinas. The difference is in the level of development—beachfront homes aren't crammed onto barrier islands, commercial fishing is strictly regulated, towering hotels and condos don't festoon every scrap of waterfront, and there simply aren't as many bustling cities, towns, and villages here, although there are certainly people.

The reasons for Georgia's less developed coast are:

- Georgia's coast took a back seat to the development of South and North Carolina back in the 1970s and 1980s because of more strict building rules;
- Commercial fishing is tightly regulated in order to protect the marine environment;
- Americans have never thought of the coast of Georgia as being a waterfront playground; the Carolinas were more popular, with the Outer Banks, Bogue Banks, Carolina Beach, Wilmington, Myrtle Beach, Charleston, and Hilton Head Island being typical areas for rapid and massive development

The result is an angler's heaven with some of the best sport fishing along the Eastern Seaboard.

Getting There

Getting to coastal Georgia can be simple and quick to painstakingly slow, all depending on the direction from which it is approached and the mode of transportation. But regardless of how it is reached, Georgia's coast is almost always well worth the effort.

By Road
Primary access to the region by land is via Interstate 95 and US 17. Obviously, I-95 offers the fastest travel via land. It is almost never crowded, but sometimes fog can be pretty thick. Because it passes through many towns, US 17 is slower.

By Air
Savannah International Airport, northwest of the city, and Jacksonville International Airport, north of the city, are by far the two largest airports serving the region. Both have plenty of jet service and several carriers servicing them, including major airlines and regional commuter airlines. It should be noted, however, that spring, summer, and fall in the Southeast mean thunderstorms, oftentimes resulting in delays. The occasional hurricane doesn't help.

Another problem can be expensive fares if you do not stay over a Saturday night. No airline can logically explain this on-again, off-again rule, but keep this in mind when checking around for the best fare.

Smaller airports in the region include Malcolm McKinnon on St. Simon's Island, Jekyll Island Airport, and St. Mary's Airport (just south of King's Bay Naval Station).

By Water
The Atlantic Intracoastal Waterway provides easy access to the region by water. During spring and fall many large pleasure craft and outright yachts use the waterway. Commercial vessels, especially barges being pushed by tugs, are also commonplace. When one of these is approaching or being overtaken, don't underestimate the bow wave created by these vessels. Barges displace huge amounts of water and can cause trouble if other boats fail to negotiate the wave properly.

Georgia Regulations
It's very important to check the latest regulations before wetting a line in Georgia. Regulations change all the time and are therefore not printed in this book. Regulations include minimum and maximum length requirements (including measurement details, such as fork length or total length), seasons, and creel limits. Visit the Georgia Department of Natural Resources website at www.dnr.state.ga.us or contact them for more information:

Headquarters
2070 US Highway 278 SE
Social Circle, GA 30025
770-918-6408

Coastal (Region 7)
One Conservation Way
Brunswick, GA 31520
912-264-7237

Game Fish Species

Game fish species of interest to flyfishers and light tackle users include:

- Amberjack
- Black drum
- Bluefish
- Bonito
- Cobia
- Crevalle jack
- Croaker
- Dolphin
- False albacore
- King mackerel
- Ladyfish
- Pompano
- Red drum
- Sheepshead
- Spanish mackerel
- Spotted seatrout
- Striped bass
- Tarpon
- Tripletail
- Yellowfin tuna

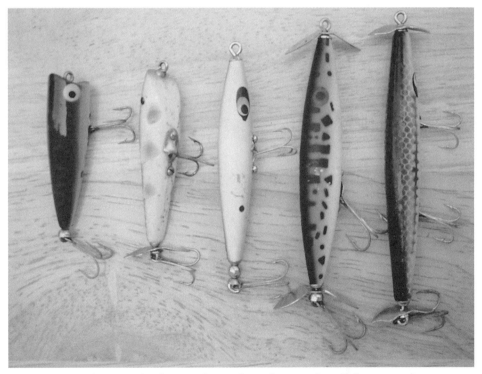

A selection of proven freshwater bass plugs that work well for spotted seatrout.

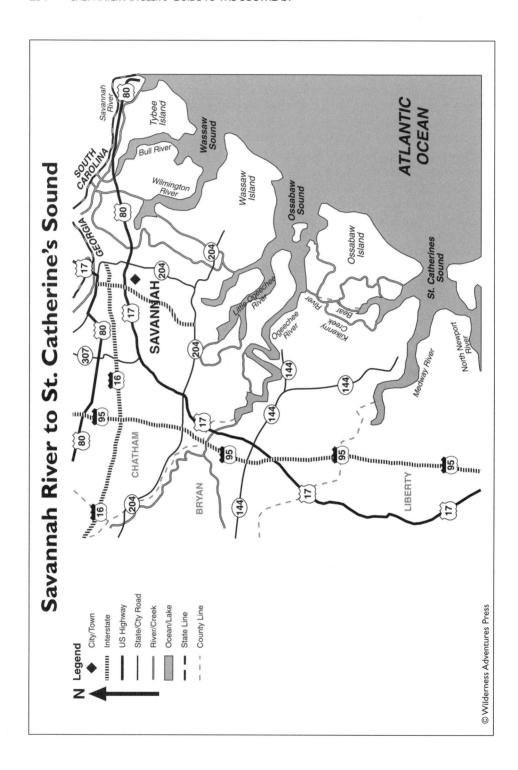

Savannah River to St. Catherine's Sound

SAVANNAH RIVER TO ST. CATHERINE'S SOUND

The Savannah River forms the boundary between South Carolina and Georgia. Savannah, that fabled city of the South now known for its antebellum architecture and gentry, as well as the novel and movie, *Midnight in the Garden of Good and Evil*, sits on this river just a ways upriver. This results in more boat traffic than all other regions along the Georgia coast. However, an angler can still find plenty of action, even right around Savannah itself—just find out where to look.

The Mouth of the Savannah River to Ossabaw Sound

King mackerel, Spanish mackerel, bonito, cobia, jacks, bluefish, and tarpon can all be found in and around the outer edges of the sounds and the Savannah River inlet. Tarpon are best brought into a chum line, and jacks can be targeted by watching for surface feeding activity, as can Spanish, blues, and bonito. By watching bird activity, these places can be targeted. Kings can be right beneath birds but seldom break the surface, unlike bonito and Spanish. Cobia can be caught near flotsam and buoys and also right on the bottom using a chum back and a dead menhaden. This advice applies to every sound and inlet in the region.

Entering the Savannah River from the sea, the first feature of note is Long Island, where Ft. Pulaski National Monument is located at the seaward terminus. Long Island is bordered on the north by South Carolina's Jones Island and on the south by Tybee Island (formed by Lazaretto Creek and Oysters Creek). Land access to the island can be made by using the bridge on US 80 (SR 26). McQueen's Island also helps form the southern shore of the river between St. Augustine Creek and Lazaretto Creek.

Like other inlets in this area, the Savannah River's mouth can become a tad tempestuous. Add the wakes of large boats, yachts, and ships, and, especially on the weekend, plenty of vessels of all sorts, and waves can stack up rather high. Use caution at all times and never expect the other boater to do what he is supposed to do according to maritime rules of the road.

Long Island breaks the river into the south and north channels. Although they try to keep it well marked and the buoys accurately placed, rivers constantly change. Boaters need to be vigilant in looking for new sandbars or sandbars that routinely change shape and sometimes location. If there aren't any boats traversing an area or there are boats using very specific routes or going slower than others outside the area, they probably have a good reason for doing so.

Game fish in Georgia's coastal waters can be just as unpredictable as the other Southeastern coastal waters—they can show up just about any time. The Savannah River is home to everything from tarpon to stripers to seatrout to redfish, and lots more.

The second navigable waterway joining the Savannah River is St. Augustine Creek, joining the river just down from the Wilmington River. St. Augustine twists and turns to the east until it meets up with the Bull River at Talahi Island (Talahi Island and Wilmington Island to the south are really only slight rises in the terrain that have been added to by man until there was enough to build on).

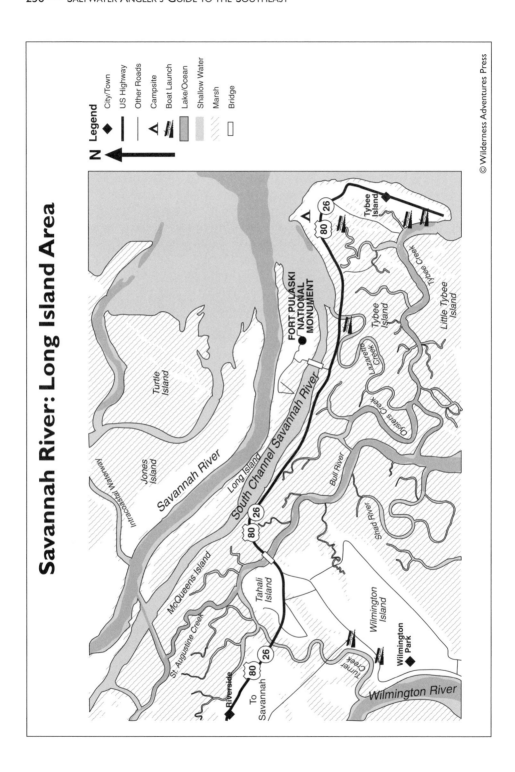

Savannah River: Long Island Area

© Wilderness Adventures Press

Wilmington River

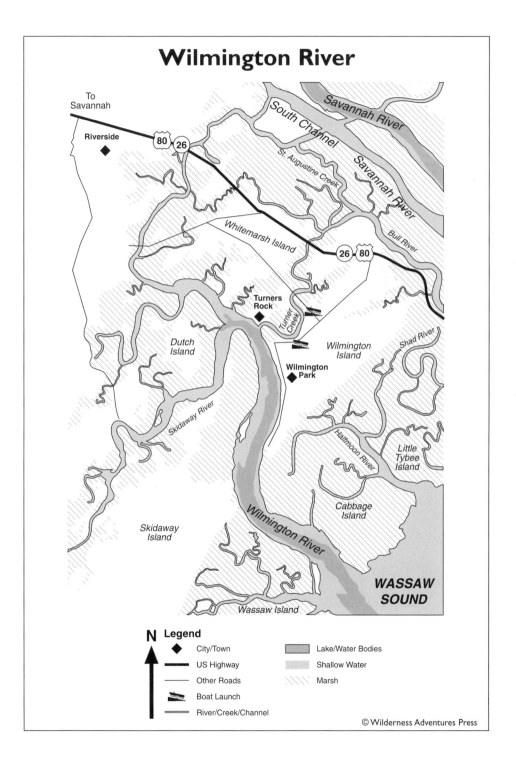

St. Augustine Creek

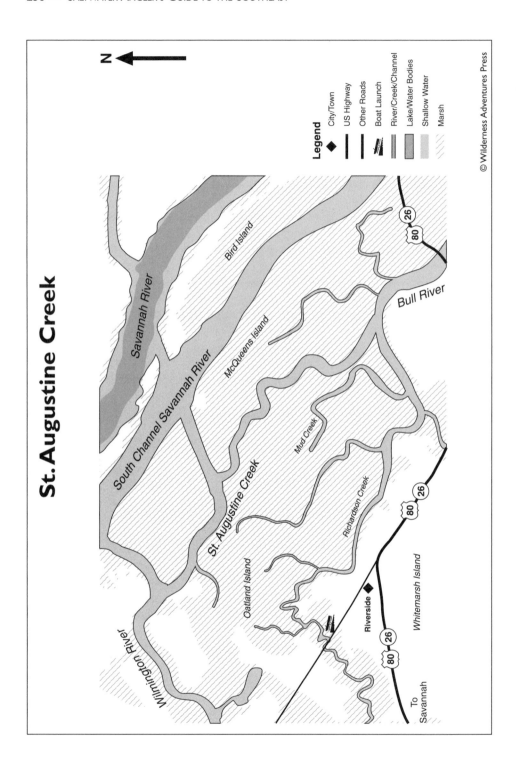

© Wilderness Adventures Press

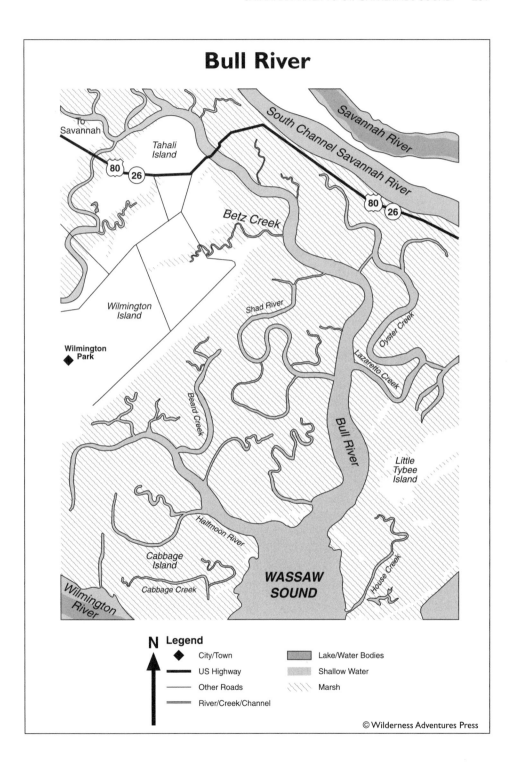

Bull River

To Savannah

Tahali Island

80 26

Betz Creek

South Channel Savannah River

Savannah River

80 26

Wilmington Island

Shad River

Oyster Creek

Lazaretto Creek

Wilmington Park

Beard Creek

Bull River

Little Tybee Island

Halfmoon River

Cabbage Island

Cabbage Creek

House Creek

WASSAW SOUND

Wilmington River

N

Legend

◆ City/Town
—— US Highway
— Other Roads
═══ River/Creek/Channel

Lake/Water Bodies
Shallow Water
Marsh

© Wilderness Adventures Press

Boat traffic comes in all shapes and sizes. Plan and act accordingly.

At the mouth of the Savannah River's south channel is Lazaretto Creek, which has a boat launch at the bridge leading to Long Island.

Off the Bull River lies the smaller Shad River on the western bank, Turner Creek at the Bull's upper end, and Tybee Creek on the eastern bank (forming the northern end of Little Tybee Island).

The Shad River is more of a creek than a river. On the falling tide specks, flounder, and reds that went up the creek in search of mullet, silversides, alligator minnows, and other types of forage begin to come out looking for deeper water. Position yourself at the mouth of the creek on the Bull River and cast live bait into the mouth. Spin fishers should try using a slip-sinker rig with live bait, which is simple to do: slide an egg sinker (¼ to ½ ounce) onto your line and then tie on a barrel swivel. To the other end of the barrel swivel, tie 18 to 36 inches of monofilament and then a live bait hook. That's the rig. This system allows a game fish to grab the bait but not feel the weight of the sinker because the line slides through it.

Kings are often found in close proximity to or right inside inlets. The Savannah River is no exception.

Flyfishers hitting the mouth of Shad River should try a Super Clouser or other heavy, sinking fly to probe the deeper water at the confluence. An intermediate or sinking line with a very short leader will work best.

On high tide, get into Turner Creek, which cuts through the marsh to the Wilmington River. Some nice specks are in here, so bring a curl-tail Mister Twister or Kalin jigs. Also try small Zara Spooks right up against the bank and over deep holes; use the "walking the dog" technique, which is done by reeling and twitching the Spook with the rod tip so that the Spook cuts back and forth on the surface. Big specks love this action.

Tybee Creek is very similar to Turner and should be worked accordingly. Also, the mouth of Tybee Creek can see some sharks, rays, Spanish mackerel, small kings, flounder, and occasionally a big red drum rooting for worms and crabs along the bottom. Once in a while a tarpon will surprise you, so when soaking cut bait on the bottom for reds, be ready for a silver king.

A red drum weighing well over 30 pounds thrashes on the surface after falling for a crab body.

Heading out of Savannah toward the ocean, the Wilmington River skirts the town's eastern edge and eventually makes its way down to Wassaw Sound. Creeks and lesser rivers join up with the Wilmington. The following are a few of the most important:

- St. Augustine Creek
- Turner Creek
- Halfmoon River
- Skidaway River

They all hold redfish, seatrout, stripers, bluefish, flounder, jacks, tarpon, ladyfish, and the rest of the gang. No special tactics are needed for these game fish as the usual methods will suffice (i.e., Deceivers, Clousers, and Bendbacks for flyfishers, and jigs and crankbaits for hardware throwers). Look for cuts, rips, oyster rocks and beds, holes in the grass, deep holes in channels, channel lips, docks, and so on. Also watch for dolphins chasing baitfish into very shallow water (sometimes the entire dolphin can be seen throwing itself up into the grass or onto the mud chasing forage).

At the mouth of the Wilmington River below Halfmoon is Cabbage Island, which offers good speck action and some flounder. Look for tarpon around here, too.

The Wilmington River, Halfmoon River, and Bull River all help form the broad Wassaw Sound, which holds rolling silver kings throughout the summer. Wassaw

This drum is a more average size, but even reds of this size put up great fights.

Sound's southern shore is Wassaw Island, home to the Wassaw National Wildlife Refuge and Cape Charlotte at the northeast tip. Rhodes Creek, Wassaw Creek, and others with no official names wander through Wassaw NWR and afford much speck (MirrOlures), bluefish (soft plastic jigs with bright lead heads), and flounder action (a finger mullet worked very slowly along the bottom can get some fat slabs here). Flyfishers might want to try streamers with a lot of flash when the water is murky but should also consider poppers and sliders. Canoes and flat-bottom skiffs can get back into these creeks all the way up into the Romerly Marshes on the southeast side of Skidaway Island.

The Odingsell River separates Wassaw Island from Little Wassaw and Pine Islands, and Adams Creek separates Little Wassaw from the southernmost tip of Skidaway Island.

The Atlantic Intracoastal Waterway is part of the Vernon River, which lies between Green Island and Petit Gauke Hammock Island. The Little Ogeechee River joins with the Vernon at Ella Island, and a boat launch is located up the Little Ogeechee at Coffee Bluff. Other launches in the region are shown on the map. I have found that the deeper water is best in this area, so when flyfishing I use sinking lines and heavy flies (a brown-and-gold or white-and-olive 2/0 Clouser being an excellent choice for

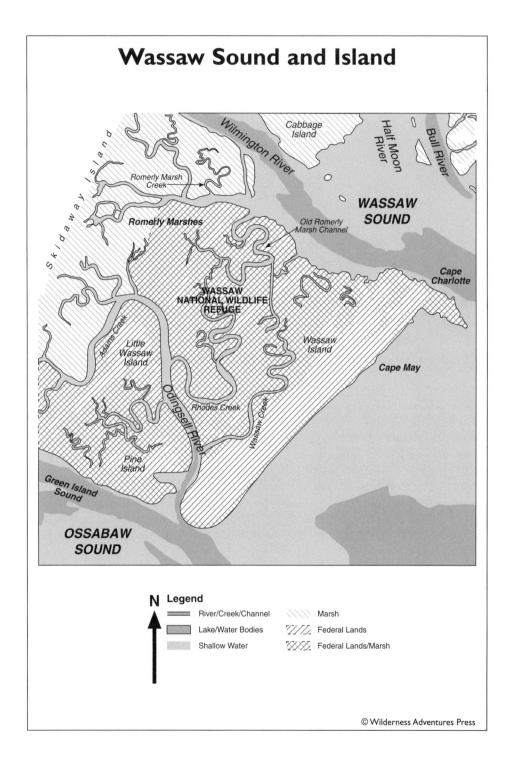

Wassaw Sound and Island

Skidaway Island

Wilmington River

Cabbage Island

Half Moon River

Bull River

Romerly Marsh Creek

Romerly Marshes

Old Romerly Marsh Channel

WASSAW SOUND

WASSAW NATIONAL WILDLIFE REFUGE

Cape Charlotte

Adams Creek

Little Wassaw Island

Wassaw Island

Odingsell River

Rhodes Creek

Wassaw Creek

Cape May

Pine Island

Green Island Sound

OSSABAW SOUND

N Legend

	River/Creek/Channel		Marsh
	Lake/Water Bodies		Federal Lands
	Shallow Water		Federal Lands/Marsh

© Wilderness Adventures Press

Green Island Sound

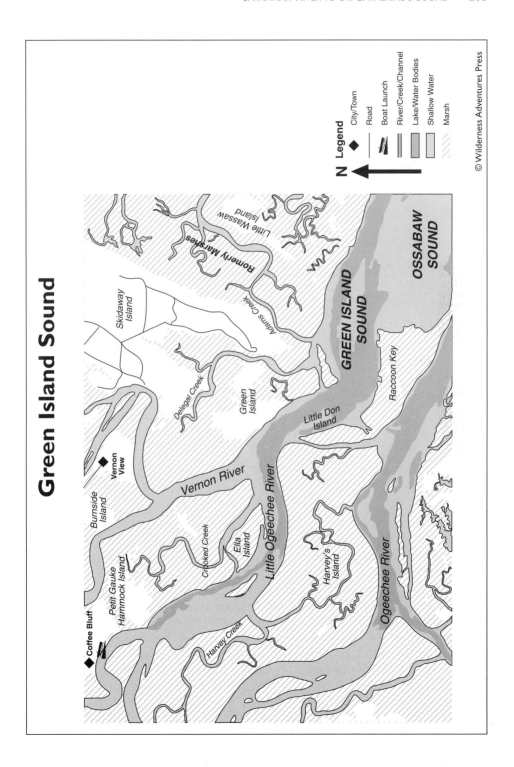

Legend

- ◆ City/Town
- Road
- Boat Launch
- River/Creek/Channel
- Lake/Water Bodies
- Shallow Water
- Marsh

N

© Wilderness Adventures Press

Skidaway Island

Romerly Marshes

Little Wassaw Island

Adams Creek

Delegal Creek

Green Island

GREEN ISLAND SOUND

OSSABAW SOUND

Raccoon Key

Little Don Island

Burnside Island

◆ Vernon View

Vernon River

Little Ogeechee River

Petit Gauke Hammock Island

Crooked Creek

Ella Island

Harvey's Island

Ogeechee River

◆ Coffee Bluff

Harvey Creek

Pelicans are only one bird species that are attracted to game fish feeding on baitfish. Bluefish, jacks, and even red drum can attract these obvious birds. Keep an eye out for their feeding activity regardless of where you are.

specks as well as flatties and puppy drum). I have also found ladyfish around here, which are always a treat.

Raccoon Key, Little Don Island, and Harvey's Island all have plenty of specks, reds, ladyfish, and jacks, plus flounder and tarpon.

Ossabaw Sound to the Medway River

Ossabaw Island is home to the bird- and fish-filled Ossabaw Island Wildlife Management Area. The Bradley River cuts deep into the island beginning on the west side of Bradley Point. Skiffs and canoes (even kayaks) can get back in here for specks and reds. There are turkey, deer, and other game species on the island, which attracts hunters, so don't be alarmed by guns going off. Try trolling a crankbait or curltail jig while motoring around Bradley Point; ladyfish are often found there and smack such offerings, and sometimes the ladies can be pretty big.

Ossabaw Island's southern shore is bordered by St. Catherine's Sound. Turning into the sound, Bear River is located on the north side. This is the Intracoastal Waterway, so watch for other boats, some of them big. Proceeding north on Bear River, one will find:

Ossabaw Island/Bear River

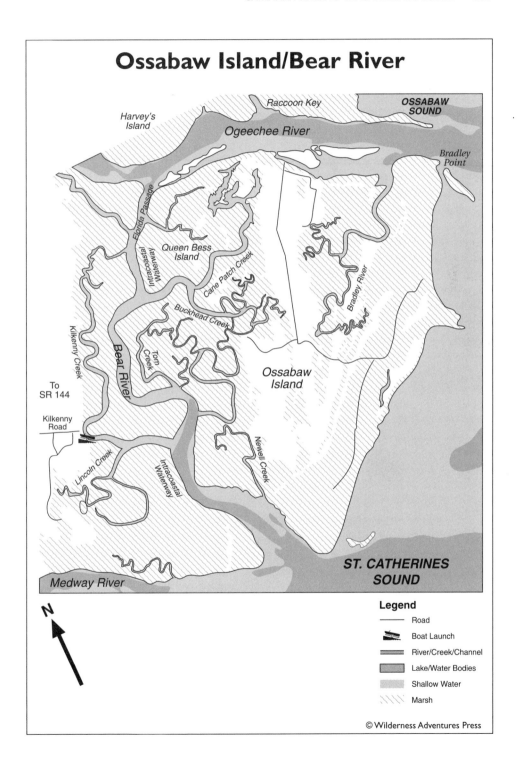

Raccoon Key

OSSABAW SOUND

Harvey's Island

Ogeechee River

Bradley Point

Florida Passage

Queen Bess Island

Cane Patch Creek

Bradley River

Intracoastal Waterway

Buckhead Creek

Kilkenny Creek

Tom Creek

Bear River

Ossabaw Island

To SR 144

Kilkenny Road

Lincoln Creek

Intracoastal Waterway

Newell Creek

ST. CATHERINES SOUND

Medway River

N

Legend

—— Road

Boat Launch

River/Creek/Channel

Lake/Water Bodies

Shallow Water

Marsh

© Wilderness Adventures Press

Medway River/Colonel's Island

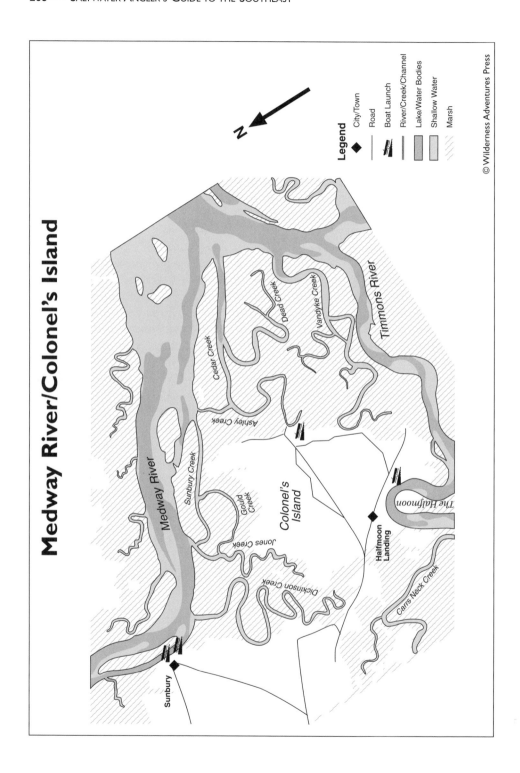

Legend

- ◆ City/Town
- Road
- Boat Launch
- River/Creek/Channel
- Lake/Water Bodies
- Shallow Water
- Marsh

© Wilderness Adventures Press

N

Timmons River

Dead Creek

Vandyke Creek

Cedar Creek

Ashley Creek

Medway River

Sunbury Creek

Gould Creek

Colonel's Island

Jones Creek

The Halfmoon

Halfmoon Landing

Dickinson Creek

Carrs Neck Creek

Sunbury

Chum slicks run in sounds during moving tides can bring all manner of game fish to your boat. Oily baitfish species such as menhaden are best.

- Newell Creek (on the right)
- Tom Creek (larger than Newell and also on the right)
- and Lincoln Creek (on the left)

Because of their versatility, I like using jigs in here. I don't often use white jigs, but one time I was working this area, and for some reason, I tied on a white jig with a red head. I pulled in a few fat specks with it and also two big flounder until a fish bit the curl-tail off. I looked in my tackle box for another white jig and found not a one left, so I switched to a white marabou jig and tipped the hook with an alligator minnow. Boom! Three more flounder.

The river is joined by Kilkenny Creek at its uppermost reaches. There is a boat ramp at the base of Kilkenny Road.

The Medway River has two ramps in Sunbury, and some very good fishing for specks and other species is available right around the ramps. Check the following creeks that surround Halfmoon Landing on Colonel's Island:

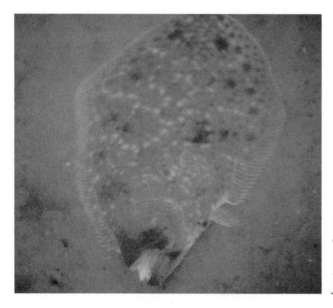

This flounder fell for a chartreuse curltail jig with an orange lead head. Flatties are suckers for these popular jigs.

- Jones Creek
- Cedar Creek
- Ashley Creek
- Dead Creek
- Dickinson Creek

Try throwing a gold spoon in these five creeks for the smallish redfish that patrol them. You might also come across specks, jacks, ladyfish, flounder, blues, and once in a while, a black drum. However, if you are after the blacks, go with a clam on the bottom because black drum adore such taste treats. Also, upgrade your line and terminal tackle since these blacks can be big (20 pounds or so).

This area is best known for specks, drum, and some flounder. Curl-tail jigs in dark green, chartreuse, and pearl with orange, red, or white heads, all work well. MirrOlures twitched along rips, seams, banks, and over oyster beds, also work well. Flyfishers should use Clousers from 1/0 to 3/0 in chartreuse and white, brown and gold, or dark green and white. Sometimes a sinktip helps to get the fly down. When you use one, go with a short leader (2 feet maximum).

Savannah
Population-139,000

ACCOMMODATIONS

The Gastonian, 220 East Gaston Street / 800-322-6603 / With rooms crammed with antiques and a fireplace in each room, this inn was built in 1868 and has maintained all of its charm / Breakfast comes with the room

Hampton Inn, 201 East Bay Street / 912-231-9700

Hyatt Regency, 2 West Bay Street / 912-238-1234 / This Hyatt is a cut above the rest, and the rest are pretty darn nice

The Kehoe House, 123 Habersham Street / 800-820-1020 / Kehoe House has lovely verandas in the Southern tradition and a complimentary breakfast

Olde Harbour Inn, 508 East Factors Walk / 800-553-6533 / Proper Southern service and hospitality are the norm in this inn overlooking the river

Dunes Inn Best Western (Tybee Island), 1409 Butler Avenue / 912-786-4591

CAMPGROUNDS

Biltmore Campground, 4707 Ogeechee Road / 912-236-4065

Bellaire Woods Campground, 805 Fort Argyle Road / 912-748-4000

River's End Campground (Tybee Island), 915 Polk Street / 912-786-5518

Waterway RV Campground (Richmond Hill), 70 Hwy 17 / 912-756-2296

RESTAURANTS

Elizabeth on 37th, 105 East 37th / 912-236-5547 / Very high quality food is served here; bring a jacket / The menu is superior, as is the atmosphere

Garibaldi's Café, 315 West Congress Street / 912-232-7118 / Seafood, pasta, and veal dishes / Nice atmosphere and decor

Love's Seafood Restaurant, 6817 Basin Road / 912-925-3616 / I love properly cooked catfish and Love's has it

The Old Pink House, 23 Abercorn Street / 912-232-4286 / Some creative and very tasty dishes

Pearl's Elegant Pelican, 7000 LaRoche Avenue / 912-352-8221 / Good Low Country seafood

The Shrimp Factory, 313 East River Street / 912-236-4229 / Different decor and good atmosphere / Delicious shrimp dishes

River's End (Thunderbolt), 3122 River Drive / 912-354-2973 / Right on the water

TACKLE AND FLY SHOPS

Cranman's Sporting World, 401 East Montgomer Xrd / 912-921-1488

Landings Harbor, 1 Harbor Street / 912-598-1901

Tackle Box (Pooler),1529 East Hwy 80 / 912-964-0790

River Supplies (Thunderbolt), 2827 River Drive / 912-354-7777

Arnie's Beach Store (Tybee Island), 725 1st Street / 912-786-5904

MARINAS

Bona Bella Marina, 2740 Livingston Avenue / 912-355-9601
Bull River Marina, 8005 Old Tybee Road
Chimney Creek Marina, D.A.V. Road / 912-786-9857
Coffee Bluff Marina, 14915 White Bluff Road / 912-925-9030
Delegal Creek Marina, 1 Marina Drive / 912-598-0023
Fountain Marina, 2812 River Road / 912-354-2283
Hogans' Marina, 36 Wilmington Island Road / 912-897-3474
Isle of Hope Marina, 50 East Bluff Drive / 912-354-8187
Landings Harbor, 1 Harbor Street / 912-598-1901
Lazaretto Creek Marina, just past Lazaretto Creek Bridge on Hwy 80 /
    912-786-5848
Lee Shore Marina, 135 Johnny Mercer Boulevard / 912-897-1154
Marlin Marina (Tybee Island), Chatham Avenue / 912-786-7508
Palmer-Jones Marina, River Drive / 912-352-4956
Riverwatch Marina, River Drive / 912-897-2896
B&B Marine, 2902 River Road / 912-355-0360
Savannah Bend Marina, Old Tybee Road / 912-897-3625
Tidewater Boatworks, Old Tybee Road / 912-352-1335
Tuten's Marina, LaRoche Avenue/ 912-355-8747
Young's Marina, off Wilmington Island Road / 912-897-2608
Fort McAllister Marina (Bryan County), GA Hwy Spur 144 / 912-727-2632
Kilkenny Fish Camp (Bryan County), Kilkenny Road / 912-727-2215

FOR MORE INFORMATION

Chamber of Commerce
222 West Oglethorpe Avenue, #100
Savannah, GA 31401
912-944-0444

Savannah Chamber of Commerce
301 Martin Luther King Jr. Boulevard
Savannah, GA 31401
912-234-0947

ST. CATHERINE'S SOUND TO ALTAMAHA SOUND

The rivers and creeks of coastal Georgia tend to run a bit wider at this point, which makes access easier.

The Clouser is great for probing the bottom and mimicking shrimp and baitfish, while poppers make noise on the surface to imitate something being eaten, or something struggling or wounded. All saltwater flyfishers need to have a selection of flies that can cover the entire water column.

St. Catherine's Sound to Altamaha Sound

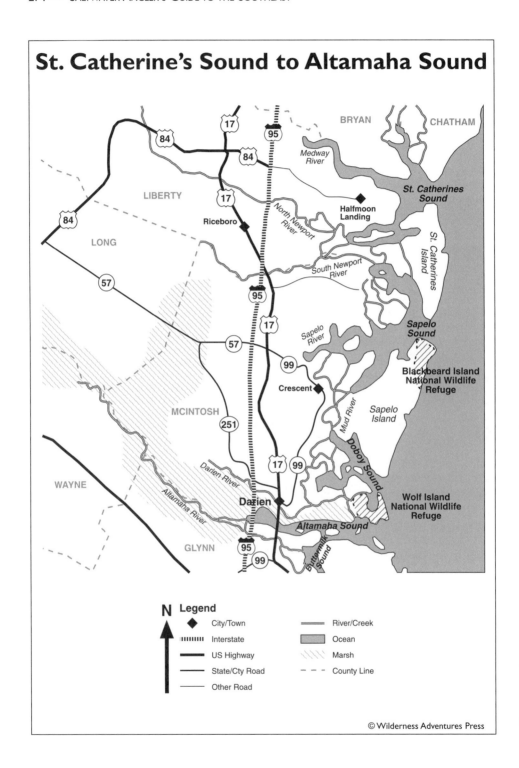

N

Legend

◆ City/Town

|||||||| Interstate

━━━ US Highway

─── State/Cty Road

── Other Road

━━━ River/Creek

�▨ Ocean

▨ Marsh

╌╌╌ County Line

© Wilderness Adventures Press

North Newport River to Doboy Sound

The western side of St. Catherine's Sound is formed by marshes in which can be found:

- Cedar Creek
- Dead Creek
- Vandyke Creek
- North Newport River (which separates Walburg Island from the Halfmoon Landing area)

Spoon flies are terrific on red drum working the grass for crabs and other goodies. A spoon fly doesn't imitate a crab in any way, but red drum don't focus on one specific forage item the way some freshwater trout do in many situations. Fluttering a spoon fly near a calm, happy, feeding redfish can bring an immediate reaction, but be quiet on the approach so you don't blow them out.

While using spinning tackle, I have tossed loud popping plugs along grass banks and come up with vicious attacks by speckled trout. If you miss the strike, don't worry about it; just keep retrieving the plug until you get a hit.

The so-called Timmons River is more of a shortcut between the Outer North Newport River and Halfmoon Landing than a river. South Newport Cut is found where the North Newport and Timmons converge below Halfmoon Landing, where Gross Tide Creek and South Hampton Creek are located.

Rat-L-Traps are one of the best lures ever devised. They are hit by drum, specks, tarpon, jacks, ladyfish, flounder, stripers, blues, and a host of other game fish.

St. Catherine's Sound: West

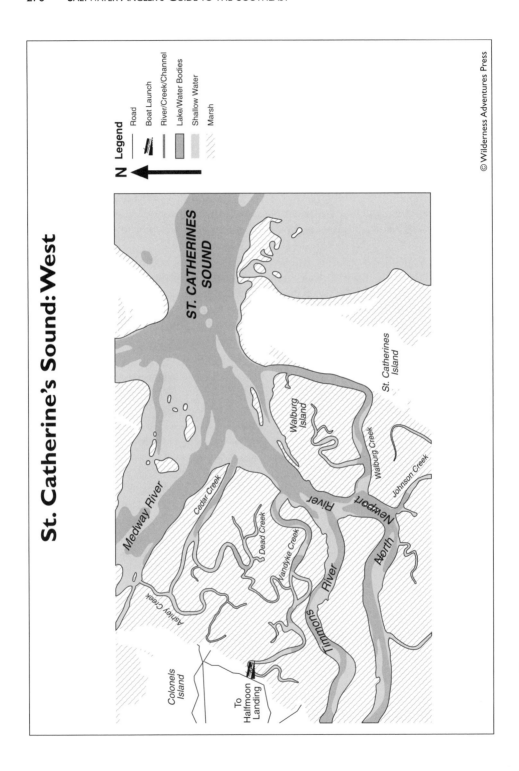

Legend
N
Road
Boat Launch
River/Creek/Channel
Lake/Water Bodies
Shallow Water
Marsh

ST. CATHERINES SOUND

St. Catherines Island

Walburg Island

Walburg Creek

Johnson Creek

Medway River

Cedar Creek

Dead Creek

Vandyke Creek

Newport River

North

Timmons River

Ashley Creek

Colonels Island

To Halfmoon Landing

© Wilderness Adventures Press

Timmons and North Newport Rivers

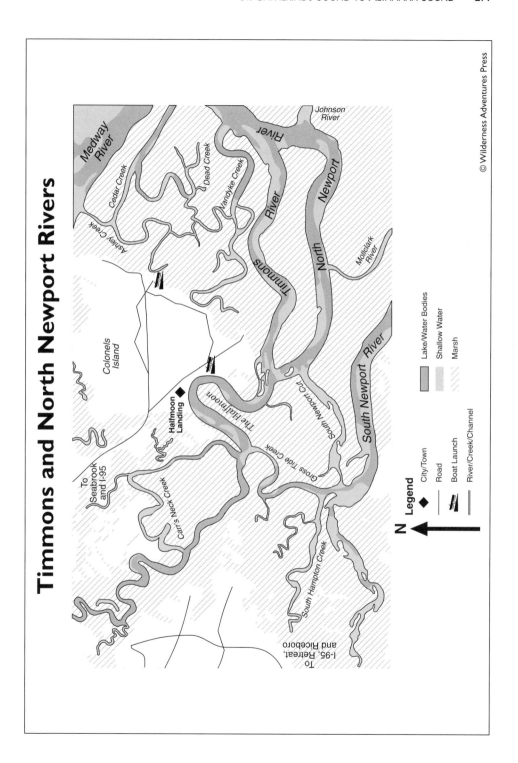

© Wilderness Adventures Press

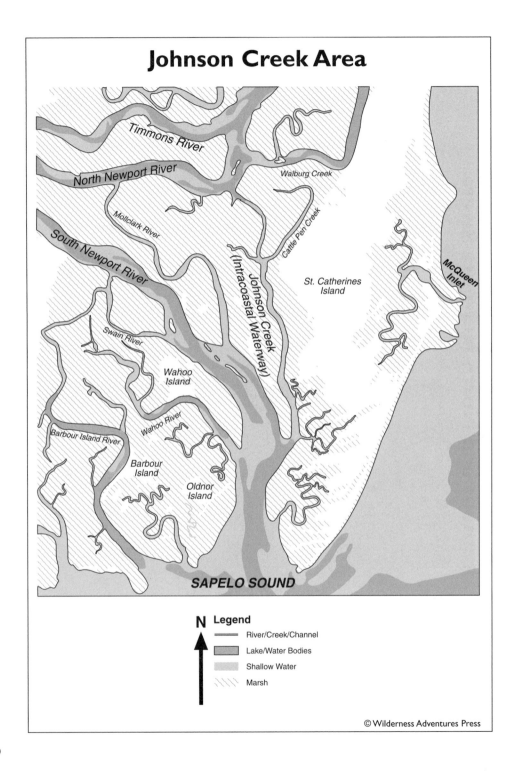

Johnson Creek Area

Timmons River

North Newport River

Walburg Creek

Mollclark River

Cattle Pen Creek

South Newport River

Johnson Creek (Intracoastal Waterway)

St. Catherines Island

McQueen Inlet

Swain River

Wahoo Island

Wahoo River

Barbour Island River

Barbour Island

Oldnor Island

SAPELO SOUND

N

Legend

— River/Creek/Channel

Lake/Water Bodies

Shallow Water

Marsh

© Wilderness Adventures Press

Twitched on the surface in an erratic (as opposed to erotic) fashion, jerk baits can bring vicious strikes. A certain color pattern may be needed at times, so have a broad selection at hand.

This area has many little nuances and intricacies that should be explored. I have found fish in here holding in tight pockets and some that show up very unexpectedly. Take your time in here. Use a light spinning rig with a small jig or very small crankbait and consider a weedless gold spoon, such as a Johnson Spoon, to get into the grass. In deep holes, make sure the jig or sinking crankbait gets all the way to the bottom. Likewise, flyfishers should use smaller flies if drum and specks aren't biting and use weedless flies (try a weedless spoon fly) to get back into spartina.

This region holds specks that like soft curltail jigs and flies that mimic shrimp. Carr's Neck Creek is also good, and the North Newport River can be followed all the way up to Riceboro.

Johnson Creek, also part of the Intracoastal Waterway, is found by heading straight south down the North Newport River (don't follow the river where it turns west). Cattle Pan Creek is off to the left, and fish can be found there, with flounder and specks being fairly plentiful. Johnson Creek dumps into the South Newport River at Sapelo Sound. Rivers to check out are:

- Mollclark
- Swain
- Wahoo

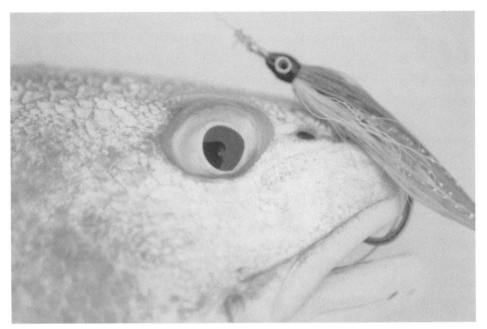

Redfish love Deceivers just as many other game fish do.
Green and yellow is a popular color combination.

I have had good results dragging jigs along the bottom around these parts. By dragging I do mean dragging, which is done by pointing your rod tip right at the jig and slowly reeling. I am not sure what the specks, flounder, reds, and sometimes jacks think the jig is when presented this way, but they seem to think it is something edible. This area sees some tarpon, too, so watch for signs of them rolling, slurping air, feeding, etc. A large, soft plastic Cotee jig in pearl can bring a wallop from a passing tarpon here, but be ready—a tarpon could easily go more than 100 pounds. I saw one guy in a giant fight with a 150-pound-plus tarpon in this area. This means that flyfishers should be ready with flies, such as the Cockroach and Tarpon Bunny and 12- to 14- weight rods.

Speaking of St. Catherine's Island, McQueen's Inlet on the ocean side offers action for jacks, tarpon, and redfish, as well as specks, flounder, stripers, blues, ladyfish, Spanish mackerel, and other worthy notables. The island has numerous trails on which to wander, but there is no vehicle access from the mainland. This makes it all the nicer, of course.

Sapelo Sound has a lot to offer, too. The Mud River runs off the sound to the south and holds flounder and Spanish mackerel, among other species. The Front River is a shortcut to the northwest of the Mud River and forms one side of Dog Hammock and one side of Creighton Island. The Sapelo River runs from the sound

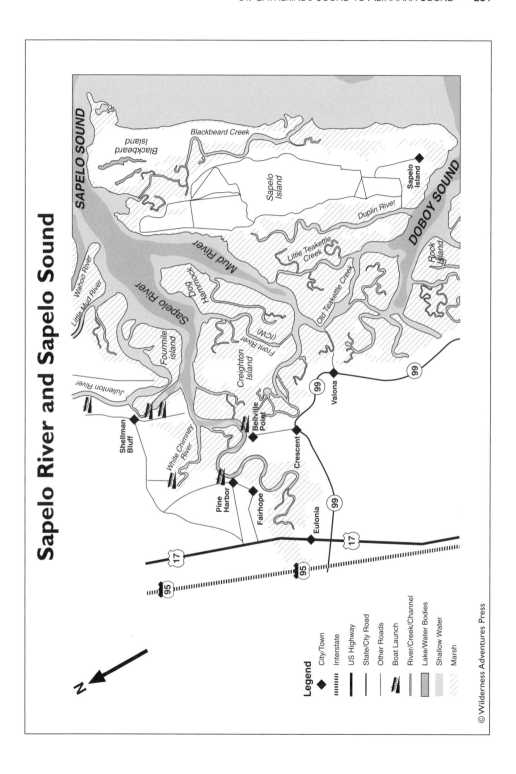

Sapelo River and Sapelo Sound

SAPELO SOUND

Blackbeard Creek

Blackbeard Island

Sapelo Island

DOBOY SOUND

Sapelo Island

Duplin River

Little Teakettle Creek

Old Teakettle Creek

Rock Island

Mud River

Wahoo River

Little Mud River

Sapelo River

Dog Hammock

Fourmile Island

Front River (ICW)

Creighton Island

Julienton River

Shellman Bluff

White Chimney River

Belville Point

Valona

99

99

99

Crescent

Pine Harbor

Fairhope

Eulonia

17

95

17

95

N

Legend

◆ City/Town

▦ Interstate

━━ US Highway

│ State/Cty Road

│ Other Roads

⚓ Boat Launch

River/Creek/Channel

Lake/Water Bodies

Shallow Water

Marsh

© Wilderness Adventures Press

A soft jig produced this pretty nice red drum. Photo by Rick Pelow.

up into Fairhope and Eulonia. There is a ramp in Bellville Point and others near Shellman Bluff.

Rat-L-Traps in chrome, silver, gold, and red and white can bring hard hits from specks in this area. I like to use the Rat-L-Traps when the water is off-color because the lures make a racket in the water. A Real Image suspending Tattlin' Minnow or Smithwick Rattlin' Rogue (an oustanding lure) are also good in murky water for the same reason, as are surface poppers designed to wake the dead. The Rattle Rouser is a good fly for these situations. If the water is fairly clear, try a Fin-S Shad in alewife (a color that looks like an alewife). For flyfishing, a white Deceiver with some strands of peacock herl for the back can be deadly.

Doboy Sound to Wolf Island National Wildlife Refuge

Sapelo Island is the big island between Sapelo Sound and Doboy Sound to the south. For some reason cartographers have said that Blackbeard Island is a separate island instead of really being part of Sapelo Island—Blackbeard being the northeast part of what looks like all of Sapelo Island. Blackbeard Creek and other smaller creeks in the area hold specks and flounder, plus reds. Blackbeard Island is home to the Blackbeard Island National Wildlife Refuge, while Sapelo Island is home to the Sapelo

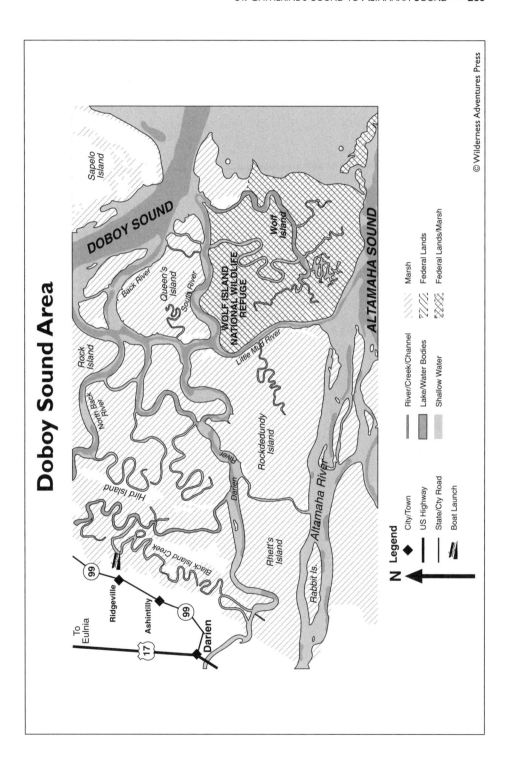

Doboy Sound Area

DOBOY SOUND

ALTAMAHA SOUND

Sapelo Island

Wolf Island

WOLF ISLAND NATIONAL WILDLIFE REFUGE

Back River

Queen's Island

South River

Rock Island

North Back River

Little Mud River

Rockdedundy Island

Hird Island

Darien River

Rhett's Island

Altamaha River

Rabbit Is.

Black Island Creek

To Eulnia

99

Ridgeville

Ashintilly

99

17

Darien

Legend

N

◆ City/Town

US Highway

State/Cty Road

Boat Launch

River/Creek/Channel

Lake/Water Bodies

Shallow Water

Marsh

Federal Lands

Federal Lands/Marsh

© Wilderness Adventures Press

The flats from North Carolina to Florida hold some surprisingly large red drum. They are one of the most exciting game fish available to flyfishers.

Island Wildlife Management Area. The Duplin River runs up the west side of Sapelo Island and should be explored with flies and jigs. Just west of Duplin is Little Teakettle Creek, which cuts from the lower Mud River down to Old Teakettle Creek.

There's a real maze of creeks southwest of Sapelo Island in which one could spend several full days exploring without really covering all the water and structure. The following areas form this warren of very fishy water:

- Hird Island
- Rock Island
- Queen's Island
- North Back River
- Back River
- Darien River
- South River

- Wolf Island (home to the Wolf Island National Wildlife Refuge)
- Rockdedundy Island
- Black Island Creek
- Little Mud River
- Rhett's Island

This is a rich area not heavily fished and simply waiting to be explored. A good approach is to think where a trout, red, flounder, jack, or what have you, would be. There are many deep holes, little sloughs, tuckaways, bars, oyster rocks, spartina beds, and channels that need attention.

Suspending Rat-L-Sticks and plastic worms that have been Carolina rigged can be very productive for working holes. In holes with a lot of current running over or through them, use heavy lead on the worms to get down to fish. Along breaks, try a surface plug, such as a Dalton Special for specks. If flyfishing, go with 3/0 Super Clousers and a sinking line in the current-laden holes and big silver or pearl pencil poppers along the breaks up top. Strangely, deer-hair bugs that are usually used for bass also work in here. (Actually, if I used them more I would probably find that they work elsewhere, too.)

There is a boat ramp on the Darien River right in the town of Darien that provides boat access to this area.

Darien
Population–1,800

ACCOMMODATIONS
Comfort Inn, 703 Frontage Road / 912-437-4200
Fort King George Motel, 1205 Hwy 17 / 912-437-4780
Hampton Inn, 610 Hwy 251 / 912-437-5558
Holiday Inn, Exit 10, Georgia Hwy 251 / 912-437-5373
Super 8 Motel, Hwy 251 & I-95 Exit 10 / 912-437-6660

CAMPGROUNDS
Tall Pines Campground, RR1 Box 1100 / 912-437-3966

RESTAURANTS
Andy's Bar-B-Que, Hwy 17 / 912-437-2763
Darien Resaturant, 1819 Northway / 912-437-6574
Archie's Restaurant, 1106 Northway / 912-437-4363
Huddle House, Hwy251 & I-95 / 912-437-5590

FOR MORE INFORMATION
McIntosh County Visitor's Center
P.O. Box 1497
Darien, GA 31305
912-437-4192

Sapelo Island Visitor's Center
P.O. Box 15
Sapelo Island, GA 31327
912-437-3224

*The unexpected arrival of a large amberjack at a pier is always
a source of great fun and stories.*

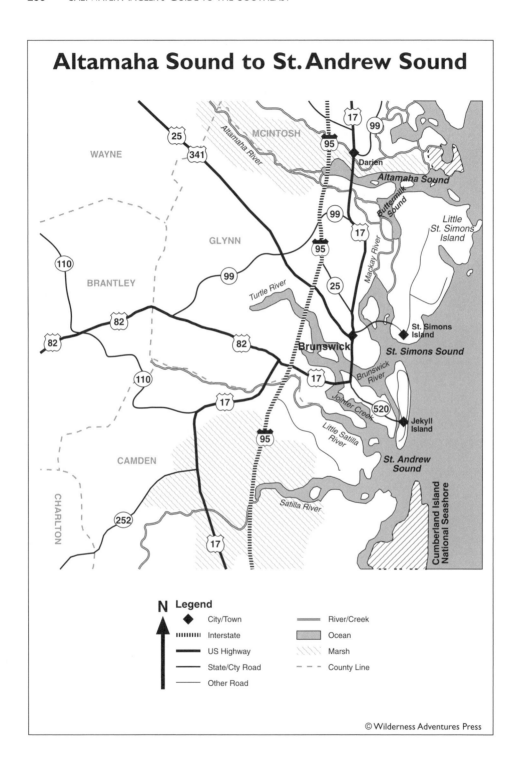

Altamaha Sound to St. Andrew Sound

N Legend

- ◆ City/Town
- ▮▮▮▮ Interstate
- US Highway
- State/Cty Road
- Other Road
- River/Creek
- Ocean
- Marsh
- County Line

© Wilderness Adventures Press

ALTAMAHA SOUND TO ST. ANDREW SOUND

Although quite a ways down the coast of Georgia, it's only here that some fairly well known waters begin to show up. There's rarely much coverage in the national outdoor press about the waters to the north of Altamaha Sound, but there are occasional articles describing the fishing available to the sound's south.

Altamaha River to Brunswick River

The Altamaha River is best fished from west of Interstate 95 at about Lewis Island east to the mouth in the sound of the same name. West of I-95 is the Altamaha Wildlife Management Area, which includes:

- Lewis Creek and River Swamp
- Butler River (it is barely a creek much less a river)
- Butler Island
- Chambers Island
- Wright's Island

The Altamaha River, according to Captain Larry Kennedy of The Bedford Sportsman South on St. Simon's Island, doesn't often see stripers like the one I

The shallows around spartina marshes must be investigated. Surprisingly large game fish can get up into very shallow water. Photo by Rick Pelow.

Saltwater catfish like cut bait just as much as drum. They live in the shallows surrounding spartina flats. Use caution when unhooking them because they have poisonous barbs that will ruin your day if allowed to puncture your skin.

apparently blundered into there a few years ago. It surprised some people who fish there all the time. Larry finds plenty of reds and specks back in here, as well.

Buttermilk Sound isn't really a sound but rather a cut between Broughton Island and the marshes of northwestern St. Simon's Island. It is part of the Altamaha and Mackay Rivers. These areas are good for specks in particular. Toward the upper end of Mackay River is a creek called Wally's Leg, which roughly parallels US 17 east of I-95. Wally's has good specks, redfish, ladyfish, and sometimes tarpon.

At Cypress Mills the Back River breaks off from the Mackay and forms a loop that runs under the Torras Causeway, which links the city of Brunswick to St. Simon's Island. Don't skip this little cut because it is close to the city—there are trout there. In fact, the cuts and creeks that wind underneath the length of the causeway are all excellent. So, too, are the winding creeks in the huge spartina marsh east and south of Brunswick just inside St. Simon's Sound.

Altamaha River and Buttermilk Sound

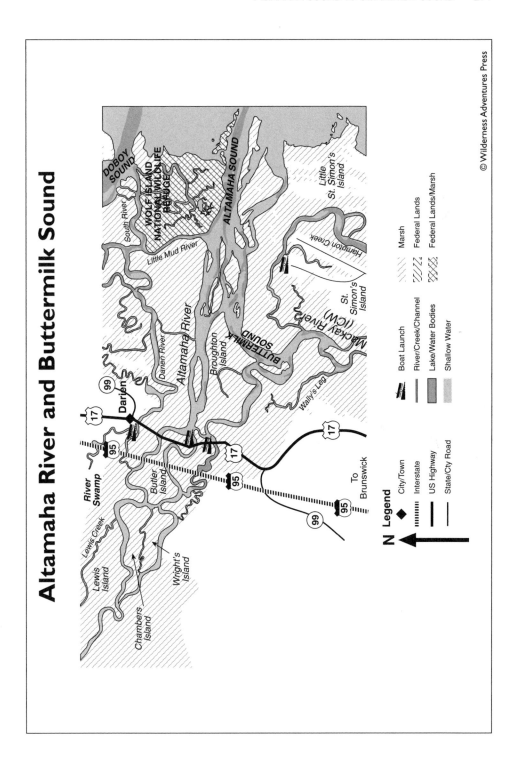

© Wilderness Adventures Press

Legend

N

◆ City/Town
▓▓▓ Interstate
— US Highway
— State/Cty Road

⛟ Boat Launch
| River/Creek/Channel
▨ Lake/Water Bodies
▨ Shallow Water

Marsh
Federal Lands
Federal Lands/Marsh

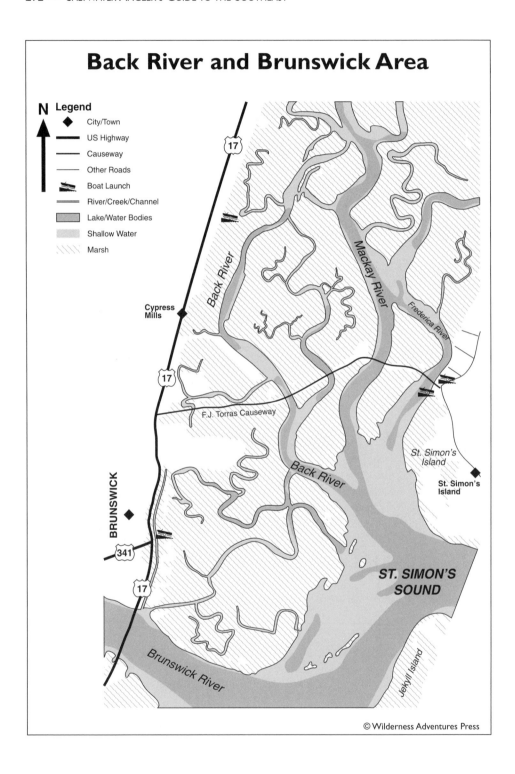

Back River and Brunswick Area

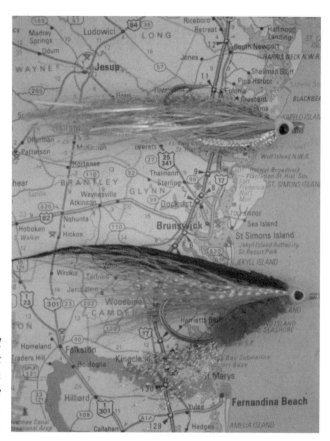

Rattle Rousers and Bendbacks are just two excellent drum and speck flies for the waters around St. Simon's Island.

But the big attractions in this area are St. Simon's and Little St. Simon's Islands. Separated by Hampton Creek, Little St. Simon's is an undeveloped barrier island except for The Lodge at Little St. Simon's, whereas St. Simon's is a resort with several golf courses (the St. Simon's Island Club, Hampton Club, and Sea Palms Golf and Tennis Resort), and other tourist attractions, although the island has managed to keep most of its charm and fish. Guides such as Captain Kennedy facilitate access to the tarpon found in some of the saltwater ponds on the golf courses. There is one town, St. Simon's Island, and four villages: Sea Island, German Village, Harrington, and Glynn Haven. Three methods can be used to get on and off the island: boat, the causeway, and the Malcolm McKinnon Airport (small planes only).

There is a ramp in Harrington and one off the causeway, plus a third at the northern end of the island at Butler Point on Hampton Creek. Little St. Simon's has no such amenities.

The Brunswick River is a major commercial river with heavy ship and boat traffic. Always keep an eye out when in the river. Specks, bluefish, jacks, ladyfish, and

St. Simons Islands

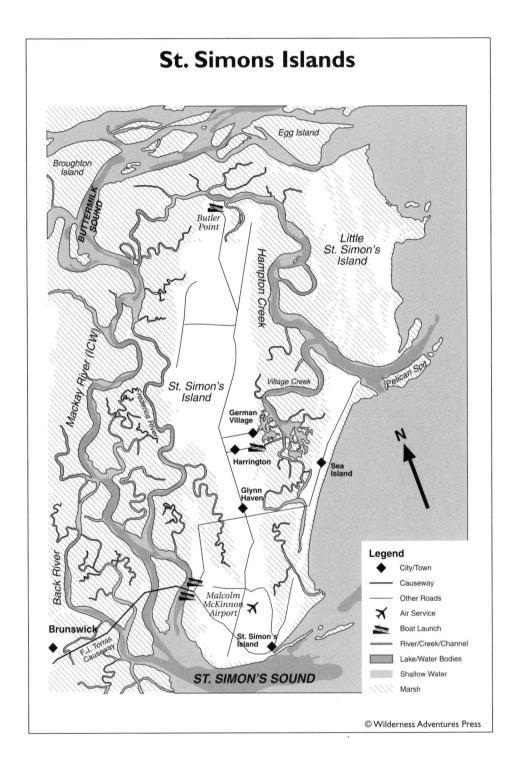

Egg Island

Broughton Island

BUTTERMILK SOUND

Butler Point

Little St. Simon's Island

Hampton Creek

Mackay River (ICW)

Frederica River

St. Simon's Island

Village Creek

Pelican Spit

German Village

Harrington

Sea Island

Back River

Glynn Haven

Malcolm McKinnon Airport

Brunswick

F.J. Torras Causeway

St. Simon's Island

ST. SIMON'S SOUND

N

Legend

◆	City/Town
—	Causeway
—	Other Roads
✈	Air Service
⚓	Boat Launch
═	River/Creek/Channel
▨	Lake/Water Bodies
▨	Shallow Water
▨	Marsh

© Wilderness Adventures Press

West Brunswick Area

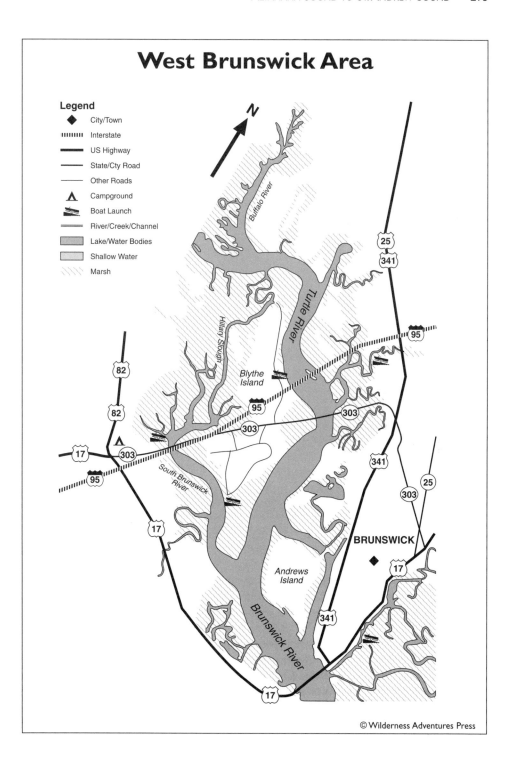

Legend

- ◆ City/Town
- ‖‖‖‖‖‖ Interstate
- ━━ US Highway
- ── State/Cty Road
- ── Other Roads
- ▲ Campground
- 🛥 Boat Launch
- ══ River/Creek/Channel
- ▨ Lake/Water Bodies
- ▨ Shallow Water
- ▨ Marsh

N

Buffalo River

Turtle River

Hillary Slough

Blythe Island

South Brunswick River

Andrews Island

Brunswick River

BRUNSWICK

25
341

95

82

82

17

303

95

303

95

303

303

341

25

303

17

17

341

17

© Wilderness Adventures Press

Ladyfish don't require anything heavier than an 8-weight, and quite often a thinner line will work.

others are found in the waters west of Brunswick, even though they might be within sight of the city and I-95. Check out:

- Blythe Island
- Turtle River
- Buffalo River
- South Brunswick River
- numerous little creeks and cuts

There are several boat ramps in the area, including two off I-95 on Blythe Island.

Brunswick River to Satilla River

Jekyll Island lies across St. Simon's Sound and helps to form the mouth of the Brunswick River. Like St. Simon's Island, there is just one land access to Jekyll Island from the mainland: SR 520, also aptly known as Jekyll Island Road. The road can be found going south out of the city of Brunswick, where it crosses the Brunswick River,

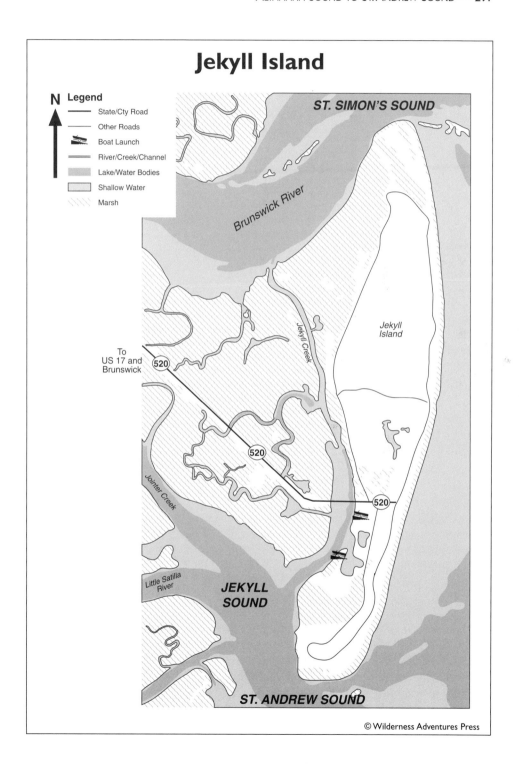

Jekyll Island

N Legend
— State/Cty Road
— Other Roads
Boat Launch
— River/Creek/Channel
Lake/Water Bodies
Shallow Water
Marsh

ST. SIMON'S SOUND

Brunswick River

Jekyll Creek

Jekyll Island

To
US 17 and
Brunswick
520

520

520

Jointer Creek

Little Satilla River

JEKYLL SOUND

ST. ANDREW SOUND

© Wilderness Adventures Press

Little Satilla River

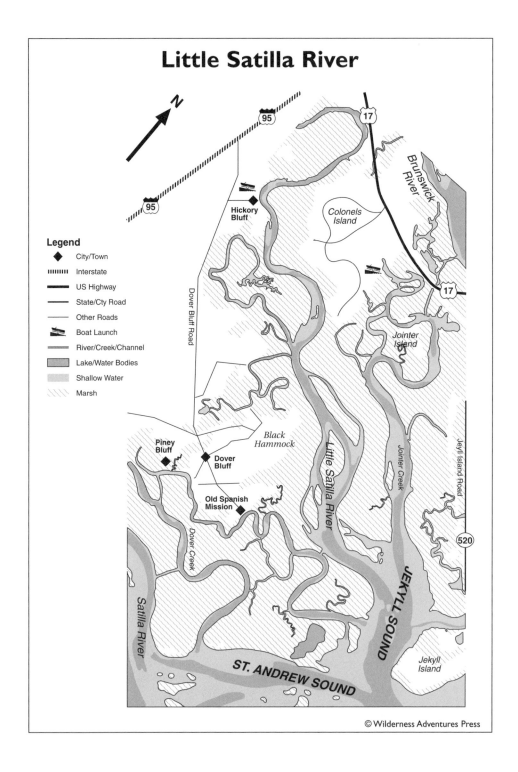

Legend
- ◆ City/Town
- ⅢⅢⅢ Interstate
- ▬▬ US Highway
- ▬ State/Cty Road
- — Other Roads
- Boat Launch
- ▬ River/Creek/Channel
- Lake/Water Bodies
- Shallow Water
- Marsh

or off I-95. Besides redfish, ladyfish, flounder, stripers, specks, sheepshead, croakers, tarpon, and so on, Jekyll Island has a golf course, hiking trails, and other attractions.

Jekyll Creek separates Jekyll Island from the mainland and has plenty of specks. If they can't be found in the main channel, try the smaller creeks that run off the main channel. Also try Jointer Creek, which breaks into several small channels near Jekyll Island Road. The northern tip of Jekyll Island offers game fish, as does the entire beach facing the ocean and the southern tip of the island.

Little Satilla River enters Jekyll Sound to the west and winds up in the Hickory Bluff area, where there is a ramp. Farther up, Little Satilla crosses under I-95. The side channels and creeks between Hickory Bluff and Black Hammock are good, as are the creeks of Piney Bluff, Dover Bluff, and Old Spanish Mission. I usually find specks back in here, but reds rooting for crabs and flounder chasing baitfish like finger mullet and lizardfish also show up.

Brunswick
Population–17,500

Accommodations
Comfort Inn, 5308 New Jesup Hwy / 912-264-9296

Embassy Suites, 500 Mall Boulevard / 912-264-6100

Holiday Inn, 5252 New Jesup Hwy / 912-264-4033

Holiday Inn Express (Darien), Interstate 95 at Exit 10 / 912-437-5373

Comfort Inn Island Suites (Jekyll Island), 711 North Beachview Drive / 912-635-2211

Holiday Inn Beach Resort (Jekyll Island), 200 South Beachview Drive / 912-635-3311

Jekyll Island Club Hotel (Jekyll Island), 371 Riverview Drive / 800-535-9547 / This is the best place on the island / Built around the turn of the century, it is quite nice

The Lodge at Little St. Simon's Island, PO Box 21078 / 912-638-7472 / email: lssi@mindspring.com / To call this lodge spectacular would be a terrible disservice; one of the best lodges on the continent in terms of service, light-tackle angling and flyfishing, meals, style, luxury, and charm, it is not to be missed in your lifetime / Private and secluded, this marvelous establishment is on a 10,000-acre barrier island

Sea Gate Inn (St. Simon Island), 1014 Ocean Boulevard / 912-638-8661

Campgrounds
Jekyll Island Campground (Jekyll Island), 1197 Riverview Drive / 912-635-3021

Blythe Island Regional Park, 6616 Blythe Island Parkway / 912-261-3805

Belle Bluff Island Campground (Townsend), RR 3, Box 3246B25 / 912-832-5323

Restaurants
Jinright's Seafood House, 2815 Glynn Avenue / 912-267-1590 / Pretty good seafood place

Matteo's Italian Restaurant, 5448 New Jesup Hwy / 912-267-0248 / Decent Italian fare

Blackbeard's (Jekyll Island), 200 North Beachview Drive / 912-635-3522 / Hearty fare including good seafood and beef / Excellent setting

Allegro Restaurant (St. Simon's Island), 2465 Demere Road / 912-638-7097 / Interesting establishment—menu is quite varied

Frederica House, 3611 Frederica Road / 912-638-6789 / Very good seafood in a nice setting / Comfortable surroundings

Tackle and Fly Shops
Altamaha Fish Camp, 1605 Altamaha Park Road / 912-264-2342

Tackle Shack, 3737 Community Road / 912-264-4665

McIntosh Enterprises (Darien), Hwy 251 West / 912-437-6679

The Bedford Sportsman South (St. Simon's Island), 3405 Frederica Road / 912-638-5454 / Owned and operated by Captain Larry Kennedy, Jr., and his two sons, Larry and Mike / As complete as a shop can get, carrying many top lines of tackle

Coastal Outdoor and Marine (St. Simon's Island),117 Marina Drive / 912-634-2848

GUIDES

Captain Wendell Harper, 107 Boyd Drive / 912-264-4459 / Captain Harper has been guiding for about 30 years / Species of expertise include tarpon, reds, spotted seatrout, large Spanish mackerel, amberjack, cobia, and kings. Wendell notes that his "bread and butter" are the reds and specks around Brunswick because they are available throughout the year

Captain Larry Kennedy, Jr. (St. Simon's Island), 3405 Frederica Road / 912-638-5454 / Kennedy is a superb guide whose sons are also guides. He has been featured in such magazines as *Fly Fishing in Salt Waters* and *Salt Water Sportsman*; he's topnotch

Captain Larry Kennedy III (St. Simon's Island), 511 Marsh Villa Road / 912-638-3214 / Gaining fast on dad is Larry the Third, who has gained a solid reputation as a clever guide who knows these waters well.

Captain Mike Kennedy (St. Simon's Island), 511 Marsh Villa Road / 912-638-3214 / The third member of the Kennedy triumvirate, Mike is also an Orvis-endorsed guide who cut his teeth in the spartina marshes, rivers, and inlets of coastal Georgia around St. Simon's Island

MARINAS

Bell Bluff Marina, off Bell Hammock Road/ 912-832-5323

Blythe Island Regional Park Marina, off GA Hwy 303, 912-261-3805

Brunswick Boat Marina, US Hwy 17 South / 912-265-2290

Brunswick Landing Marina, 2429 Newcastle Street / 912-262-9264

Credle's Complete Marine, 1455 US Hwy 17 South / 912-262-6003

Dallas Bluff Marina & Campground, off Shellman Bluff Road/ 912-832-5116

Fisherman's Lodge, Broro River Bluff/ 912-832-5162

Pine Harbor Marina, Pine Harbor Marina Road/ 912-832-5999

Troupe Creek Marina, 375 Yacht Road / 912-264-3862

Two-Way Fish Camp, 1400 Darien Hwy / 912-265-0410

Jekyll Harbor (Jekyll Island), 1 Harbor Road / 912-635-3137

Jekyll Wharf (Jekyll Island),1 Pier Road / 912-635-3153

Golden Isles Marina (St. Simon's Island), 206 Marina Drive / 912-634-1128

Village Creek Landing (St. Simon's Island), 526 South Harrington Road / 912-634-9054

FOR MORE INFORMATION

Chamber of Commerce
4 Glynn Avenue
Brunswick, GA 31520
912-265-0620

St. Andrew Sound to St. Mary's Entrance

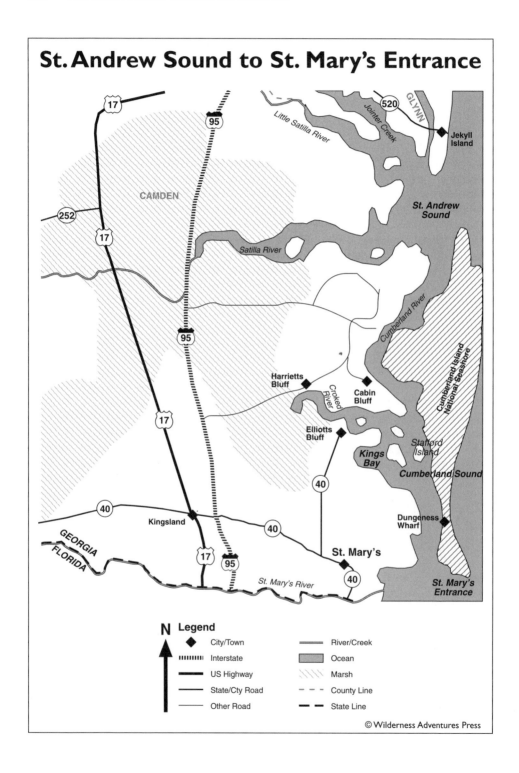

GLYNN

520

Jekyll
Island

Little Satilla River

Jointer Creek

CAMDEN

St. Andrew
Sound

252

17

17

Satilla River

Cumberland River

95

95

Harrietts
Bluff

Croked
River

Cabin
Bluff

Cumberland Island
National Seashore

Elliotts
Bluff

Stafford
Island

Kings
Bay

Cumberland Sound

17

40

40

Dungeness
Wharf

Kingsland

40

40

St. Mary's

GEORGIA

FLORIDA

17

95

St. Mary's River

40

St. Mary's
Entrance

N

Legend

◆ City/Town

River/Creek

Interstate

Ocean

US Highway

Marsh

State/Cty Road

County Line

Other Road

State Line

© Wilderness Adventures Press

St. Andrew Sound to St. Mary's Entrance

This region of coastal Georgia is just north of Florida's Fernandina Beach, which is the northernmost town on Florida's east coast. There isn't as much boat traffic and angling pressure as one might think in this area, even though sprawling Jacksonville is just a bit south.

Satilla River to Stafford Island

This area has probably never been written up in the national angling press, but locals know that there are many flyfishing and light-tackle opportunities here. The area does not get heavy tourist pressure—nothing like Jacksonville Beach or the Cocoa Beach region. One big reason for this is that spartina marshes are still the norm, with the white, sandy beaches of Florida still a ways south. The sand beaches that are here are part of the Cumberland Island National Seashore, which means that development is prevented with a long, pointy stick. Good news, indeed.

Along the south shore of the Satilla River are Todd Creek and Floyd Basin. Speck lovers will find that jigs, crankbaits, and hard jerkbaits like MirrOlures all work well in here, and flyfishers can get after the specks with Clousers in such traditional colors as brown, copper, chartreuse, white, silver, and gray. Take a canoe up into Barrel Head Swamp, and you probably won't see another soul.

Black drum are found around the northern tip of Little Cumberland Island and can be caught using shrimp, cut bait, and clams right on the bottom. In the Cumberland

A variety of lures will improve your chances in southernmost Georgia

Lower Satilla River/Northern Cumberland Island

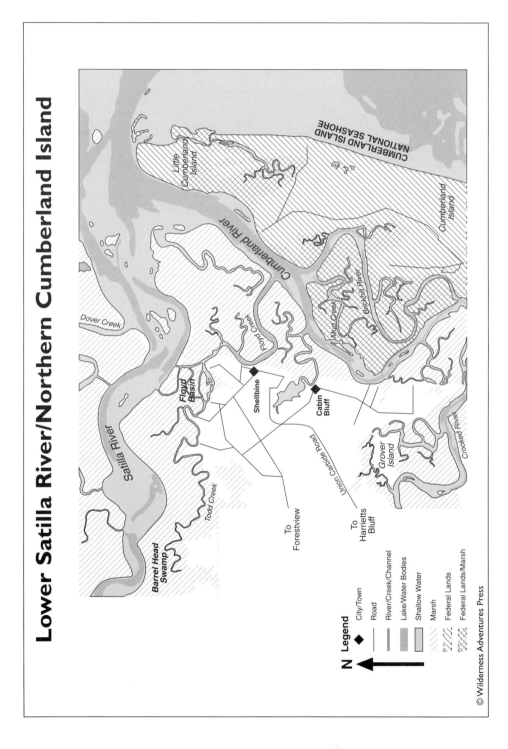

Little Cumberland Island

CUMBERLAND ISLAND NATIONAL SEASHORE

Cumberland Island

Cumberland River

Brickhill River

Dover Creek

Floyd Creek

Mud Creek

Floyd Basin

Shellbine

Cabin Bluff

Crooked River

Satilla River

Grover Island

Union Carbide Road

Todd Creek

To Forestview

To Harrietts Bluff

Barrel Head Swamp

N Legend

◆ City/Town

Road

River/Creek/Channel

Lake/Water Bodies

Shallow Water

Marsh

Federal Lands

Federal Lands/Marsh

© Wilderness Adventures Press

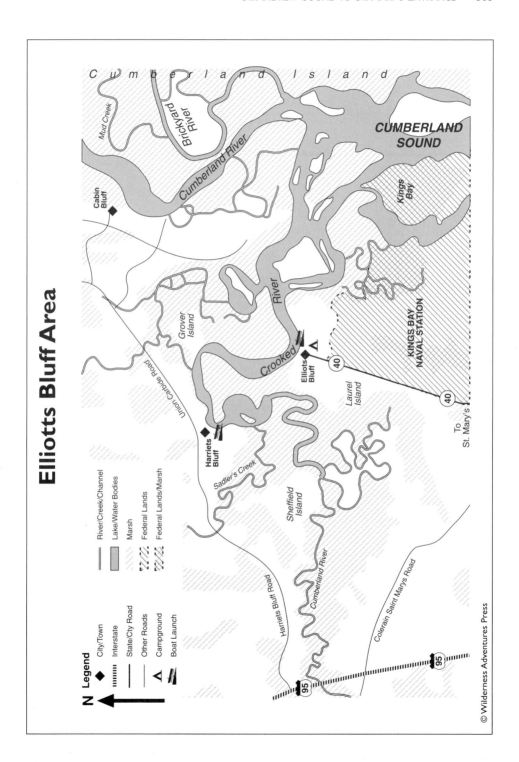

Elliotts Bluff Area

Cumberland Island

Mud Creek

Brickyard River

Cumberland River

CUMBERLAND SOUND

Cabin Bluff

Kings Bay

KINGS BAY NAVAL STATION

River

Grover Island

Crooked

Elliots Bluff

40

40

Laurel Island

To St. Mary's

Union Carbide Road

Harriets Bluff

Sadler's Creek

Sheffield Island

Cumberland River

Harriets Bluff Road

Colerain Saint Marys Road

95

95

N

Legend

◆	City/Town
▪▪▪▪▪	Interstate
—	State/Cty Road
--	Other Roads
△	Campground
🚤	Boat Launch

—	River/Creek/Channel
▦	Lake/Water Bodies
⁄⁄	Marsh
⁄⁄	Federal Lands
⁄⁄	Federal Lands/Marsh

© Wilderness Adventures Press

Southern Cumberland Island

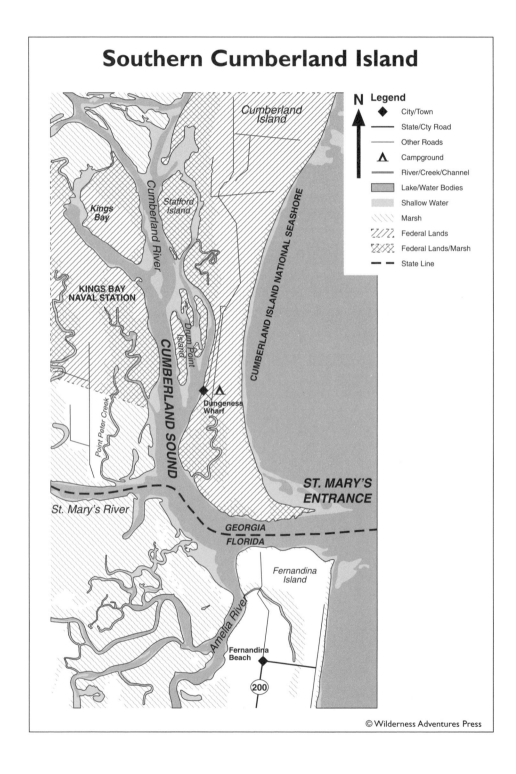

N

Legend
- ◆ City/Town
- —— State/Cty Road
- —— Other Roads
- ⋀ Campground
- —— River/Creek/Channel
- ▨ Lake/Water Bodies
- ░ Shallow Water
- ⧄ Marsh
- ⧄ Federal Lands
- ⧄ Federal Lands/Marsh
- – – State Line

Cumberland Island

Kings Bay

Stafford Island

Cumberland River

CUMBERLAND ISLAND NATIONAL SEASHORE

KINGS BAY NAVAL STATION

Drum Point Island

CUMBERLAND SOUND

Point Peter Creek

◆ ⋀ Dungeness Wharf

ST. MARY'S ENTRANCE

St. Mary's River

GEORGIA
FLORIDA

Fernandina Island

Amelia River

◆ Fernandina Beach

(200)

© Wilderness Adventures Press

River, which forms the western side of Little Cumberland and Cumberland Islands, stripping Clousers and shrimp patterns along the bottom with a sinking line can dredge up big specks that are plenty fat. Try Mud Creek and the Brickhill River off the Cumberland.

Around Elliott's Bluff, focus on:

- Sadler's Creek
- Sheffield Island
- Laurel Island
- Grover Island
- Crooked River

From time to time I have found cobia in the deeper water around here, so try soaking a chunk of cut mullet on the bottom with a chum back resting near it. This is how many cobia are caught in North Carolina, especially around Morehead City.

Kings Bay Naval Station is here, so watch out for Navy vessels coming and going. This includes submarines, which should be given a wide berth as they are not very maneuverable while on the surface and can churn up massive bow waves and wakes.

Stafford Island to Southernmost Cumberland Island

East of Kings Bay is Stafford Island, a large island with decent angling around it. However, I have found that by heading farther south past Drum Point Island to the Dungeness Wharf area, better luck can be had most of the time. There is a boat ramp on the St. Mary's River at the south end of town.

On the beach side of Cumberland Island, drum, stripers, seatrout, pompano, and bluefish are available.

St. Mary's
Population–8,200

ACCOMMODATIONS
The Lodge at Cabin Bluff (northeast of St. Mary's) / 912-638-3611 (Sea Island, GA) / This Orvis-endorsed lodge sits just north of the Florida border / Well run by Karen Cate, it is recommended by those who insist on comfortable surroundings, good service, delicious meals, and plenty of fish in the neighborhood
Spencer House Inn, 200 Osborne Street / 912-882-1872
Cumberland Kings Bay Lodges, 603 Sand Bar Drive / 912-882-8900
Guest House Inn and Suites, 2710 Osborne Road / 912-882-6250
Hampton Inn (Kingsland), 1363 Hwy 40 East / 912-729-1900
             (Fernandina Beach, FL), 2549 Sadler Road / 904-321-111
Days Inn (Kingsland), 1050 East King Avenue / 912-729-5454
Quality Inn (Kingsland), 985 Boone Street / 912-729-4363
Comfort Inn (Kingsland), 111 Edenfiled Drive / 912-729-6979

CAMPGROUNDS
Jacksonville North KOA (Kingsland), 1521 Srubby Bluff Road / 912-729-3232
Country Oaks Campground and RV (Kingsland), 6 Carlton Cemetery Road / 912-729-6212

RESTAURANTS
Borrell Creek Landing, 1101 Hwy 40 East / 912-673-6300
Huddle House, 103 Spur 40 / 912-673-6691
Angelo's of Point Peter, 944 Point Peter Road / 912-673-7007
Breaux's Cajun Cafe, 2710 Osborne Road / 912-882-6250
Bonzai Japanese Steak House, 2714 Osborne Road / 912-882-8600
Wood's Seafood Market, 2202 Osborne Road / 912-882-1056
Sin Far Chinese Restaurant, 133 City Smitty Drive / 912-882-1800
St. Mary's Seafood & Steakhouse, 1837 Osborne Road / 912-882-6875
Applebee's Neighborhood Grill (Kingsland), 113 The Lakes Boulevard / 912-729-9515
Angelo's of Kingsland, 1369 Hwy 40 East / 912-882-7676
Waffle House (Kingsland), 1075 Boone Road East / 912-729-2506
Cracker Barrel Old Country Store (Kingsland), 900 Boone Street / 912-576-1991

TACKLE AND FLY SHOPS
Bait House (Fernandina Beach, FL), 1620 North 14th Street / 904-277-0503
Hall's Beach Store (Fernandina Beach, FL), 2021 South Fletcher Avenue / 904-261-7007
Island Hardware (Fernandina Beach, FL), 5210 First Coast Hwy / 904-277-4111
Orvis Tidewater Outfitters (Fernandina Beach, FL) / 904-261-2202

Brown's Bait and Tackle (Jacksonville, FL), 5672 Timuquana Road / 904-772-1046

Fishin' Buddy Bait and Tackle (Jacksonville, FL), 13642 Atlantic Boulevard / 904-221-0865

Julington Creek Bait and Tackle (Jacksonville, FL), 12807 San Jose Boulevard / 904-262-8826

GUIDES

Hot Ticket Charters (Fernandina Beach, FL) / 904-321-1668

Golden Isles Charter Fishing (St. Simons Island), Lawrence Road / 912-638-7673

Captain Mark D. Noble (St. Simons Island), Lawrence Road / 912-634-1219

Amelia Island Charter Boat (Fernandina Beach, FL), 3 South Front Street / 904-261-2870

Tradewinds Charter Fishing (Fernandina Beach, FL), 1901 Highland Drive / 904-261-9486

MARINAS

Hickory Bluff Marina, Hickory Bluff Road / 912-262-0453

Lang's Marina, off St. Mary's Street / 912 882-4452

Ocean Breeze Marina & Campground, off Ocean Breeze Drive / 912-265-8280

FOR MORE INFORMATION

Camden County Chamber
of Commerce
1411 Hwy 40 East
Kingsland, GA 31548
912-729-5840

Fernandina Beach Chamber
of Commerce
102 Centre Street
Fernandina Beach, FL 32034
904-261-3248

Offshore Action

A guidebook such as this just wouldn't be complete without some good information regarding offshore angling opportunities for light-tackle anglers and flyfishers. By "offshore" I mean not inshore, that is, anywhere outside an inlet or more than a few casts' distance from the beach. True, the more traditional sense of the word means out of sight of land, I suppose, but let's broaden it a bit this time.

Before we look into this, I want you to seriously consider using your fly rod and light spinning or trolling tackle offshore, provided you don't already. Put down that heavy trolling gear with the massive Penn 130ST International II and have some real fun by picking up a much smaller Penn 16S International II.

You might be very pleasantly surprised to learn that flyfishing out in the ocean can be incredible, as can using light tackle. Imagine the thrill of nailing a huge yellowfin tuna or wahoo on the fly or with your bass rod. Yes, it can be done, and then some. This chapter will tell you how and give you some places to try, too.

Kings are found just off the beach and miles out of sight of land.
They are wonderful light tackle and fly tackle targets.

*By going with a lighter jig-
ging rod, the author man-
aged quite a few more
snapper than most of the
other anglers on this party
boat. Photo by Rick Pelow.*

Zones of Action

Offshore angling is a world consisting of two zones: the green water near shore and the blue water far enough offshore not to be colored by suspended particles being carried out to sea by rivers and creeks through inlets, which helps make the water appear greenish (the shallowness of the water also helps it appear to be a hue of green). Some game fish seldom venture into green water. These include:

- Dolphin
- Gray triggerfish
- Grouper (although young can be inshore)

- Vermilion snapper
- Wahoo
- Yellowfin tuna

Normally found in blue water near the surface, dolphin are big fans of flyingfish. They are also suckers for flies, jigs, spoons, crankbaits, and live bait.

This isn't to say that these fish never come close to shore, because from time to time, when the conditions are right, they will. But they prefer the blue water well out of sight of land for the most part. Green water species include:

- Bluefish
- Black drum
- Crevalle Jack
- Croaker
- False albacore
- Gray trout
- Pompano

- Red drum
- Sheepshead
- Spanish mackerel
- Spotted seatrout
- Tarpon
- Tripletail

John Nuckolls of Newport, North Carolina, found this fat grouper in 130 feet of water. He used a cigar minnow soaked with menhaden oil to trick it.

Then there are species that can go both ways, such as:

- Amberjack
- Black sea bass
- Bluefin tuna
- Bonito
- Cobia
- King mackerel

This is important information because far too many opportunities are missed by anglers who don't understand what species could be in an area and why. For example, anglers who only fish a couple of times out of the year and only on party boats might think that cobia, king mackerel, and amberjack are only found well offshore in the blue water, but these species can be found just outside the inlet quite close to shore, even from piers.

The speedy wahoo is rarely found in green water. The author caught this one while fishing aboard the Sunrise *out of Atlantic Beach, North Carolina, with Captain Robert Freeman in command. Photo by Ken Wiles.*

How Light?

Now, a word about how light your tackle should be (spinning, trolling, and fly tackle).

Your tackle should be as light as *safely* possible—this means that your tackle should allow you to get the fish to the boat in a reasonable amount of time without undue effort. In other words, if you have to play the tuna for three hours, you went too light. The jury is still out on exactly how long you can play a fish and still be able to release it alive if you want to, but it is known that the longer you play a fish, the more it is stressed. Stress can kill a fish as fast as a gaff can, so use tackle that allows you to handle the fish quickly without being overly heavy.

The houndfish isn't targeted by many anglers, but this fish of green water can be fun on light tackle and on the fly. It is related to the much smaller needlefish. Photo by Fred Kluge.

Fighting Skills

It is also important to remember that your fighting skills are just as important as the tackle you use. You must be up to your tackle. I have seen many anglers with the right tackle but poor fighting skills kill fish inadvertently because they couldn't handle it properly during the battle. Practice and coaching from those who know how to fight big fish quickly and safely go a long way toward this end.

Good fighting skills also allow you to fish confidently with light tackle in waters where large, powerful game fish such as amberjack and grouper are mixed in with much smaller game fish like gray triggerfish and snapper. It is generally no problem hauling up the triggers and snapper, but when the brute arrives and inhales your squid or cigar minnow, it is a whole new ball game. I have seen many trophy fish lost that simply outfought the angler who was expecting a 3-pound fish but ended up fighting a 30-pound fish. These mixed-bag situations need not be disappointing.

It really is all about tackle and tactics, and you are going to catch far fewer fish if you only understand and know how to use one of the two.

Choosing Offshore Tackle

It is so easy to go so wrong. So where do you start? Begin by selecting only tackle brands that have been around long enough to be proven time and again. The test of time

Large yellowfin tuna can show up at any time in almost any offshore situation. Light tackle and the right fighting techniques can beat such a fish quite quickly. Or, if you or your tackle are lacking, the fight could last more than an hour.

is the best test possible. Tackle manufacturers with names like Shimano, G. Loomis, Thomas and Thomas, Penn, Sage, Harris, Fly Logic, Orvis, L.L. Bean, Lamson, Scott, St. Croix, R.L. Winston, and the like are successful because they have withstood the test of time. Don't ever buy an $8 reel—you will get just what you paid for. Is this to say that a $15 Shimano spinning reel is a bad choice? No. Such a reel is fine for smaller game fish and wasn't designed for 100-pound tuna.

This is where common sense comes into play. Just as you wouldn't put Estelle Getty in the ring with Mike Tyson, you wouldn't put a reel meant for specks up against a 350-pound bluefin.

Sometimes large game fish live side by side with smaller game fish, such as greater amberjack and vermilion snapper. What do you do when the big guy shows up?

The same applies to fly tackle. For the majority of flyfishers, the most important feature of the reel is its drag. The best drags engage instantly and are smooth with no skipping or catching. They can take great heat (through friction) because the disc system is designed to deal with repeated runs from powerful fish. I doubt whether one design system is always better than another, however, because there really are many excellent reel models available that do well under pressure. Nevertheless, I have found that some of the best are the Harris Solitude, Orvis Odyssey and Vortex, Scientific Anglers System 2, and, surprisingly perhaps, the affordable Fly Logic FLP.

Top-of-the-line tackle is of limited use unless you know how to use it.

Remember that line capacity can be a determining factor. You don't want to run out of line. This has happened to me on only one occasion while trolling from a party boat off North Carolina. We were moving from one spot to another and there was a lot of sargassum around. I flipped out a large bucktail jig with a curltail trailer to see if I could pick up a dolphin , wahoo, yellowfin, or king, and sure enough, one of those nailed the jig and began a screaming run in the opposite direction the boat was moving. By the time someone ran up the ladderwell to the wheelhouse to tell the captain to stop the boat so I could fight the fish—about 20 seconds—the fish had emptied my reel and was long gone.

When it comes to rods, think efficiency. The type of graphite used for the rod, its taper, scrim, length, and resulting action are all factors to be considered. No one rod does it all in all situations, and this applies to fly rods, spinning rods, trolling rods, and jigging rods. My two favorite spinning/trolling/jigging rod manufacturers are Penn and Shimano. Fly rod top choices, at least in my experience, include the major manufacturers:

- Scott (truly superior rods)
- St. Croix (one of the best around)
- Winston (lovely rods made by Joe Begin up in Montana)
- Sage (the classic rod favored by Lefty Kreh)

The same tackle used to take the black sea bass would be badly strained against this large amberjack and might fail altogether.

- Thomas and Thomas (very good rods)
- Orvis (a huge selection and all high quality)
- and L.L. Bean (topnotch)

Newcomers to the rod field include three winners:

- Raven (very, very nice)
- Fly Logic (outstanding for so new a rod)
- and the upstart Talon

More so than inshore rods, offshore rods must have the ability to deliver very large, bulky wet flies distances of 80 feet or so, and they must have lifting power to handle game fish that sound and slug it out down deep, such as tuna. You must have faith in the rod at this point, that is for sure. Loading the rod with the weight and strength of a 100-pound yellowfin directly below you that is trying to go as deep as it can is best done if you aren't worried about the rod breaking. If you are afraid to "put

Light spinning tackle means light line, too. Captain George Beckwith of Down East Guide Service used this tackle and 6-pound test monofilament to handle this pretty seatrout. But George has also handled much larger game fish with the same rig, including some very large red drum in Pamlico Sound. The key is knowing how to use what you have and selecting quality tackle to begin with.

Clousers and other flies that can mimic shrimp and baitfish near or on the bottom are terrific for working deep holes in the winter, where trout "hole up" and get lazy during cold spells.

the rod to the fish," then you either have the wrong rod or need to learn how to use the rod properly.

Tactics

As is the case with all fishing, structure is the foundation of what tactics you choose to use. After all, you must first find the fish before you select and employ your tactics, right? Of course.

Structure is anything in the water, on the surface, or on the bottom other than fish and other types of forage. Offshore, this includes sargassum, wrecks, rocks, buoys, boats, debris, bottom variations, and so on. All game fish associate in one way or another with structure, so find the structure and find the fish.

Once the structure is located—let's pick sargassum, for example—begin looking for signs of game fish possibly (or definitely) being in the area. Look beneath the

Troll something that looks tasty close to and through sargassum. If something takes, stop the boat and begin casting.

sargassum. Are there lots of little baitfish and other forage items on the underside? That's a good sign; if there is nothing there, then there are probably few if any game fish around. Are their birds working the sargassum? Good sign. Any sign of feeding activity by game fish?

If you see good signs, use a prospecting fly (a fly that is generally good in a variety of situations), such as a Clouser or Deceiver to see if anything is hungry. Prospecting lures include spoons in gold or silver, splashy jerk baits, and noisy crankbaits. Throw chunks of chum and the occasional live baitfish into the water. Use a Judas stick to whack the surface by the boat to make the game fish think that a feeding frenzy is happening. Whack the fly or lure hard on the water, too, to make the game fish react instantly to it and not take the time to think about whether it is edible or not.

Salt Water Sportsman's *George Poveromo is known as one of the top dolphin specialists in the world. Yes, you too can wrestle large dolphin like this on spinning tackle and even on the fly. Photo courtesy of George Poveromo.*

To quickly see if there are any game fish hanging out in sargassum that is spread out, try trolling through it and around the edges, getting the lure or bait as close as possible to the individual mats.

I don't want to get into any more tactics details here because it is all contained in my book, *Flyfishing Structure* (available from Wilderness Adventures, Inc., at 800-925-3339). This book teaches you everything you need to know about where game fish live and how to catch them. It covers salt and fresh water and a huge array of species.

Planning a Trip

Booking Guides, Airline Tickets, and Hotel Rooms

The first thing you must do when planning a fishing trip is to determine what species of fish you would like to catch and how much money you can afford to spend to do it. Start this process by calling a few guides who have the species you want in their region and asking when the best time would be to come and how much they charge. In the Carolinas, a flyfishing and light-tackle guide is going to run you anywhere from $250/day (wickedly cheap) to about $350/day (more like it). If the guide is charging much more than that—and some of them are—do not patronize him.

Once those details are settled and after you have found what transportation is going to cost and determined that you can afford it, book the guide (be prepared to send him a deposit, although not all guides require one; deposits vary widely and make sure you are clear on his refund policy should you have to cancel or postpone). If you'll be flying, make you airline reservations immediately after booking the guide, along with rental car and hotel reservations. Get preassigned seating when you make your reservations. This is often forgotten and is annoying when you show up and find that you forgot to ask for an aisle seat toward the front of the plane and have been assigned a window seat in the emergency exit row, which of course does not recline.

Plan your trip correctly and this will likely be the result.

It is always best to book a guide first and then make airline reservations because a hefty penalty may have to be paid for canceling or changing a flight should the guide not be available during the days you have scheduled your trip for.

Make sure you get reservation numbers of the hotel and rental car. Verify all reservations before you leave, and verify your airline reservation at least 22 days prior to leaving—if the airline has botched your reservation, it's likely you will be able to get a discounted ticket if you book three weeks prior to departure. Give them your frequent flyer number if you have one. Also, get the full name of every person who books a reservation for you.

When booking a hotel room, check on discounts (the same applies on rental cars). Many hotel chains offer great discounts if you belong to certain organizations such as the American Automobile Association (AAA; join them today if you are not already a member). However, some dates are blacked out, so once in a while you won't be able to get a discount. If you do book with a discount, make sure you have some proof that you qualify for the discount when you check in and verify the price as quoted. If you are a member of a frequent flyer program, book a room at a hotel that gives miles for staying with them (the same goes for rental cars). Your guide might recommend a certain hotel or inn and that is fine, but make sure you are get- ting a discount on the room at the place suggested.

Rental Cars

Rental car prices, unlike most airline ticket prices, can vary quite a bit. I usually rent through Hertz because they screw up reservations less often than many other agencies and I never rent a car through an agency that isn't national. Still, you have to be careful when booking through an agency that you haven't used before, even if that agency is nationwide. For example, on a recent trip to Florida I rented a car in Orlando through Payless, which didn't work out very well. Although they are a nationwide agency, it took 40 minutes for the bus to show up (it showed up after three calls to the agency) that took us to the offsite lot (all the agencies are offsite at the Orlando airport), and then it took us another 30 minutes just to get the vehicle, and we were the first ones in line. The man who rented us the car asked us if we wanted to upgrade slightly for only a few dollars more and we said yes because we liked the vehicle he offered (a sport utility vehicle). We filled out the paperwork and then he went to get the vehicle, but returned without it saying that it had been mis- placed and no others like it were available. You can imagine how the rest of the trans- action went.

Check to see if one of your credit cards or your personal auto insurance covers rental car insurance—this saves money. When you make a reservation, check on dis- counts for members of certain organizations, such as Trout Unlimited, Ducks Unlimited, and so on; some rental agencies give such discounts.

Selecting a Guide or Charter Captain

For our purposes, let's call professional anglers who take people fishing for money guides, even though many are certified captains.

*Quiet backwaters are known to the locals but often missed
by the angler in a rush.*

There are a great many saltwater guides between Currituck and the mouth of the Savannah River. How many is a great many? Well, no one really knows, since the number changes practically on a daily basis. Suffice it to say that you would probably go broke trying to fish with them all, although that is certainly a worthy goal. So, the trick is to find the right guide for you, and that means finding a guide who is personable (most are) and knows how to find the fish you would like to catch in the way you would like to catch them, i.e., red drum on the flats, Spanish mackerel off the capes, tarpon in the channels, specks in the river, and so on. Whereas the guides and outfitters listed in this book are all professionals, you might hire a guide who isn't listed herein, and you have to do your homework if you are to increase your chances of a good trip.

Guides are funny and no two are alike. I like asking guides what they think about another guide in their area because sometimes I get the oddest responses. For example, recently I was speaking with a guide and I asked him about another guide I know who works the same water. He replied that the guide I asked about was brand new to guiding, having only been at it for a year. He didn't say that his competition was a bad guide, mind you; only that he was new, the implication (often an inaccurate one) being that a new guide was to be avoided because he is inexperienced. When I told the man that he was mistaken and that I had been fishing with the "new" guide for several years and always had a good trip (drum up to 34 pounds), the fellow really started backpedaling. This is a clear sign of a guide worth avoiding.

Whenever I am going to be fishing in an area where I don't know any guides personally, I start by asking friends and fellow writers if they can recommend anyone in the area. If they can't, I make some cold calls to guides who run ads in magazines, such as *Fly Fishing in Salt Waters*, *Salt Water Sportsman*, *Sport Fishing*, and *Fly Fisherman*. When I get a guide on the phone, I ask him if he knows so and so, whose name I picked from an ad in the same magazine. If that guide slams the other guide in any way, I end the conversation without booking him. I suggest you do the same.

Guides with whom you are unfamiliar should be asked for references, and you should call several of those references. Questions that should be asked include:

- Did you enjoy the trip?
- Was the guide on time?
- Was the guide's boat clean and set up properly for flyfishing and light tackle (recessed cleats, etc.)
- Did the guide ask about your accommodations?
- Did he recommend any restaurants?
- Did he aggressively seek fish?
- Were those fish the species you were primarily interested in, or did the guide seem to have his own agenda?
- Did he ask for any money up front other than for a booking deposit at the time you booked him? If he asks for payment in full prior to leaving the dock, do not go out with him because he suspects that he isn't going to find you any fish and he is worried that you are going to stiff him.
- Was lunch provided? Drinks? The guide should make clear what food and drinks you are expected to provide and what will provide before you show up at the dock.
- Did he ask about your experience level?
- Did he position the boat so that you were able to make the easiest possible cast to the fish?
- Was he treated with respect by other guides?
- Was he clearly safety conscious?
- Did he offer to help with your casting if you were in need of help?
- Did he have a selection of flies and lures that he favored for that area? Or did he simply suggest flies and lures you had along?
- Was his tackle in excellent condition and did he have plenty of it?
- Did he spot more fish than you?
- Did he have an obvious knowledge of the environment?
- Did he insult other anglers he had taken out or other guides he knows?
- Did he have rain gear along? Extra sunglasses, film, band aids, and so on?
- When you returned home, did he call or drop you a line to remark on your trip?

These are just some of the questions you should ask. You can also check with the local Better Business Bureau and Coast Guard to see if any complaints have been lodged against him.

Checklist

Here is a list of things that you may want to bring with you when fishing saltwaters in the Carolinas and Georgia. Bring this book with you when you go on each trip and use a pencil to check off each item as you pack it. Remember that there will be certain special items you want to take that aren't on this list.

Before you depart, make sure you leave your itinerary, location (including your hotel, lodge, etc.), and useful phone numbers with someone at home who might need to contact you, such as your Labrador.

Tackle

- ____ Rod(s)
- ____ Reel(s)
- ____ Extra spools
- ____ Extra line(s)
- ____ Extra backing
- ____ Flies/lures
- ____ Leaders
- ____ Tippet
- ____ Hook removers
- ____ Knot tool
- ____ Nippers
- ____ Magnifying glass
- ____ Scissors
- ____ Waders/hippers
- ____ Vest/chest pack
- ____ Net
- ____ Rod tube(s)
- ____ Chest/hat light
- ____ Hook file
- ____ Leader straightener
- ____ Wader patches
- ____ Booties
- ____ Leader stretcher
- ____ Stripping basket

Clothing

- ____ Fishing pants
- ____ Fishing shorts
- ____ Fishing shirts
- ____ Waders/hippers
- ____ Vest/chest pack
- ____ Booties
- ____ Other fishing footwear
- ____ Hat
- ____ Sunglasses

Miscellaneous

- ____ Camera
- ____ Film
- ____ Pocketknife
- ____ First aid kit
- ____ Sunblock
- ____ Rags
- ____ Maps
- ____ Important phone numbers
- ____ Itinerary and reservations

The Self-guided Trip

Experienced anglers shouldn't automatically shy away from a self-guided trip, even to completely new areas. Such trips are often fun and very enlightening. Then again, you might die on the trip because of some heinous mistake you made, so you make the call.

But seriously folks, self-guided trips can be very rewarding if you just ask questions and follow up on things before you leave. Here's how.

Call the local marinas and bait and tackle shops about recent fishing conditions and general conditions to expect during the time you are there.

Call AAA if you are a member and get their travel guides for the state/region. These are updated all the time and contain a lot of information. Call the city halls in the area as well to gather information.

Contact the Environmental Protection Agency (EPA) to see if there have been any serious environmental problems in the region recently. This is important because accidents happen, such as the time one of North Carolina's 6,000 corporate hog farms spilled tens of millions of gallons of hog waste into the New River. No, as a matter of fact that wasn't a pleasant sight, nor smell. And *Pfiesteria* could be a problem, too, so check on it. Now, two hurricanes back to back in 1999 have destroyed hundreds of such lagoons. The destruction of and damage to coastal waters has been called "catastrophic;" only time will tell.

The Often Forgotten and Sorely Missed

One of the most often forgotten items are sunglasses. These crucial items help you find fish, provided they are high quality and offer 100% ultraviolet protection and are 100% polarized. Three excellent brands are Action Optics, Bollé, and Costa Del Mar, which can cut glare like no other sunglasses. Whatever you buy, don't forget them!

State Agencies and Other Resources

North Carolina Department of Environment and Natural Resources

Division of Marine Fisheries
Headquarters
3441 Arendell Street
Morehead City, NC 28557
252-726-7021

South Carolina Department of Natural Resources

Marine Resources Division

Headquarters
217 Ft. Johnson Road
P.O. Box 12559
Charleston, SC 29412
843-762-5000

Bluffton Office
Waddell Mariculture Center
P.O. Box 809, Sawmill Creek Road
Bluffton, SC 29910
843-837-3795

Georgia Department of Natural Resources

Wildlife Resources Division / Law Enforcement Section

Headquarters
2070 US Highway 278 SE
Social Circle, GA 30025
770-918-6408

Region VII (Coastal)
One Conservation Way
Brunswick, GA 31520
912-264-7237

Map Sources

The best source available, in my opinion, for maps that show the most important land and coastal features is Delorme. They make the very popular and extremely useful *Atlas and Gazetteers* that are available in many places.

DeLorme
P.O. Box 298
Yarmouth, ME 04096
207-846-7000

Chart Sources

Maptech sells NOAA charts (including the new photocharts) and software.
Maptech
888-839-5551
Website: www.maptech.com
E-mail: marinesales@maptech.com

Also check out:
Seastore at www.seastore.com

Navigation
Website: www.safenav.com

Boats, Navigation, and Safety

Boats and Boating Safety for the Southeast Coast

Spend a day along the Southeast coast and you will see all manner of fishing vessels, ranging from kayaks to big offshore cruisers. However, what you will see the most are center consoles, skiffs, and cuddy cabins. The reason these types of boats are so abundant is that they are more affordable than larger boats designed for offshore use and they can get into shallower water without the hull finding the bottom. Also, these boats are very versatile, easy to operate safely and maintain, and don't kill you at the gas pump.

Center Consoles

Of all the boat designs I have experienced while fishing, the center console is the most flexible. They take their name from the fact that the control console is located amidships, usually a bit more aft than dead center lengthwise. What this setup allows is excellent visibility and the ability for anglers to easily move around the boat, which comes in very handy when fighting something like a tarpon, cobia, yellowfin, king, or false albacore.

Center consoles run from 14 feet or so well into the 30-foot range, so how much to spend depends on how many banks you feel you can safely rob. All kinds of outboards are used on these boats, with Evinrude, Johnson, Mercury, Yamaha, and Honda all being popular. I am especially impressed with the Yamaha outboards, particularly when run on such extremely high quality boats as those made by John Stamas of Stamas Yachts (the Stamas Tarpon 270 is a world-class center console) and Donnie Jones of Jones Brothers Marine (their Cape Fisherman Series is unsurpassed).

Skiffs

These are flat-bottomed boats meant for inshore and calm near-shore waters. Especially well suited for working the Intracoastal Waterway and adjoining waters, such as rivers and creeks, skiffs from 12 to more than 20 feet are available. Many are wide and very stable in protected waters. Center-console skiffs are seen with great regularity because of their stability as well as being very affordable and easy to maintain. Two of the most common makes are Carolina Skiff and Jones Brothers.

Cuddy Cabins

Cuddies are also popular and are made by many manufacturers. Although a bit more expensive, generally speaking, than a center console of the same length, cuddy cabins (walkarounds, in particular, which are designed to allow someone to move from aft to forward along a narrow walkway lining both sides of the cabin) do offer a lot of space aft for fighting fish and moving about. They also have the advantage of a protected space, usually equipped with a forward V berth(in the bow), and some have marine heads and even little galleys. One drawback is that they need more water, so the shallowest waters can't be reached by them. Sea Ray makes some nice ones.

Navigation and Safety

Southeastern saltwaters have taken more than their fair share of boats and ships to their respective graves, with the Outer Banks being somewhat infamous for the destruction of innumerable vessels of all shapes, sizes, and purposes. I won't turn this guidebook into a boating safety manual, but a few important points do need to be made here regarding safety.

The fact is that the more you venture out onto the water in boats, the greater the chances of your having an accident or breakdown. Remember, to the other guy, you are the other guy. Given this, you need to plan ahead so that you are prepared for most eventualities.

Learning Marine Navigation

To learn maritime Rules of the Road, I highly recommend the U.S. Coast Guard Auxiliary's Boating Skills and Seamanship Course. This is a fun, inexpensive, and very educational course that teaches things that the vast majority of recreational boaters do not know. It will help keep you alive. The course includes reading buoys and other markers, how to tell which direction another vessel is traveling at night by reading lights, navigation, how to read charts, determining who has the right of way, and so on.

In any case, the best way to operate a boat is to err on the side of caution. If you see another boat coming and you have the right of way, never, never assume that the other guy sees you and knows that he has to give way. In fact, assume that he is a moron, has no idea that you are there, and is surely going to ram you unless you get out of his way. This attitude will help keep you alive.

Safety Equipment

The Coast Guard can give you a detailed list of safety equipment you must have and should have on board, but to start make sure that you have:

1. Coast Guard certified personal flotation devices (PFDs), one for each person on board and preferably two or three extras.
2. A fire extinguisher rated for use on fuels and electrical equipment.
3. A horn for use in fog and at night.
4. A bright flashlight.
5. Extra dry clothing.
6. Fresh water.
7. A complete first aid kit.
8. A marine band radio.
9. Charts of the area.
10. A cellular telephone.
11. Binoculars.

12. Bullhorn.
13. Extra lines (ropes for you landlubbers) in good condition.
14. Sea anchor.
15. Bottom anchor (there are different designs for different bottoms and sizes of vessels).
16. Extra fuel.
17. Tools (spark plug wrench, adjustable wrench, lever, pliers, and so on for working on a motor).
18. Sunscreen.
19. Wet weather gear (full).
20. Extra personal medications.

And this list is just for starters.

General Safety Guidelines

Following are some general safety guidelines that will help keep you out of trouble. The bottom line, however, is that you should always err on the side of caution. If you do that, the chances are good that you will never be faced with a serious problem while boating.

Assume the other guy is dangerous and unpredictable. The vast majority of boating accidents are caused by operator error. If you assume that every other boater has the potential for causing an extremely dangerous situation with little or no warning, you will likely stay afloat and out of harm's way longer.

• When in doubt, give way. In other words, even if you know that you legally have the right of way, if you think or suspect for even a moment that another boater may not understand this or may not care, give way to him.

• Never drink alcoholic beverages while operating a boat and never allow those in your boat to drink excessively. Need I say more?

• Keep an eye on the weather at all times—Mother Nature can get cranky very quickly, and she does not suffer fools gladly. Before you put to sea, get a weather forecast and monitor the local weather channel on your marine radio.

• Keep your boat shipshape at all times with the best possible safety and navigation equipment you can afford. This should include: personal flotation devices for everyone on board, a fire extinguisher, a whistle, an air horn, a marine radio, a heavy duty flashlight with extra batteries, good ropes (at least 100 feet), foul weather gear, a good anchor, a sea anchor, a cellular phone (charged), a GPS unit (know how to use it, too), fresh water, a complete first aid kit, wool blankets (for keeping a person in shock warm or for use if it gets cold), extra eyeglasses if you wear them, a flare gun, plenty of fuel, spare spark plugs and a plug wrench, charts, and so on. Remember: the item you leave behind is the item you will need the most to save your life and your vessel. Count on it.

• Be watchful at all times.

• If the inlet looks too rough to get through, it is. Stand off and wait for things to settle down. Just because one fool runs the inlet and makes it doesn't mean you can too.

- If you are truly lost and out of sight of land, stop. This also applies to running in dense fog. Use your radio or cell phone to get help from other boaters or the Coast Guard. If you see a buoy, stay near it and call the Coast Guard to assist you if you feel the need. Do not tie up to the buoy since this can be not only illegal but dangerous.
- Learn every nuance of your vessel, including its hydraulics, mechanics, and electronics.
- If you are unfamiliar with the waters within sight of land, slow down and use caution —there may be obstructions or shallows in the area.
- Know every symbol on your charts. The illustrations in this section will help.
- Spend a lot of time in your vessel—the more time you spend, the better you will know your boat's idiosyncracies. If you don't know your boat well enough, you will eventually put it abeam in an inlet or other tall water and capsize or be swamped. This is not good, folks.
- Before you cut back on the throttle, look aft; there may be another boater riding your stern who isn't able to stop in time to avoid a collision. Likewise, stay off the other boater's aft.
- Watch out for lunatics operating personal watercraft, i.e., those jet-ski things. Many of the people operating these water rockets are extremely careless and, like many boat operators, are drunk.
- Finally, always wear a PFD while running at high speed and know how to swim well. You might be surprised to learn how many boaters can't swim a lick.

If you follow the aforementioned rules and take the Coast Guard Auxiliary's Boating Skills and Seamanship Course, your time on the Southeast's coastal waters will be all the more fun and safe.

Danger Areas

The sea will attempt to kill you if you act foolishly in general, head out unprepared, drink lots of alcohol while boating, or fail to pay attention and think defensively. For instance, chart features don't always tell the whole story: an inlet that is flat at 7:00AM can be stacked with 10-foot rollers at 8:00AM; shoals (try running onto a rocky shoal at 20 knots some time); debris (flotsam and jetsam that can rip your lower unit off or go straight through the hull); sandbars (driving your boat up onto a sand bar at full throttle isn't funny). And then there are the squalls and water spouts with minds of their own (and they do have minds, I tell you). Those who ignore safety, common sense, and preparation at sea often pay with their lives.

AIDS TO NAVIGATION ON NAVIGABLE WATERWAYS
except Western Rivers and Intracoastal Waterway

LATERAL SYSTEM AS SEEN ENTERING FROM SEAWARD

PORT SIDE
ODD NUMBERED AIDS
GREEN OR WHITE LIGHTS

FIXED
FLASHING
OCCULTING
QUICK FLASHING
EQ INT

LIGHTED BUOY
"9"
Fl G 4sec
Ra Ref

CAN
C"7"
Ra Ref

SG

DAYMARKS
G "I"
RG

MID CHANNEL
NO NUMBERS—MAY BE LETTERED
WHITE LIGHT ONLY

MORSE CODE
Mo(A)

CAN
BW
C"T"
Ra Ref

LIGHTED
BW"N"
Mo (A)
Ra Ref

NUN
BW
N"B"
Ra Ref

MB
BW
"A"
DAYMARK

JUNCTION
MARK JUNCTION AND OBSTRUCTIONS
NO NUMBERS—MAY BE LETTERED
INTERRUPTED QUICK FLASHING

WHITE OR GREEN | WHITE OR RED

RB"M"
IQk Fl G
Ra Ref

LIGHTED
RB"D"
IQk Fl R
Ra Ref

CAN
PREFERRED
CHANNEL TO
STARBOARD
TOPMOST BAND
BLACK
RB
C"N"
Ra Ref

NUN
PREFERRED
CHANNEL TO
PORT
TOPMOST BAND
RED
RB
N"L"
Ra Ref

JG
A
RG
"A"

B
RG
"B"

STARBOARD SIDE
EVEN NUMBERED AIDS
RED OR WHITE LIGHTS

RED
FLASHING
OCCULTING
QUICK FLASHING
EQ INT
GROUP FLASHING (2)

LIGHTED BUOY
R"8"
Fl R 4sec
Ra Ref

NUN
R
N"6"
Ra Ref

DAYMARK
TR
R "2"

BUOYS HAVING NO LATERAL SIGNIFICANCE—ALL WATERS

SPECIAL
PURPOSE
W Or
C
Ra Ref

QUARANTINE
ANCHORAGE
Y
C
Ra Ref

SHAPE HAS NO SIGNIFICANCE
NO NUMBERS—MAY BE LETTERED
MAY BE LIGHTED
ANY COLOR LIGHT EXCEPT
RED OR GREEN

FIXED
FLASHING
OCCULTING

ANCHORAGE
W.
C"N"
Ra Ref

FISH NET
AREA
BW
C
Ra Ref

DREDGING
GW
C
Ra Ref

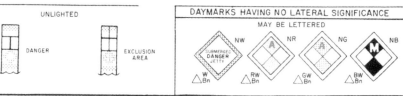

UNLIGHTED

DANGER

EXCLUSION
AREA

DAYMARKS HAVING NO LATERAL SIGNIFICANCE
MAY BE LETTERED

SUBMERGED
DANGER
JETTY
W
Bn
NW

A
RW
Bn
NR

A
GW
Bn
NG

M
BW
Bn
NB

Buoys and Beacons

#	Symbol	Description	#	Symbol	Description
1	.	Position of buoy	17	RB RB	Bifurcation buoy (RBHB)
2		Light buoy	18	RB RB	Junction buoy (RBHB)
3	BELL	Bell buoy	19	RB RB	Isolated danger buoy (RBHB)
3a	GONG	Gong buoy	20	RB G	Wreck buoy (RBHB or G)
4	WHIS	Whistle buoy	20a	RB G	Obstruction buoy (RBHB or G)
5	C	Can or Cylindrical buoy	21	Tel	Telegraph-cable buoy
6	N	Nun or Conical buoy	22		Mooring buoy (colors of mooring buoys never carried)
7	SP	Spherical buoy	22a		Mooring
8	S	Spar buoy	22b	Tel	Mooring buoy with telegraphic communications
†8a	P	Pillar or Spindle buoy	22c	T	Mooring buoy with telephonic communications
9		Buoy with topmark (ball) (see L-70)	23		Warping buoy
10		Barrel or Ton buoy	24	Y	Quarantine buoy
(La)		Color unknown	†24a		Practice area buoy
(Lb)	FLOAT	Float	25	Explos Anch	Explosive anchorage buoy
12	FLOAT	Lightfloat	25a	AERO	Aeronautical anchorage buoy
13		Outer or Landfall buoy	26	Deviation	Compass adjustment buoy
14	BW	Fairway buoy (BWVS)	27	BW	Fish trap (area) buoy (BWHB)
14a	BW	Mid-channel buoy (BWVS)	27a		Spoil ground buoy
†15	R "2" R "2"	Starboard-hand buoy (entering from seaward)	†28	W	Anchorage buoy (marks limits)
16	"1"	Port-hand buoy (entering from seaward)	†29	Priv maintd	Private aid to navigation (buoy) (maintained by private interests, use with caution)

Dangers

1 Rock which does not cover (elevation above MHW)	**11** Wreck showing any portion of hull or superstructure (above sounding datum)	**27** Obstr Obstruction
		28 Wreck (See O-11 to 16)
2 Rock which covers and uncovers, with height in feet above chart (sounding) datum	**12** Masts Wreck with only masts visible (above sounding datum)	**29** Wreckage Wks Wreckage
	13 Old symbols for wrecks	**29a** Wreck remains (dangerous only for anchoring)
	13a Wreck always partially submerged	**30** Subm piles Submerged piling (See H-9, L-59)
3 Rock awash at the level of chart (sounding) datum		
When rock of O-2 or O-3 is considered a danger to navigation	**†14** Sunken wreck dangerous to surface navigation (less than 11 fathoms over wreck) (See O-6a)	**30a** Snags Stumps Snags; Submerged stumps (See L-59)
†4 Sunken rock dangerous to surface navigation	**15** Wk Wreck over which depth is known	**31** Lesser depth possible
		32 Uncov Dries
		33 Cov Covers (See O-2, 10)
	†15a Wk Wreck with depth cleared by wire drag	**34** Uncov Uncovers (See O-2, 10)
5 Rk Shoal sounding on isolated rock (replaces symbol)	**16** Sunken wreck, not dangerous to surface navigation	**35** Rep (1958) Reported (with date) Eagle Rk (rep 1958) Reported (with name and date)
†6 Sunken rock not dangerous to surface navigation (more than 11 fathoms over rock)	**17** Foul Foul ground	**36** Discol Discolored (See O-9)
		37 Isolated danger
6a Rk Wk Obstr Sunken danger with depth cleared by wire drag (in feet or fathoms)	**18** Tide Rips Overfalls or Tide rips *Symbol used only in small areas*	**†38** Limiting danger line
7 Reef Reef of unknown extent	**19** Eddies Eddies *Symbol used only in small areas*	**39** rky Limit of rocky area
	20 Kelp Kelp, Seaweed *Symbol used only in small areas*	**41** P A Position approximate
		42 P D Position doubtful
8 Sub Vol Submarine volcano	**21** Bk Bank	**43** E D Existence doubtful
	22 Shl Shoal	**44** P Pos Position
	23 Rf Reef	**45** D Doubtful
9 Discol Water Discolored water	**23a** Ridge	**†46** Unexamined
	24 Le Ledge	**(Oa)** Subm Crib Crib (above water) Crib
10 Coral Co Co Coral reef, detached (uncovers at sounding datum)	**25** Breakers (See A-12)	**(Ob)** Platform (lighted) HORN Offshore platform (unnamed)
Coral or Rocky reef, covered at sounding datum (See A-11d, 11g)	**26** Sunken rock (depth unknown) When rock is considered a danger to navigation	**(Oc)** Hazel (lighted) HORN Offshore platform (named)

Light Symbols and Their Meanings		
Symbol	**Meaning**	**Description**
F	Fixed	A continuous, steady light.
F Fl	Fixed and flashing	A fixed light at regular intervals by a flash of greater brilliance.
F GP Fl	Fixed and group flashing	A fixed light varied at regular intervals by groups of 2 or more flashes of greater brilliance.
Fl	Flashing	A single flash showing at regular intervals, the duration of light always less than the duration of darkness.
Gp Fl	Group flashing	Groups of 2 or more flashes showing at regular intervals.
Qk Fl	Quick flashing	Shows not less than 60 flashes per minute.
I Qk Fl	Interrupted quick flashing	Shows quick flashes for about 5 seconds followed by a dark period of about 5 seconds.
E Int	Equal interval	Duration of light equal to that of darkness.
Occ	Occulting	A light totally eclipsed at regular intervals, the duration of light always equal to or greater than the duration of darkness.
Gp Occ	Group occulting	A light with a group of 2 or more eclipses at regular intervals.

Flyfishing and Light Tackle

The flyfishing and light tackle selected for use in the Southeast's saltwaters plays an important role in success. Reels, rods, lines, and even leaders are continually evolving, with new and improved products showing up on the market seemingly daily. Outdoor writers like me are fortunate to have an "in" within the industry, which allows us to test new products as they become available. Yes, we are basically prostitutes at heart, but most of us test the gear honestly and report the same way.

In any case, what follows are my recommendations based on *my* experiences. In the end, you should take what I say and consider it, but when you do reach for your wallet (or pocketbook), you should buy the product that *you* like best. After all, I am not going to be using it; you are. If I didn't recommend it but you like it, then have at it. I hope you catch more fish with it than you ever thought possible.

FLYFISHING TACKLE

This section covers fly rods and reels by manufacturer, with both basic and specific information that might be useful when selecting fly tackle.

Fly Rods

I have a couple dozen or so fly rods from various manufacturers, such as Scott (always a favorite; my Labrador, Rocky the Deranged Lunatic, recently bit my Scott STS right in half, but Scott replaced it at no charge), Sage (certainly topnotch and highly respected), Orvis (beautiful things that could pass for good artwork), Elkhorn (a solid rod made by Tom Clinkenbeard), L.L. Bean (more people should own Bean fly rods), St. Croix (very good rods that are less expensive than others of like quality), R.L. Winston (absolutely gorgeous things that all other rods aspire to be like), Raven (very good rods with class), Fly Logic (for a new series of rods, these are very good indeed), Talon (an upstart company that should do well), G. Loomis (good utility rods), J.C. Rods (great custom-made rods), and others.

From time to time I break one, and I cry. I cry because my fly rods are more like works of art to me than tools of my trade. Of course, I don't cry for long, since all my rods come with good guarantees. For example, if I were to lay one of my Scott, Orvis, Sage, Winston, or other good rods beneath a launching space shuttle and the rod were to be melted, I could send the goo back to the factory with an explanation of what happened, and they would send me a new one, perhaps even with an apology for their rod not standing up to the heat. I just love those guys!

But just because I have a fairly serious collection of fly rods doesn't mean that you have to have a bunch, too, although you certainly deserve to. The truth is, you can flyfish for all the species listed in this book with four, perhaps three fly rods, those being an 8-weight, 9-weight, and a 12-weight. However, you will most likely find that a tip-flex 8- or 9-weight, a midflex 8- or 9-weight, and a midflex 12-weight will cover a huge array of flyfishing situations. Of course, if you want to get into game fish that far fewer flyfishers target, such as croakers and ladyfish, a midflex 6/7-weight can be just the ticket (maybe an 8-weight for the ladyfish). The only reason I have so many rods is because I am a glutton.

Graphite
All good saltwater rods are made of graphite, which is a soft carbon that is flexible but also remarkably strong. The degree of stiffness in a graphite fly rod is called the rod's *modulus*—generally speaking, the higher the modulus, the stiffer and stronger the rod—and stiffness and taper dictate how the rod performs (56 million modulus is high and 57 million is very high). This information should play a crucial role in rod selection.

Taper
One of the most common mistakes a novice or uninformed flyfisher makes when selecting a rod is not considering the rod's taper. For example, she might pick up an 8-weight, 9-foot rod that says it is made of 56 million modulus graphite and wiggle it a few times in the shop, and think, Hey, I like this rod. Then she gets it out on the water and loads the rod to deliver a bulky fly in to a 12-knot wind and her cast floats out 30 feet. As she strips in to recast, a false albacore grabs her fly and takes off for Madrid, emptying the reel of its contents or popping the leader should she try to apply serious pressure. The problem is often the rod's taper, which she learned too late gave the rod a midflex, thus not generating enough line speed for the conditions and fly used and not being nervy enough to turn the albacore.

Taper refers to how the rod's diameter is reduced from directly in front of the grip to the tiptop. An almost imperceptible difference in taper can make a noticeable difference in performance. When buying a fly rod, don't just wiggle it around a few times—cast it with a variety of flies under assorted conditions. Try different lines, too. (Good fly shops let you do all this. The performance differences between some lines can be staggering. For example, I've found that Orvis' Wonderline casts farther with less effort than all other lines.) Talk to a knowledgeable member of the shop's staff or, if buying from a catalog, call the company.

Let's take a look at various brands and models of rods so that you can make the right selection the first time around.

The Orvis Company
Orvis, which has been around since 1856, has made some major changes in much of their rod line-up since they began refining their Trident Series. Orvis upped the ante considerably when they introduced these rods, which are constructed using technology developed and employed in the building of the U.S. Navy's Trident submarines. What they gleaned from the subs was damping technology. Damping is the reduction of vibration, and vibration has been a problem with fly rods for as long as there have been fly rods. The longer a rod vibrates as it unloads (either in the back cast or fore cast), the more vibration (wiggle) is transmitted into the line. Wiggles in

a line that is being cast increases a loss in efficiency in the form of reduced possible distance and reduced accuracy, and distance and accuracy can be two absolutely crucial factors when fishing the waters covered in this book. The Trident TL rods, which are the second generation of Trident rods, substantially reduce vibration and therefore allow for a much improved cast.

It takes a little while to get used to a Trident TL rod when casting one for the first time since most flyfishers have become accustomed to vibration and have adapted to it during the casting stroke. However, after adapting to this rod, the feel and results make it worthwhile. They are surprisingly light for the power they generate, i.e., a Trident TL 908-4, which is a 9-foot, 8-weight, 4-piece, tip-flex rod, weighs only 5 ounces.

There are far too many Trident rods to discuss here (43 models or so), but I make some suggestions in Chapter 2. Remember, however, that you should be the one who picks the rod because of what you like about it, not what I say I like. My suggestions should only be a starting point in the selection process. This advice applies to every rod I recommend in this chapter.

Scott High Performance Fly Rods

Scott makes some of the very best fly rods in the world, and I have used them extensively. Besides being very high quality rods, Scott rods come with an uncondi-tional lifetime warranty, and that is certainly a consideration every flyfisher should think about. As I mentioned earlier, when my Labrador, Rocky the Socially Unaccept-able, ate one of my Scott rods recently, it was replaced quickly and without any shouting or threats of serious bodily harm.

Besides the great warranty and high quality, Scott rods are premium rods because of their internal ferrules (the rod bends right through the ferrule, which makes it stronger) and more than 100 models to choose from. Their tapers are excel-lent, too, because Scott rods are made with lay-ups designed specifically for a certain model and weight of a rod. This painstaking process results in rods that are almost custom made.

Scott's Eclipse Series is in such demand that the factory can hardly keep up. Introduced in 1998, Eclipse rods are constructed with soft tips and medium-fast tapers, high-modulus graphite, and a butt section that can put tremendous pressure on a fish. These are critical features when dealing with tarpon, snook, stripers, blues, and tripletail, to name a few tough guys.

St. Croix Rod

In north central Minnesota, there are many St. Croix rods in better tackle shops—mostly spinning and bait casting rods and far fewer fly rods. This is because St. Croix was first known as a maker of high quality muskie and pike rods in these parts. However, over the years, and especially since flyfishing took off in the 1980s, more and more flyfishers are using these excellent rods that cost quite a bit less than comparable rods from other manufacturers. For example, their top-of-the-line

Legend Ultra UF9010 is a 9-foot, 10-weight rocket launcher that weighs in at just over 4½ ounces and costs $270. This is a marvelous midsized tarpon and yellowfin rod that can shoot a bulky fly straight into a 15-knot wind with weird ease. It is certainly the equal to some makers' rods that run twice that price. St. Croix's UF908 is a 9-foot, 8-weight that I use a great deal on redfish and seatrout and also costs $270. St. Croix's IFT9067 is a 9-foot, 6/7-weight that is perfect for croakers, small jacks, and ladyfish when there isn't much of a breeze ($150).

R.L. Winston Rod Company

R.L. Winston is synonymous with very high quality fly rods. The company has been around for nearly seven decades and began making graphite fly rods in 1975. It didn't take long for flyfishers to realize that a Winston fly rod built by Joe Begin is not only beautiful to behold but performs extremely well on the water. Still, R.L. Winston is much better known as a manufacturer of fly rods for trout than anything else, and they aren't seen anywhere near as often on the salt as Sage, Orvis, Penn, Scott, and the like. This is a shame, because Winston's saltwater rod line (XDLT Series) is top shelf. The butt is beefy, the tip stiff, and the action quite fast for handling large flies in the wind. I suspect that more and more Winston fly rods will be see on saltwater in the coming few years.

Penn

The name Penn has long been associated with saltwater tackle for nearly seven decades, and although Penn is certainly best known for its International Series of trolling reels, it has been gaining some ground in the flyfishing field recently. Still, the company isn't putting all that much effort into getting the word out that its fly rods are pretty darn good.

Penn now offers two lines of fly rods: the Gold Series and Silver Series, with the latter being less expensive. For inshore game fish, such as specks and puppy drum, the Silvers are fine. However, go with the Gold Series when after more serious game fish, such as large crevalle jacks and dolphin.

Salt Water Sportsman's Mark Sosin uses Penn fly tackle extensively. A man with Mark's qualifications and reputation can pretty much get sponsored by any tackle company he wants, but Mark went with Penn and tells me privately that Penn tackle is everything it is cracked up to be.

Sage

Sage sells staggering numbers of fly rods because of its reputation over the years for making fast, powerful saltwater rods that receive praise and honest endorsements from such famous flyfishers as Lefty Kreh. Now, Lefty can go with any fly rod manufacturer he wants, but he likes Sage. That should tell you something.

Based on Bainbridge Island in Washington, Sage has two series of rods that can work in saltwater, the RPL+ and RPLXi, and I use them both. However, the RPLXi is specifically designed for saltwater use and has features that make it very durable and useful under a variety of situations, such as a narrow taper and a strong butt. These rods are like fly cannons.

Raven

Many flyfishers haven't even heard of Raven, but I have a Raven rod and like it immensely. They are made of the highest quality components and are built with great pride. Raven knows it will never be a Sage or Orvis or Scott but has carved out a niche, and I suspect more of them will be seen on saltwater in the future.

Talon

Little Talon is barely a blip on the radar screen but is slowly getting noticed. I have two of Talon's lighter rods and like them and expect to go heavier in the future. Try one out.

Thomas and Thomas

The Mercedes of fly rods, Thomas and Thomas has earned a wonderful reputation for making absolutely flawless rods. I have only fished them occasionally and do not own one, but hope to in the future. The T&T rods I have used cast beautifully and otherwise performed perfectly.

G. Loomis

I own one G. Loomis rod and have found it to be well suited for general near-shore and offshore use. It develops pretty good line speed without all that much effort and can handle a good number of feisty game fish. On false albacore it does very well.

J.C. Rods

Although not well known, J.C. Rods has been crafting quality fly rods for more than 30 years. Master rod builder John Christlieb designs and constructs very good rods in both graphite and fiberglass. His line includes rods up to 12-weight, and he makes two 4-piece travel rods (an 8-weight and a 9-weight, both 9 feet long).

One might expect to pay quite a bit more than for these rods, but John's top-end rod is only $299.

Fly Reels

New fly reels are popping up on the market with great regularity. Newer companies like C.A. Harris and Fly Logic offer dependable reels for considerably less than many other manufacturers, which makes saltwater flyfishing more affordable for everyone. And old standby reels, such as Scientific Anglers, are perfectly good reels that don't necessitate a second job. Is this to say that an Abel, Orvis, or Billy Pate reel that costs several hundred dollars isn't worth the money? Absolutely not, because they are. What this means is that you don't have to empty your savings account to get a good reel. You can even buy an excellent Orvis saltwater reel with a disc drag for

$135. I have used just such a reel for several years and have beaten it senseless, but it has yet to fail me.

Unfortunately, from time to time a good reel will go out of production for no good reason, at least from the perspective of the flyfisher. For example, Sage used to make the Sage 5000 series of reels, which were very good, but stopped making them recently to focus entirely on rods. Nevertheless, Sage 5000 reels can be found on internet flyfishing auction sites and flyfishing resale sites.

Drags

Without question, the most important primary feature of any reel designed for use in saltwater is the drag system. Many, if not most, of the fish caught on the Southeast coast will have the ability to engage a drag, and many of these fish do so with gusto. Don't expect to efficiently fight a tarpon, giant bull red, yellowfin, or wahoo with a reel that has a cheesy drag, because the drag will melt, fry, fuse, explode, implode, have a stroke, crap out, burn up, or any of the other colorful adjectives that flyfishing writers have used over the years to describe what happens to a bad drag when a mean fish gets hold of it. If your reel can't stop a 40-pound jack in the middle of Charleston Harbor, get another reel. Save yourself the heartache and buy reels with excellent drags. You'll thank me later.

The better saltwater reels have disc drags, many of which are made of cork, but some newer models now feature Teflon. Of particular importance is the drag's ability to start up smoothly, thus protecting the tippet. A drag that sticks just prior to engaging is going to lose fish, especially such fish as drum, tarpon, jacks, and bluefish, which make several runs during the course of a fight.

Fly Logic

I first met Rex Bledsoe, Fly Logic's general manager, in Denver at a flyfishing trade show. We struck up a conversation at the Fly Logic booth, where he told me about Fly Logic reels, which were fairly new to the market. I hadn't fished one before but ended up leaving with one to test on a scheduled trip to Costa Rica and Belize. I was skeptical of the drag's ability to put the brakes on tarpon in Belize and bonito in Costa Rica at only $119. I needn't have been concerned.

The tarpon I caught while fishing out of the venerable Belize River Lodge and the many bonito I caught while a guest at the Golfito Sailfish Rancho all failed to kill the drag. In fact, the drag never even skipped. With plenty of line and backing capacity and a nice light weight, the Fly Logic Premium reel is a super choice in less-than-expensive reels that I strongly recommend. Since those tarpon and bonito, I have put trevally, red drum, tripletail, and several other species on the reel and have never had a problem.

C.A. Harris

The Harris Solitude fly reel is one of the best reels available, and it isn't very expensive considering the reel's quality, which is odd for a reel of this caliber. I seldom venture into saltwater without my Solitude IV, and I have put it up against some serious game fish in the Southeast. I think what I like most about it is the drag, which combines the two major disc drag materials—Teflon and cork—to produce a silky smooth system that is slicker than opossum grease on a ball bearing.

The bottom line on the Harris Solitude fly reel is that it is absolutely outstanding in every sense of the word. It won a 1999 Editor's Choice Award from *Fly Fish America*, which is a difficult thing to do given the steep competition. The Harris Solitude is certainly one of my top choices when it comes to tough saltwater reels.

The Orvis Company

Orvis offers a large selection of saltwater reels in a tremendous price range, from $115 for their Battenkill disc 7/8 to their Odyssey+ IV at $490. With proper care, Orvis' Clearwater and Rocky Mountain reels can also be used on the salt and are quite inexpensive (the Clearwater starts at about $29). My first saltwater Orvis reel was an Odyssey III, which I still have and trust after extensive use (it perfectly matches my PM-10 9-foot, 9-weight).

Orvis' newest entry is the Vortex, a large-arbor reel that promises to become a favorite quickly. The drag appears completely dependable, which is what we have come to expect from Orvis.

Scientific Anglers

I have been flyfishing with Scientific Anglers reels for quite a few years now and have found them to be excellent reels that don't require taking out a second mortgage on the house. Besides being just plain good reels with reliable drags, they have what is surely one of the easiest right- to left-hand conversions available, which takes about one second and requires no tools and not even a brain, the latter feature being of particular importance to me. I received two Scientific Angler System 2 reels recently, which came from the factory set up for right-hand retrieve, but I retrieve with my left hand. All I had to do was lift out the center drag gear and replace it upside down. Yes, that's all there is to it.

The first fish I ever caught on an SA reel was a false albacore. I stopped that rascal by cranking down the drag and palming him to a complete stop in a matter of about 4 seconds. I wasn't sure if the reel was going to be able to handle such blatant abuse, but it did, and I have been a fan of Scientific Anglers reels ever since. I really like their lines, too—I now use SA Mastery Series lines more than any other lines.

Ross

Ross is a Colorado-based reel company that is getting more and more attention these days. I use two of their reels in the salt, although one isn't really made specifically for saltwater use. Ross makes the Colorado (a low-end reel for line weights 2 through 7); Cimarron (designed with fresh water in mind, I use this reel for specks sometimes); Gunnison (at $235 for the G4, which takes 8- and 9-weight lines, this reel is a solid bargain for game fish like red drum); San Miguel (a high-end reel mainly for freshwater use); Saltwater (a new addition that will certainly become very popular very quickly).

Ross reels are known for high quality at an affordable price. If you are in the market for such a reel, this is one good option.

Lamson

I am very fond of this company's reels. They don't cost a fortune but are very smooth and fully reliable. When fishing inshore I never shy away from a Lamson, such as the DCA-4 and LP-3.5, and when offshore with a 10-weight, I often go with the LP-4.

Other Reels

The following reels have good reputations, however, I don't have extensive time using them:

- Abel (a very expensive reel that comes highly recommended by many who use it, but one which is simply too costly for many flyfishers)
- Tibor
- Bauer (fly tier, material manufacturer, and guide Steve Hazlett praises this reel's drag)
- Tioga (recipient of a *Fly Fish America* Editor's Choice Award)
- Billy Pate (a great reputation with a legend's name on it)
- Loop
- Loomis
- Hardy (very well known for classy reels)
- R.L. Winston (I have just received my first Winston reel, which is made by Hardy, and will be using it extensively in the near future; if this reel is anything like Winston's rods, it is sure to become a prized possession)
- Phos (their Yukon Big Game reel is superb; also a winner of *Fly Fish America's* Editor's Choice Award)

LIGHT TACKLE

It should first be noted that the "term light" tackle is relative by its very nature. Therefore, what one angler's idea of light tackle is may be different from another angler's. For our purposes, we will consider light tackle to be spinning rods and reels rated to handle no heavier than 30-pound test line.

The 30-pound test figure is purely arbitrary on my part. I could just as easily have said 25-pound test or 12. I selected 30 because, in my experience, most lines, rods, and reels rated for more than this become cumbersome and "heavy." Remember, though, that other anglers have different experiences and opinions. And besides, experienced saltwater anglers can defeat the vast majority, if not all of the game fish covered in this book, with line rated above 30-pound test with relative ease, and many can do it with 20 and no problem at all. Some I know can do it with 10.

But we must go further with our definition of light tackle. For example, "light" in the term "light spinning" does not refer to how the rod loads, that is, how it bends when under pressure. A rod designed for 15-pound test line at the max might have a medium-heavy action, meaning it is stout and does not bend far down the blank, whereas another rod rated for the same line may have an action termed medium light, which bends more under pressure. So the "light" in "light spinning" (or trolling or jigging) is really a broad definition for tackle that transfers the fighting quality of the fish for which it is intended to an angler in a challenging fashion and revealing the fish's strength, agility, size, and spirit.

Could there be even more to the definition? Certainly. We can look at fish weight as compared to line rating. Is the term "light tackle" a misnomer if the average fish being caught weighs two pounds and the line is rated at 8? No, not at all. If the fish's qualities are readily evident in the fight, then the fish-weight-to-line-rating is irrelevant. Again, an inexperienced angler who wins a fight with a 10-pound striped bass on 30-pound test and says it was a great fight may not have a frame of reference, i.e., he obviously has never fought a 10-pound striper on 8-pound test.

What follows are recommended spinning rods and reels by manufacturer. I intentionally do not list rods and reels from every manufacturer because: 1) there are far too many manufacturers out there to cover them all here; 2) I haven't used all of them; and 3) some I have tried I do not recommend, which are not listed herein.

Note that in this section I recommend only certain series of rods and by manufacturer rather than specific models, as those recommendations are made in Chapters 4 through 6. Each series has different attributes (action, line and lure weight ratings, price, and so on), so check each series out in a local tackle shop. (Websites and catalogs are fine for general information, but a rod should be handled before purchase.)

Spinning Rods

Spinning rods are what most anglers think of when they hear "light tackle." Advances in design, engineering, materials, and production have resulted in some spinning rods that are far superior to even the rods of 10 years ago. Here are some manufacturers that produce assorted high-quality, light-tackle spinning rods.

Shimano

I own more Shimano spinning rods than any other brand, as is the case with my spinning reels. It is just that I have found Shimano spinning tackle to be precisely what I am looking for in overall performance, and the quality of their rods and reels —even the very inexpensive stuff—is right up there. I have never been in a situation where a Shimano rod has failed to allow me to do what I wanted to do—reach a certain fish or fight a certain fish correctly. No Shimano rod has ever failed me in performance, in other words.

Shimano has many rods from which to choose, among them the Carbomax, SG, FX, Calcutta, Talavera, Socorro, Tejera, Saragosa, and TDR.

Daiwa

One of my most poorly treated and treasured spotted seatrout rods is a Daiwa Inshore Series rod I have been using for years and years. It has a fast action and a level of sensitivity that I find nearly perfect for fishing jigs. When fishing for specks with jigs, I always grab this rod first. I trust it.

I have other Daiwa rods but have found that they are best for freshwater situations, which is what they are designed for, as opposed to the Inshore Series, which is meant for the salt.

Abu Garcia

I hadn't fished with an Abu Garcia rod until 1991 or so when a guide (Captain Rodney Smith of Satellite Beach, Florida) on the Abu Garcia professional program handed me one to try on some big red drum (flats bulls in the 30- to 40-pound class). The rod was longer than I was used to and I wasn't sure I was going to like it, but a moment or two after I hooked my first red, I found the rod to be very well suited for the situation. Abu Garcia's Morrum and Conolon Premier Series are both worth investigating.

Penn

When one thinks of the classic, time-tested saltwater rod, one thinks of Penn. This company was a leading force in saltwater tackle long before most of the others even showed up on the scene. Their rods are first-class and dependable in every way. Penn offers an intimidating selection, too.

Penn rods are known for their durability and fish-fighting power. Their Power Stick, Power Graph (an excellent inshore rod), and Sabre rods are well worth consideration. Of course, Penn may be most respected for their lineup of offshore trolling rods, which are seen on thousands of charter boats around the world.

Spinning Reels

My first spinning reel was a Mitchell 300, a classic and timeless reel that unfortunately isn't in use as much today, no doubt because it has remained simple and functional without bells and whistles. It just isn't sexy enough for many of today's eye-candy buyers, who are influenced by tournament bass anglers with their own Saturday morning television shows rather than what actually works best and what is really needed. They forget that those guys are paid huge sums to plug a company's tackle (you might be surprised just how much money those guys get from tackle companies).

Shimano

I would have to take both shoes off to figure out how many Shimano spinning reels I have. That is how satisfied I am with their performance. I've used them religiously for more years than I can remember and am still surprised how Shimano is able to keep many of their prices very low.

Shimano manufactures the superior Sustain, Stradic, Symetre, and Sedona, as well as the Spirex, Solstace, Syncopate, Sidestab/Sienna, CX, AX, and FX, and the excellent live-bait reel series, Baitrunner.

Daiwa

One of the giants in the industry, especially along the B.A.S.S. tournament trail, Daiwa also manufactures some good saltwater reels. The Long Cast X-Treme models have features that make up the Gyro Seven-Point System. Two important parts of the system are a micro-adjustable drag and an anti-reverse mechanism that completely eliminates reel handle back-play. This latter feature is particularly useful when slack-lining a jig for spotted seatrout and the trout hits the jig on the fall.

Daiwa spinning reel models to consider are the Emblem-X-T, BG, Regal-Z-T, Regal-X-T, Regal-S-T, and the Apollo.

Penn

One is never surprised to see a Penn spinning reel doing battle with some enraged saltwater game fish. They are the choice of innumerable saltwater anglers, many of whom were brought up with a Penn Spinfisher in their hands. But Penn hasn't been resting on its laurels when it comes to new ideas and innovations.

The recent past has seen two new Penn reel series hit the market, and I haven't heard anyone complaining about them. These are the Prion and Power Graph reels, which don't look at all like the traditional Spinfisher. They are, however, quite up to par when it comes to the quality one expects from Penn. Both are rugged, with the Prion having a tough titanium nitride finish and the Power Graph finished in a graphite housing, hence the name. Both also have no back-play.

You would be hard pressed to go wrong with the Spinfisher, Prion, or Power Graph.

Abu Garcia

I should probably fish more often with Abu Garcia reels. Naturally, if I had one, I would offer you an excuse as to why I don't, but I don't. The truth is that Abu Garcia makes some outstanding smooth reels with topnotch drags. I've beaten some gigantic game fish on Abu Garcia reels and had no trouble doing so, despite the proverbial screaming runs and smoking drags.

Three Abu Garcia reels in particular should be considered by light-tackle saltwater anglers in the Southeast. These are the Suveran (great drag and gear system, very tough), Tournament (smooth as silk), and Ultracast (for making casts to distant fish that you might not be able to reach otherwise).

Consider one of these Abu Garcia reels the next time you are in the market. I don't think you will be disappointed.

That is all I want to say in this chapter on tackle. "Game Fish" and "Forage Species" as well as the chapters covering the states have additional specifics and recommendations.

The Future of the Southeast's Inshore Fisheries

The only state in the Southeast with major environmental threats is North Carolina. South Carolina and Georgia have things under control in comparison to North Carolina. Given this, let's look at North Carolina's problems.

Once a state that boasted vast, clean coastal wetlands and saltwater fish populations that boggled the mind, North Carolina has become the laughing stock of coastal states, but it is no laughing matter. The Tar Heel state's coastal waters are a shocking disaster when compared to other coastal states, and it isn't going to get better any time soon. The state's politicians are deep in the pockets of a very powerful commercial fishing industry that has decimated the fisheries as well as commercial agriculture that poisons North Carolina waters with near impunity.

North Carolina's coastal waters are under virtual attack. Baitfish reared in these waters are crucial to the survival of species like the king mackerel.

The knockout combination: rampant commercial overfishing
(this page and the next in the background) and coastal water pollution
from industry (next page in the foreground).

For example, incredibly destructive commerical fishing vessels, such as trawlers, are allowed to lay waste to the state's largest and most diverse marine ecosystem, Pamlico Sound. The industry is authorized to drag its lethal wares right across extremely sensitive bottom structure that is crucial to the health of the sound, which covers 1.25 million acres. A trawl net dragged over delicate bottom rips it up and destroys it. The net sweeps up everything, including countless juvenile fish that use the sound as a nursery. All unwanted fish are tossed back into the sound, and most of these are dead. The carnage includes baby trout, drum, flounder, croaker, and innumerable other fish and crustaceans.

I believe the problem originates with Governor Jim Hunt and his self-appointed Marine Fisheries Commission. It has been granted authority to not only create rules that directly affect how commercial fishermen are allowed to do business, but also the power to dictate the state's Division of Marine Fisheries agenda. This is indeed an outrageous conflict of interest, but so long as politician's coffers are being filled with money from the commercial fishing industry, North Carolina's marine fisheries will remain in dire straits.

The North Carolina Fisheries Association

Names can be misleading, which is precisely the case with the North Carolina Fisheries Association (NCFA). The NCFA is not a conservation organization but rather the extremely powerful and ruthless lobby of North Carolina's commercial fishing industry, whose apparent job, many conservationists feel, it is to deplete fish stocks to the point of no return with ruinous high-tech equipment and brutal, lethal efficiency. The industry is vigorously supported by Governor Jim Hunt, Senator Jesse Helms, and the state legislature, who have formed a protective wall around the netters in return for campaign contributions. The clearest evidence of this is how equipment and practices outlawed or severely restricted by other coastal states have the full approval of Hunt, Helms, and the rest of North Carolina's elected and appointed anticonservation politicians and are allowed to continue unabated, regardless of indisputable evidence of the precipitous decline in many of the state's fish populations. Even indiscriminate gill nets (the equivalent of firing a shotgun into a flock of mixed ducks with no regard whatsoever for the species that falls) and habitat-destroying nets that mangle critical bottom structure (akin to burning a town to the ground in order to flush out a burglar hiding in one of the buildings) are happily approved.

North Carolina has long been the target of conservationists who, backed by hard science, have been exposing the nature and true agenda of the NCFA. However,

Spartina marshes and coastal creeks hold juvenile baitfish. North Carolina's environmental threats include the loss of these precious wetlands.

despite national attention being focused squarely on North Carolina's wanton vandalism of its marine resources by netters, the tragic fact remains that the NCFA will continue to plunder fish stocks for as long as the current regime stays in power, and that, sadly, is almost surely to be for some time.

If it seems that I speak rather emphatically about North Carolina's horrifically destructive commercial fishing industry, it is because I lived on North Carolina's Coast and am very familiar with the netters' practices, attitudes, and crimes against nature. No other state in the nation allows what North Carolina allows, and there really is no end in sight to the devastation of fish and habitat that belong to us all. The carnage brought upon the waters is gruesome and baleful, with seemingly incalculable tons of by-catch being willingly destroyed by the netters every year, a loathsome and sickening practice.

Coastal rivers like North Carolina's New River and its tributaries could be home to many more game fish. Here, Britta waits for some action.

The National Marine Fisheries Service

The National Marine Fisheries Service is supposed to be the agency that protects our fisheries for future generations in such a way that everyone benefits from their actions. Incredibly, the NMFS has become little more than a weapon for the commercial fishing industry to wield against conservation-minded recreational anglers who have the gall to cry out against the devastation being visited upon our waters. This agency is literally at the beck and call of the nation's commercial fishing industry.

One of the favorite ploys of the NMFS is called redirected emphasis. This was a technique used by communist interrogators questioning American prisoners of war that deftly fools the prisoner into thinking that there really isn't any harm in answering the inquisitor's questions because that question is clearly harmless. The NMFS uses the technique by pointing out that things could be worse and that gains are being made to protect the fisheries. A classic example of this is when Richard Parry, chief of intergovernmental and recreational fisheries, answered conservationists' outcry by stating that back in 1980 recreational anglers caught 42 million pounds of weakfish (gray trout). He conveniently fails to mention that this figure pales in comparison to what commercial fishermen used to catch in a year. He then tried to mislead conservationists by telling them that the NMFS recently adopted new regulations that require juvenile weakfish to be returned to the water if caught in shrimp or crab trawls in an area where juvenile weakfish are *known* to overwinter. The problem, of course, is that so many of these young fish are already dead when they are shoved back into the water. The other part of the problem is that most weakfish overwintering areas are unknown, which means the netters can drag their gear right through these very sensitive areas with impunity.

Agriculture

While living in the coastal town of Jacksonville, I witnessed firsthand the detrimental agricultural practices allowed by North Carolina. The commercial hog farm industry is one of the most powerful entities in the state, and as such, it can and does dictate to the government. This dangerous situation has led to more than 6,000 sprawling corporate hog farms springing into existence in North Carolina, each with thousands of hogs. Now, imagine the effluent produced by hundreds of thousands of hogs. You get the picture. Now situate every hog farm, with its massive waste lagoons, on the banks of or adjacent to a creek, stream, or river. Throw in politicians who accept huge sums of money from the industry, and you get a very dangerous industry that is nearly unregulated.

The result? Hideously toxic hog waste lagoons that burst with terrible regularity, with millions of gallons of feces and urine spilling into the creeks, streams, and rivers that lead to the ocean. The results are catastrophic.

In the past few years, gigantic hog waste lagoons have burst and flowed into important coastal rivers like the New, killing countless fish and other life forms. I lived not far from the New River when a completely preventable spill of titanic proportions nearly killed the river. Massive mats of dead fish clogged the water, but the cries of environmentalists went unheard and unanswered by Governor Hunt, who knew that to challenge the commercial hog farm industry was to invite a serious reduction in campaign funds. The lagoons are still there and multiplying at a staggering rate.

But the hog farms aren't the only dire threat to North Carolina's coastal waters, because other types of farms—tobacco, corn, soy, cotton—are coating fields with lethal pesticides, herbicides, fungicides, and fertilizers, which find their way into the bordering creeks, streams, and rivers to begin their short journey to the coast. Known as runoff, these poisons foster algae growth, which reduces oxygen levels in the water, resulting in far fewer baitfish, and therefore, far fewer game fish. No better example of this can be seen than the Neuse River, which is born in the hinterlands near Deep Run and empties into Pamlico Sound between Drum Point and Maw Point. The Neuse used to be a fine striped bass (rockfish locally) and red drum river, but agricultural pollution and heavy commercial fishing pressure have reduced the catchable populations of these once teeming game fish to a fraction of what they once were.

One of the most serious side effects of runoff is a particularly nasty single-celled organism called *Pfiesteria piscicida*, which has 24 life stages and the bizarre ability to alternate back and forth within these stages (11 of which are deadly) like some horribly virulent chameleon. While I was living in North Carolina, Dr. JoAnn Burkholder of North Carolina State University, a research scientist studying the effects of agriculture on coastal waters, became seriously ill after working with *Pfiesteria* in her lab and on coastal rivers and other waters. This was one of the first indications that humans could become the victims of an organism that has the ability to kill and feed on billions of baitfish, primarily Atlantic menhaden, perhaps the most important baitfish for game fish along the entire Atlantic coast. Soon thereafter, watermen and just plain folks near the water started getting very sick. The outbreak was tracked to *Pfiesteria*. The cell thrives in waters rich in nitrogen and phosphorus, two major components of runoff.

Governor Hunt and Wisconsin Tissue

As we were about to go to press, word reached me through a highly respected guide who works the Roanoke River striper fishery that one of Governor Jim Hunt's pet projects, the establishment of a huge paper mill adjacent to a critical striper spawning ground, is about to go through. The toxins this mill could release into this fragile ecosystem are some of the most deadly known to man. It appears that construction on this horrific facility will begin in the summer of 1999—without an environmental impact statement being required.

This brutish plant will likely use up to 9 million gallons of water a day from the river and, in return, dump untold toxins into the river. The fact that this river's water levels are already tenuous due to usage by cities evidently means nothing, nor does the undeniable fact that this river, through its striper and shad fisheries, brings in huge sums of money to the tiny communities surrounding it.

The Bottom Line

So, there must be no fish left in North Carolina, right? Not at all. North Carolina is merely the state in this region with the fewest game fish available when compared to South Carolina and Georgia. What this means is that you often stand a better chance of catching more and larger fish elsewhere in the region; it certainly does not necessarily mean that you are wasting your time casting flies into the Tar Heel salt. Truth is, I have caught many fish along the North Carolina coast and have had many very good days fishing. But just imagine what the fishery *could* be like with responsible use and regulation of its marine resources. If recreational anglers and conservationists organize and make themselves heard, perhaps we can reverse the serious situations mentioned above.

Conservation Organizations

You have to be very careful when joining a conservation organization—some of them are staffed by closet animal rights activists who have sworn to abolish fishing altogether. These three can be trusted.

Coastal Conservation Association
4801 Woodway, Suite 220W
Houston, TX 77056
713-626-4234

Established in 1977, this is an outstanding coastal resources protection organization. They were the driving force behind Florida's net ban. Join today.

Ducks Unlimited
One Waterfowl Way
Memphis, TN 38120
800-45DUCKS

DU is important not only for ducks but wetlands in general because they preserve, protect, and restore wetlands, many of which are coastal, Due to DU's efforts, we have more marine bait fish and game fish.

American Rivers
1025 Vermont Avenue NW, Suite 720
Washington, DC 20005
202-347-7550

American Rivers is a great organization devoted to saving our rivers. They are a force to be reckoned with and need your support.

About the Artists

• *Duane Raver, Game Fish illustrations.* A native of Iowa, Duane was educated in central Iowa schools and received a degree in Fisheries Management from Iowa State University in 1949. He was employed as a fishery biologist with the North Carolina Wildlife Resources Commission in 1950. In 1960, Duane transferred to the Education Division of the Wildlife Commission and was on the staff of *Wildlife in North Carolina* magazine. He was Managing Editor of the magazine until 1970, when he was appointed Editor.

Wildlife artwork has always been a major activity in his life, and Duane completed over 200 cover paintings for *Wildlife in North Carolina* during his 30 years with the Wildlife Commission. He retired in 1979 to do wildlife artwork full time.

Duane works primarily in acrylic and opaque watercolor. He does only wildlife subjects with emphasis on fish and gamebirds. He welcomes inquiries and visits at his home studio at 910 Washington Street, Cary, NC 27511. Duane can be reached at 919-467-9277.

• *Susan Newman, Forage Species illustrations.* Susan Newman's illustrations have graced several books (including the award-winning *Flyfishing Structure: The Flyfisher's Guide to Reading and Understanding the Water*) for a variety of publishers. The forage illustrations herein are her first for Wilderness Adventures Press and she will be illustrating others in this series in the years to come. Her paintings of North American waterfowl have been auctioned at Ducks Unlimited events and have fetched considerable sums.

Index

NOTES

NOTES

NOTES

NOTES

NOTES

WILDERNESS ADVENTURES GUIDE SERIES

If you would like to order additional copies of this book or our other Wilderness Adventures Press™ guidebooks, please fill out the order form below or call **800-925-3339** or **fax 800-390-7558.** Visit our website for a listing of over 2500 sporting books—the largest online: **www.wildadv.com**

Mail to: Wilderness Adventures Press™, 45 Buckskin Road, Belgrade, MT 59714

☐ **Please send me your free catalog on hunting and fishing books.**

Ship to:

Name _____

Address _____

City _____ State_____ Zip_____

Home Phone_____ Work Phone_____

Payment: ☐ Check ☐ Visa ☐ Mastercard ☐ Discover ☐ American Express

Card Number _____ Expiration Date_____

Signature_____

Qty	Title of Book and Author	Price	Total
	Flyfisher's Guide to Oregon	$26.95	
	Flyfisher's Guide to Washington	$26.95	
	Flyfisher's Guide to Northern California	$26.95	
	Flyfisher's Guide to Montana	$26.95	
	Flyfisher's Guide to Wyoming	$26.95	
	Flyfisher's Guide to Idaho	$26.95	
	Flyfisher's Guide to Colorado	$26.95	
	Flyfisher's Guide to Northern New England	$26.95	
	Total Order + shipping & handling		

**Shipping and handling: $4.00 for first book,
$2.50 per additional book, up to $11.50 maximum**